Language Policy Evaluation and the
Charter for Regional or Minority Languages

Language Policy Evaluation and the European Charter for Regional or Minority Languages

François Grin

with contributions by

Regina Jensdóttir and Dónall Ó Riagáin

First published 2003 by
PALGRAVE MACMILLAN
Houndmills, Basingstoke, Hampshire RG21 6XS and
175 Fifth Avenue, New York, N.Y. 10010
Companies and representatives throughout the world

PALGRAVE MACMILLAN is the global academic imprint of the Palgrave
Macmillan division of St. Martin's Press, LLC and of Palgrave Macmillan Ltd.
Macmillan® is a registered trademark in the United States, United Kingdom
and other countries. Palgrave is a registered trademark in the European
Union and other countries.

ISBN 1–4039–0032–9

This book is printed on paper suitable for recycling and made from fully
managed and sustained forest sources.

A catalogue record for this book is available from the British Library.

A catalogue record for this book is available from the Library of Congress.

10 9 8 7 6 5 4 3 2
12 11 10 09 08 07 06 05 04

Printed and bound in Great Britain by
Antony Rowe Ltd, Chippenham and Eastbourne

To FRF

Contents

Preface and Acknowledgements   ix

Part I   Core Issues and Concepts   **1**

1   Introduction and Overview   3
The need for this book: filling a gap   3
Approach and structure of this book   11

2   Language Policy   19
A note on terminology   19
What is language policy?   27
The policy analysis perspective   38
A framework for language policy   40

**Part II   The European Charter for Regional or
Minority Languages**   **53**

3   The Charter: an Overview   55
A brief history of the drafting and adoption of the Charter   55
The document   58

4   Implementing the Charter: Organisational Issues   69
The pre-ratification stage   69
Setting up the monitoring   73

Part III   Application   **79**

5   From Legal Texts to 'Good Policy'   **81**
Negative rights, positive rights, and results   81
Defining 'good policy'   86
Three basic principles of good policy: a preview   91

6   Effectiveness   99
Examination of goals   99
Analysing cause-and-effect relationships   101
Output and outcome measurement: basic indicators   104

Generalised effectiveness comparison 109
Assessment of policy-specific effects 113

7   Costs and Cost-Effectiveness 117
Understanding and measuring costs 117
Cost-effectiveness evaluation 132

8   Democracy 147
Democracy and policy choice 147
Participatory democracy and the evolutionary
     character of democracy 149
Participatory democracy and language policy 153

**9   A Walk-Through Example: Language
     Education Policy 163**
Methodology 163
Linguistic environment 164
What works? 167

Part IV   Conclusions 191

10   Assessment and Perspectives 193
Summary 193
Implementation of the Charter in practice 196
The role of language planning bodies 199
The way forward: diversity through *'normalització'* 201

*Appendix I   Text of the European Charter on Regional
     or Minority Languages* 207

*Appendix II   Text of the Explanatory Report on the
     European Charter* 221

Appendix III   The 'Flensburg Recommendations' 246

Appendix IV   Selected Internet Resources 252

Bibliography 265

Subject Index 275
Name Index 279

Preface and Acknowledgements

The ambition of this book is to sit astride some of the customary categories of academic disciplines.

First, it clearly focuses on language issues, and more precisely, on 'language-in-society', to use the felicitous expression once proposed by Joshua Fishman. However, it does not study languages *per se*: it is not a 'language book' or a sociolinguistics digest. Second, this book makes frequent reference to a legal instrument, namely, the European Charter for Regional or Minority Languages, and raises the question of its implementation, but it does not rest on a legal approach – in fact, it deliberately attempts to steer clear from it. Third, although the notion of 'policy evaluation' appears in the title of this book and provides its chief guiding thread, this volume makes no claim to being a fully-fledged policy analysis textbook. Fourth, the design of this book is mainly rooted in an approach to language policy that owes much to two sub-fields of economics, namely language economics and education economics; however, the reader will find relatively little of them in this book – and it contains virtually no economics, apart from a few fundamental concepts such as 'opportunity cost' or 'cost-effectiveness'.

At the same time, this book, in a large or small way, draws on all these disciplines, which have supplied the various conceptual tools and analytical angles that I use. They are, however, combined in a targeted way, with specific goals in mind – in particular, that of building bridges between distinct strands of scholarship, and to contribute to more effective policy approaches for the protection and promotion of linguistic diversity.

In my opinion, there is an urgent need for such bridges. This need is evidenced by the fact that there are notable gaps, first of all at the analytical level, between the work being pursued in these various disciplines with separate sets of analytical concepts, networks of scholars, academic journals, and lecture circuits. This results not only in distinct, but also somewhat disconnected academic cultures. However, the issues at hand are complex; hence, they require more integrative approaches. For example, the discourse on 'linguistic human rights' needs to be reconciled with the discourse on 'efficient resource allocation', and such reconciliation starts with a clarification of the logical relationships between the respective ways in which these two types of discourse address language issues. Therefore, I would like to think of this book as a sincerely transdisciplinary one.

Giving coherent substance to this transdisciplinary ambition poses a number of challenges on the strictly academic plane; in particular, the net has to be cast wide to pick and accommodate concepts developed in distinct disciplines. This requires taking account of the discipline-specific construction of these concepts; serious effort is necessary to ensure that their meaning is rendered properly, and I leave it to the reader to judge the extent to which I have been successful – or not – in this enterprise.

The concerns just described could certainly result in an ambitious scholarly enterprise focusing on the epistemological and methodological articulation of different disciplines. This, however, is not the goal I am pursuing here. While such a book would certainly be worthwhile, my main ambition is a different one – namely, to offer a contribution which practitioners may find directly useful. This is why this volume, although its underlying logic remains an academic one, does not emphasise scholarly analysis as such, but the application of abstraction to reality. It is a practice-oriented presentation of how a novel integrative approach can be put to use in language policy and, in particular, for the implementation of the Charter for Regional or Minority Languages.

Consequently, this book is not a primer in sociolinguistics, language law, policy analysis, language economics or education economics. I have deliberately selected some concepts and methods from these fields of study, and combined them together with a view to proposing some key elements of an integrative, yet operational approach to the implementation of minority language policies. My presentation, therefore, is necessarily (and deliberately) incomplete; however, my goal in this book is not to be exhaustive, but to help the reader structure his or her own analytical treatment of language policy implementation, as such questions may arise in the practical contexts with which he or she is confronted.

While I have attempted to make sure that the simplifications and shortcuts used here do not result in misinterpretations or incorrect statements, I take full responsibility for any such shortcomings, and thank readers in advance for any comments and suggestions that may serve to improve future versions of this text or other work in this area.

One more bridge-building ambition of this book ought to be mentioned. Just like the international instrument to which it often refers, namely, the Charter for Regional or Minority Languages, this book is concerned with linguistic diversity in Europe. 'Europe', in this context, must be understood as the 'Pan-European Community' (to use a term often put forward by the Council of Europe). This includes East and

West, North and South, and countries as diverse as Norway, Italy, Georgia, Ireland or Lithuania. Scholars and practitioners who have worked in various parts of Europe often notice that approaches to 'minority' issues, including language, can look quite different depending on the country considered, and that one of the most noticeable divides remains an East–West one. With exceptions, Eastern European scholars and practitioners are more likely to take ethnicity as given, to view language as a marker of ethnicity, to reason in terms of 'national minorities' and to worry about the rights accorded to them. With exceptions, Western European scholars and practitioners tend to adopt a more constructionist view of 'minority', identity, and language. Relatedly, they are more likely to focus directly on policies affecting some dimensions of minority experience (in particular, language policies) than (as Eastern European analysts or practitioners are more likely to do) on 'minority rights', of which 'language rights' would be a sub-section, and language policies an offshoot. While I essentially hail, for personal and professional reasons, from the perspective characterised here as 'Western', I have attempted to develop my line of argument with very different types of readers in mind, and to offer materials that can make sense and be relevant to persons with very different backgrounds and horizons.

The manuscript has gained very much from the advice and suggestions of a number of people, in particular Camille O'Reilly, Jean Rossiaud, Claudio Sfreddo, François Vaillancourt and Sue Wright. I would like to express my deep gratitude to these readers, whose comments have significantly helped this volume to come into existence, or guided me in successive revisions. Factual information and reading suggestions on particular points have been supplied by Michael Byram, Andrew Girle, Nancy Hornberger, Robert Phillipson and Tove Skutnabb-Kangas, to whom I am also indebted.

I have benefited from the opportunity to bounce ideas off colleagues at a number of conferences and workshops that have taken place over the period when I was working on this book. I am indebted to participants at the ECMI Conference on 'Evaluating Policy Measures of Minority Languages in Europe' held in Flensburg in June 2000, in particular Philip Blair, the late Kas Deprez, Viv Edwards, Smaranda Enache, Kjell Herberts, George Schöpflin, and Judith Solymosi – in addition to other colleagues who have also taken part in the event but are already thanked elsewhere in this Preface. This conference, which has played a seminal role in the decision to write this book, was organised as part of research project of the European Centre for Minority Issues supported by the Directorate General for Education, Arts and Culture of the

European Commission in Brussels, whose financial assistance is gratefully acknowledged. This conference then gave rise, albeit indirectly, to another research project supported by the same institution; this project was un-officially known as 'SMiLE' – for 'Support for minority languages in Europe'. There are a number of close links between this book and the SMiLE project. The analytical instrument developed in this text provided the structure for the evaluation work of the SMiLE project; reciprocally, the SMiLE project, which is reaching completion at the time of writing of this Preface, provided an opportunity to confront analytical tools with terrain realities. Thus, it offered an effective way to reconsider critically some of the concepts developed in this book and to increase their usefulness for the practitioner. In this process, I have been very fortunate to be able to discuss many of these matters with the co-authors of the SMiLE report, and in particular with Tom Moring, during intense but always pleasant working sessions in Finland.

For the most part, the writing of this book has taken place in my office at the European Centre for Minority Issues (ECMI) in Flensburg, and I would like to thank my colleagues for their support and for the very pleasant working environment they offered me throughout. Special thanks are due to my assistant Marguerite Sitthy, who patiently retrieved documents, tried out language policy examples and checked their pedagogical value, and put together most of the 'list of internet resources' provided at the end of this volume. Final revisions took place later, in my office at the Education Research Unit (SRED) in Geneva, where I also enjoyed very favourable working conditions, for which thanks.

Finally, I have been privileged to work in regular contact with two persons who have made essential contributions to this book. One is Regina Jensdóttir from the Council of Europe in Strasbourg, in charge of co-ordinating the activities of the Committee of Experts monitoring the implementation of the Charter. The other is Dónall Ó Riagáin, an independent consultant on language planning and a former President and Secretary General of the European Bureau for Lesser-Used Languages – and certainly one of the persons with the most intimate and profound knowledge of the Charter for Regional or Minority Languages. Regina and Dónall have contributed Chapters 3 and 4 of the book respectively, and have provided throughout deeply appreciated encouragement and moral support – for which, *ab imo pectore*, 'þakka þér fyrir' and 'go raibh maith agat'.

F.G.
Geneva

Part I

Core Issues and Concepts

Summary of Part I

Part I includes two chapters. Chapter 1 introduces the main issues addressed in this book; it identifies gaps in the literature and explains why these gaps need to be filled in order to facilitate the development of language policies for the implementation of standards, particularly those reflected in the *European Charter for Regional or Minority Languages*. The main function of this book is to build bridges between the sociolinguistic and the 'legal-institutional' perspectives on minority language policy.

There are, of course, many different ways to build bridges. The approach adopted here relies on *policy analysis*. Its core concern is with the ways in which choices are made, and the reasons why certain choices are made. In Chapter 1, I also explain why this book is not primarily intended as a scholarly volume, even though it draws on various strands of scholarship. Rather, its aim is to present a set of analytical and methodological tools in a targeted fashion, in order to help practitioners think about language policy matters in a policy perspective.

Chapter 2 presents the main analytical sources used to structure this enterprise, namely, 'language policy' and 'policy analysis'. These are combined into a 'policy-to-outcome path' which guides the approach developed in subsequent chapters.

1
Introduction and Overview

The need for this book: filling a gap

The challenge of minority language policies

This book initially grew out of the general observation that language issues, over the last decade, have been attracting increasing attention in the media, in the public debate, and in the concerns of national governments and international organisations. In some cases, language issues may be but one dimension of a more complex system, in which 'ethnicity' or 'nationalism' are in the foreground. However, even in those situations where language is, at first sight, not central, closer scrutiny often reveals the presence of a language question – or at least, of a language-related question.

Depending on the analytical angle chosen, different reasons may be invoked to explain the importance of language in a growing number of contexts. Let me begin by stressing two reasons pointing to something of a paradox: language is important because it is a potential source of conflict, even if, at the same time, the survival of many languages is threatened.

On the one hand, language is often associated with inter-group tensions, sometimes with conflict, which requires some form of concerted and organised intervention. Much of the international policy of European governments and a sizeable share of the involvement of international organisations in geopolitical matters – particularly since the demise of the USSR – is guided by the concern to prevent this conflictuality from becoming a threat to peace and stability. Even if such involvement is viewed in terms of ethnic groups and nationalities rather than languages, the type of measures that have to be taken to give substance to this involvement often address language issues. Recognition of

3

the legitimacy of a minority often implies granting its associated language a higher legal and political status than before; at the same time, it is important to ensure that the correlative majority does not feel threatened by such improvements, lest conflict, instead of quieting down, be fuelled by a new set of grievances. Finding appropriate solutions for tension-reduction, therefore, is not easy, and requires attention to be paid to the position of different languages in society.

However, the conflictual character of language issues is not the only reason why they have, in recent years, gained so much visibility. The second reason is related to the dynamics of language spread, maintenance and decline. It is now an established fact that small languages are disappearing at a strikingly rapid pace. Although estimates vary, many observers expect half of the world's 6,000 languages to have dropped out of use by the end of the twenty-first century – roughly one every fortnight. In other words, many languages are threatened, and diachronic analyses of language shift strongly suggest that threats originate a long time before a language is down to a clutch of speakers.

To this day, remarkably little is known about how to influence these dynamics, for example in order to prevent some languages from dying out, to revitalise other languages in order to guarantee their continuing presence as elements of mankind's cultural heritage, or to restrict the extent to which certain languages, seen as predatory, render other languages obsolete and squeeze them out of existence as living languages. The causal links that result in languages surviving, spreading or declining are complex, making any type of intervention difficult. At any rate, enough experience has been accumulated in the past decades to make one thing clear: the protection and promotion of threatened languages requires some careful planning.

Of course, this reference to a 'plan' must be understood in general terms. The fortunes of particular languages cannot be mandated, and the allocation of roles in a partnership of languages can only be regulated in a limited way. 'Planning' essentially means two things: first, that intervention in the sphere of language reflects given *intentions* – or the striving towards certain objectives, which can be formulated in different terms, from human rights to welfare theory; second, that intervention is not a haphazard one, that it is based on some knowledge of 'language-in-society' and that it is meant to be effective. In other words, intervention in the realm of language requires more than an ad-hoc collection of measures; language matters need not merely be administered; they need to be *managed*, and national governments (as well as international organisations) display a rising awareness of this requirement.

Consequently, language policies are becoming a significant field of government intervention.

Yet authorities (whether national, regional or local) often are surprisingly ill-equipped to deal with the questions that arise in the course of such management. When governments are confronted with the need to develop policy measures in the field of language (that is, to formulate a language policy), they face the difficulty that little is known about several key aspects of language policies. Practitioners in charge of language policies often have to make do with analytical instruments, empirical information, and normative principles from a set of disciplines, which, though indispensable, often fail to provide some of the necessary tools. Since language matters remain an area of competence of states, this problem is most apparent in the action of national or, as the case may be, regional or local governments.

As a starting point, governments usually have at their disposal a considerable body of legal expertise which is, of course, a necessary ingredient at specific stages of policy development, in particular when the implementation of policy goals has to be given a legal basis, and when the legal conformity of these goals with other legal norms has to be checked. This legal perspective is also relevant in the implementation of international treaties and covenants to which a state becomes party, including those that refer to language. Experience indicates that states rely heavily on such legal expertise in the drafting of language policy plans, particularly when such developments occur as part of the effort that states make to meet their obligations under some legally binding international convention.

However, the legal perspective, though necessary, is not sufficient for effective implementation. Several additional inputs are needed.

First, it is certainly indispensable to draw on expertise from the language disciplines. A distinction may be made here between the closely-related disciplines of 'sociolinguistics' and the (somewhat less strongly established in the academic world) 'sociology of language'. Deliberately simplifying this distinction, we might say that sociolinguistics is primarily a discipline in the language sciences whose concern is to account for social dimensions in patterns of language use, language learning, language reproduction, etc. – for example, a sociolinguist (or a sometimes indistinguishable 'applied linguist') might study the relationship between a person's social class and his or her tendency to, or preference for using certain syntactical forms. The sociology of language is closer to the family of core social sciences and also to the concerns of this book. It studies language in its social, political, or economic context, investigating, for example, how inequalities between groups in access to the levers of state power may affect the fortunes of the languages respectively spoken by these groups. Over the years, a considerable literature has developed in these areas. Just like the legal-institutional approach to language matters mentioned earlier, it provides essential ingredients for language policy and language planning, particularly with respect to the issues most directly relevant here, namely, the protection and promotion of regional or minority languages, which I shall sometimes call 'RMLs' for the sake of brevity.

A second set of perspectives on language matters is directly rooted in the 'core social sciences'. These extremely varied perspectives are usually developed by sociologists, political philosophers, or political scientists – who may be specialists of 'political theory' or 'rational choice'. Work hailing from these disciplines may, at times, be closer to the legal-institutional approach described earlier, and at other times, more closely connected with the language disciplines mentioned in the preceding paragraph. They sometimes blend almost seamlessly into 'sociology of language'. This line of work is rich in fundamental concepts that can help to analyse (some would say 'deconstruct') various approaches to language, ethnicity, nationhood, identity, difference, and so on.

However, even when taken together, the three broad strands of scholarship just described may not be enough. Legal expertise about standards applying to regional or minority languages, sociolinguistic knowledge of language processes, and 'core social science' contributions on language-in-society certainly constitute a necessary, but still not a sufficient basis for moving to action – as we have seen that governments increasingly must. The usual approaches, whether taken in isolation or used in combination, tend to leave an analytical and practical gap between two poles. These are, on the one hand, the legal and political obligations of states towards regional or minority languages and, on the other hand, a set of procedures for the implementation of measures giving substance to those obligations. To fill this gap, we need tools for the selection, design, implementation and evaluation of policy measures adopted on the basis of legal texts, and affecting regional or minority languages.

Let us take a closer look at the logical reasons for this gap – and hence at the functions that this book can serve.

First, why are legal approaches not sufficient? After all, many governments and international organisations give legal experts a central, sometimes hegemonic role in the production of discourse about language issues generally, and language policy issues in particular.

Yet the need for a 'positive' approach to decision-making clearly implies that policies cannot be formulated on the basis of a purely legal perspective. Almost by definition, legal texts constitute the codification of a normative discourse, stating or reflecting what a society considers to be just (and in accordance with the law) or unjust (and therefore banned by law, for example: discrimination on the basis of religious belief).[1] However, two problems arise at this point. One may question, to begin with, the very legitimacy or appropriateness of an approach based on norms and standards. People differ in their notion of what norms are just. The rejoinder to this observation, however, is that the norms being implemented have been adopted as a result of a democratic debate, and that they form, as a result, a proper basis for policy. However, criticism of an approach based on legal standards may also be the logical consequence of choosing a different analytical angle on language issues. Such criticism is usually found in the writings of political scientists hailing from the 'rational choice' side of their discipline, or in the writings of economists. For them, the case for some norms against other norms needs to be argued with explicit reference to the welfare gains that different sets of norms promise to deliver. It follows that even society's most general norms cannot rest on a moral argument alone, and that they should be derived from a theory of welfare.[2] I shall steer clear of this fundamental debate. Yet it stands to reason, no matter what position is chosen, that even the most enlightened norms do not tell us much about the *specific* measures that should be adopted in order for social reality to abide by those norms: a quasi infinite range of practical questions arise, not all of which can simply be dismissed as narrowly technical.

This is, of course, a problem that governments are confronted with in their various fields of jurisdiction. In each of them, general principles embodied in legal texts must be transposed into actual policy measures. Therefore, devoting attention to the selection, design, implementation and evaluation of policies is a normal task of modern states. However, governments' approach to language policy remains, in many ways, different from the approaches developed towards policies in other areas. More precisely, the former is far less developed than the latter. For decades, there has been sustained development in diverse policy areas such as health, transport, energy, or the environment. In those fields, decision-makers have at their disposal a growing apparatus of models and data, or at the very least a stock of historical experience generating, if nothing else, rules of thumb as guides for action. However, there is comparatively little of this kind in the field of language policy. When they have to select, design, implement and evaluate measures dealing with language, governments are venturing in what remains, to a large extent, a *terra incognita*.

As regards political philosophy (or the very closely related field of normative political theory), it offers analytical distinctions that are extremely useful to tease apart the various aspects of a very complex set of issues. Yet exercises in conceptual clarification do not amount to a set of guidelines for policy evaluation, and the normative perspective logically associated with the contributions in this area present, albeit in a different form, some of the same limitations as the legal approach. Quite apart from the fact that normative arguments are often too close to moral admonitions to carry much weight with people holding different views, they do not provide precise guidelines for policy development – nor, in fact, are they meant to.

Let us finally briefly return to the contributions of sociolinguistics, applied linguistics, and related work in the education sciences. In those disciplines, the evaluative issues that are essential to policy development have been receiving increasing attention in recent years. However, the findings derived from sociolinguistic work generally do not amount to the formulation of a fully-fledged language policy, because policy development has other, specific requirements that the language sciences or the education sciences often ignore. These requirements, indeed, are not limited to the linguistic (or educational) dimensions involved; they include some perspective on the weighing of policy alternatives and decision-making.

Procedures for the weighing of alternatives and subsequent decision-making are central to the discipline of policy analysis, but they are usually absent from the disciplines on the basis of which much of the official and academic discourse on language policy is formulated. This is, of course, not an absolute rule, and a few authors explicitly address the decision dimensions involved in any language policy, and specifically mention the public policy aspects involved.[3] However, a significant proportion of actual language planning seems to go on without much of a concerted plan. The conviction reflected in this book is that it is useful to add to the existing body of literature a contribution that makes 'choice' the organising concept of the analysis.

Summing up the points made so far, what is still largely missing is a structured, coherent approach to fill gaps between disciplines and concepts usually brought to bear on language matters. Resorting to another metaphor, one could say that the first aim of this book is to build bridges between bodies of knowledge and their associated frames of reference, or the intellectual cultures (usually organised around specific disciplines) in which they are embedded. Moreover, in addition to tackling the intellectual challenge of bridge-building, the structured, coherent approach which this book is intended to further should also pave the way for application, and offer tools for the selection, design, implementation and evaluation of actual policy measures. Building bridges and presenting tools to assist in decision-making in the field of language policy are the main motivations for this book.

The *European Charter for Regional or Minority Languages* and the issue of choice

The problem of choosing language policy measures (and the difficulty of doing so, given the relative lack of concepts and tools for this enterprise) arises precisely because languages, including regional and minority languages, are receiving more attention nowadays than they ever have. This attention, being reflected in the development of national legislation and international legal instruments, certainly is a welcome development for all those who set store by linguistic and cultural diversity. The need for clearly formulated policies, however, gives rise to a new set of questions.

It is useful, at this point, to make a distinction between two types of approach underpinning this renewed interest. In order to go straight to the heart of the matter, this point can be explained by comparing the philosophy implicit in different international legal instruments.

On the one hand, some are fundamentally legal and political texts, whose emphasis is on human rights or minority rights. This, for example, is the case of the *European Convention for the Protection of Human Rights and Fundamental Freedoms* (adopted in 1950), or the *Framework Convention for the Protection of National Minorities* (adopted in 1992).[4] In addition to a focus on rights, these instruments are often characterised by what could be described as their 'aspirational' nature: they sketch out broad, normative principles, setting standards which indicate what governments should or should not do regarding, for example, the treatment of national minorities living under their jurisdiction. Clearly, the focus of these instruments is on what is considered just. However, even if norms tell us what should be, they do not tell us, given how the world *is*, how we can select measures to implement these norms – and, consequently, which measures should be selected.

A common variant (or associated perspective) of this 'rights' argument calls upon the notions of conflict prevention, peace and security. It is found in many legal instruments, and frequently invoked in documents produced by organisations such as the OSCE (Organisation for Security and Cooperation in Europe; see e.g. OSCE, 1999), or the Office of the OSCE's High Commissioner on National Minorities.[5] This variant stresses the importance of granting and respecting minority rights not only *per se*, but also as a *condition* for peace, security and stability. The 'rights' argument and the 'peace and security' argument have many traits in common, in particular their roots in normative discourse; they jointly constitute an example of what I have just above called a specific 'frame of reference' with its associated intellectual culture and professional networks.[6]

On the other hand, attention to regional or minority languages can reflect an epistemologically different approach, whose focus is on *diversity*. Diversity is a concern that runs throughout this book. More importantly, it has inspired the *European Charter for Regional or Minority Languages* (hereafter, simply 'the Charter', presented in Part II and reproduced in full in the Appendix), which must be considered a particularly novel legal instrument.

The Charter is not about rights. It is not about standards. It is not about national minorities. It is not even about the members of minorities. It does not mention peace and security either.[7] The Charter is about *languages* – more precisely, the regional or minority languages of Europe – and about the measures required for safeguarding their existence in the long run. The Charter, as we shall see in the following chapters, represents a step beyond the essentially legal approach that characterises standard-setting instruments.[8] By the same token, it takes us closer to the problems of implementation mentioned earlier. However, the Charter raises a double set of questions related to choices.

First, the Charter does not only require states to apply certain provisions; it also proposes a wide range of options from which to choose. States signing the Charter have to pick a minimum of 35 'measures' out of the 68 proposals spelled out in Part III of the text. Many of these 68 proposals come in distinct variants. This implies that decisions must be made as to which measures will be adopted – and for what reasons. Let us for example consider paragraph 8.1.a, which offers four different options for the promotion of regional or minority languages in pre-school education: what reasons would a government have to choose one instead of another? This is a typical problem of choice, as it normally occurs in policy-making.

Second, once a decision has been made to apply a certain measure as formulated in the Charter, the question of the *specific measures* to be designed raises further problems of choice. These also arise in cases where a particular provision of the Charter is mandatory, or because given the particular situation of the regional or minority language concerned, only one option makes sense. Consider once again paragraphs 8.1.a.i to 8.1.a.iii, which require states to make available pre-school education, or a substantial part thereof, in the regional or minority language.[9] *How much* of pre-school education, or what parts thereof, should actually be available in the language? Furthermore, paragraph 8.1.a.iii makes reference to the number of families 'considered sufficient' for providing pre-school education in the relevant regional or minority languages – if they have requested it. But what does 'sufficient' mean? Or, more to the point from the standpoint of policy analysis, which criteria should be used to regard a number as sufficient – or not? Is 'sufficient' defined with respect to the goals pursued, or with respect to the resources to be invested? Again, these are typical policy analysis issues.

In short, the Charter is an instrument of great originality and cunning design, yet it raises problems of choice, which have to be solved. The need for a compass to help decision-makers navigate these issues and make coherent choices in the context of the Charter constitutes a further motivation for the writing of this book. Of course, owing to the almost limitless variability of practical cases, I do not attempt to provide simple answers or to recommend specific measures; such an ambition would be doomed from the start. Rather, my aim is to provide relevant concepts and tools to help actors approach the problem of choice in a structured way.

Approach and structure of this book

A tool for bridge-building

This book is intended as a practical tool for users, in particular civil servants, NGOs officers, or scholars involved in language planning matters, particularly in relation to the Charter. Some basic familiarity with the Charter is assumed, and the general focus of the book is on implementation issues, with particular emphasis on the evaluation of policy alternatives.

This book is therefore intended as a primer for approaching *decisions* to be made in language policy, and its approach to decision-making is rooted in policy analysis. It departs from the two dominant perspectives usually encountered in the literature related to the Charter, namely, the 'legal-institutional' perspective, whose main thrust is the formulation of a normative discourse (typically, stating standards or analysing some of the implications of such standards), but which does not offer tools to select between policy options. It also differs from the sociolinguistic perspective, which provides knowledge about language issues and a corresponding set of analytical concepts and models, but, most of the time, no general theory of choice.[10] Inputs from sociolinguistics and law are indispensable, and I shall be making frequent reference to them. However, they mostly provide the backdrop for the language policy analysis framework developed here, which intends neither to replace nor to replicate existing contributions, but to provide a useful complement to them.

This book is not a crash-course in law-making or language rights,[11] an essay on minority rights in the perspective of political philosophy,[12] a treatise on the sociolinguistics of regional or minority languages in Europe,[13] or language policy, or policy analysis.[14] Even though I draw on these different fields of specialisation, I do not intend to replicate or summarise what amounts to an enormous body of scholarship; doing justice to all the areas of expertise just listed would amount to writing whole series of volumes. Again, the emphasis is on helping the reader to establish logical and operational connections between strands of scholarship and intellectual perspectives which are pertinent to the formulation of language policies, and to equip him or her with some of the concepts needed for moving confidently between certain theoretical concepts on the one hand, and practical policy evaluation work on the other hand. Practically, this book should help the practitioner confronted with the preparation or evaluation of policy alternatives to *think about language problems in a policy-oriented way*, to ask some of the right questions, to reformulate them in a more precise and targeted way, and to select the appropriate tools to start answering them.

Finally, I wish to point out that this book is not a piece of official literature, and its tone does not necessarily echo the politically cautious formulations found in the official publications produced in conjunction with the Charter, or in similar documents published by various international organisations. The usefulness of this book rests precisely on its ambition to address language policy choices in a way not proposed elsewhere. If nothing else, I therefore hope that readers will find one virtue in this book, namely, the originality of its approach, because it brings together issues and concepts which, to my knowledge, are generally not addressed jointly in the scientific literature or in official documents – necessary though such a combination is.

Emphasis on methods, criteria and principles

A guide to the implementation of the Charter could not confine itself to a catalogue of policies, let alone specific recommendations. It would indeed be unrealistic to suggest specific measures for the implementation of the Charter, because a measure that is appropriate in one case may not be in another case. For example, the type of measures that make sense for the protection and promotion of Sorbian in Germany is likely to be ill-suited to the protection and promotion of Sámi in Finland; policies that have already produced significant achievements in the revitalisation of Welsh in Wales could not simply be replicated in *a priori* comparable cases – such as Breton in Brittany, even though Breton and Welsh are closely related languages, or Scottish Gaelic in Scotland, even though Wales and Scotland are both part of the same larger political entity. The variability of contexts is such that each case is a special case, and that measures have to be tailor-made for each. Accordingly, this book is not a review of the policies already implemented by parties to the Charter.

However, one of the fundamental assumptions made here is that there are some commonalities in the problems encountered by those in charge of formulating (or commenting on) language policies, in particular for the implementation of the Charter. These commonalities can be expressed in terms of methods, criteria and principles.

The core concept underpinning them is, of course, 'choice'. When several options can be envisaged, *methods* are needed to formulate and compare these options in order to make a good choice. These methods necessarily require some *criteria* for comparing options. These specific criteria can be generalised in terms of broad *principles*, which include in particular *effectiveness*, *cost-effectiveness* and *democracy*. This book is largely devoted to the interpretation of these principles and to their application to language policy problems, in the context of the implementation of the Charter. Rather than telling the reader that a particular policy measure would be effective whereas some other would not, I stress the technical approach with which the features of a policy measure can be assessed in terms of effectiveness, cost-effectiveness and democracy. It is then up to decision-makers, in each particular case, to assess the respective advantages and drawbacks of different options.

It is important, however, to caution the reader from the start against a purely mechanistic application of these tools. There is no simple recipe that can be applied to solve all decision-making problems. I am not claiming that a rational policy approach should (or indeed could) be applied in a simplistic way, and yield ready-made solutions. A methodology for decision-making in language policy, however, applying clearly formulated criteria embodied in general principles, can simply be *convenient* and provide useful inputs in the political process through which policy options are discussed and selected. In other words, I view decision-making in a pragmatic perspective, and in this volume, I am primarily concerned with whether a concept is helpful to solve the problems at hand.

Finally, this emphasis on methods and decision criteria does not take place in an ideological vacuum. At all times, my approach is in sympathy with the ideology which lies at the root of the Charter, namely, the recognition that linguistic diversity is an essential element of cultural heritage, in Europe as elsewhere, and that it is appropriate to devote symbolic and material resources in order to nurture it.

Intended readership

At the outset, this volume was primarily intended for one group of readers, namely, civil servants and analysts in charge of designing language policy, in the context of the Charter, and who have to prepare (if not make) a number of decisions. Such decisions start when preparing the formal ratification instrument of their country, in which the list of articles chosen, as well as the languages to which they apply and the regions in which they do, has to be specified (see Chapters 3 and 4). Similar questions also occur at subsequent stages, when actual policy measures have to be selected in order to give substance to the obligations a state undertakes as party to the Charter.

Yet this book is not intended exclusively for this core readership. I hope that the tools it provides can prove relevant for civil servants in charge of language policy independently of the context of the Charter. For example, several states may not, for a variety of reasons, be in a position to ratify the Charter, but yet be willing to adopt a set of measures with similar goals and intended effects.[15] In such cases, much the same problems of selection, design, implementation and evaluation arise.

Whereas decision-makers are likely to be most directly concerned by the topics discussed here, others may also find some use in this book. This may be the case, in particular, for non-governmental organisations, for example if they have to propose or comment on measures proposed by the authorities. Non-governmental organisations representing residents (particularly users of regional or minority languages) may experience the need to evaluate whether a particular measure, which may come under attack from some political parties or segments of majority opinion as 'wasteful', is really as costly as its opponents claim. Organisations confronted with this type of questions are likely to find some useful tools in Chapters 6 and 7. Another group of actors who may find this volume useful is made up of officers in international organisations or large non-governmental organisations, who are often called upon to advise national, regional and local authorities on education policy matters, in which language issues often play a major role.

Finally, this book attempts to relate different strands of scholarship in a targeted way, and it proposes some novel applications of policy evaluation tools to language policy questions. It contains constant references to the work of others, underlining, as the case may be, convergence or divergence, and constantly engaging in a form of dialogue with other scholars. I therefore hope that some scholars will also find some of the following chapters useful.

More generally, because language issues are gaining prominence as an increasingly important area of intervention by the state, and hence as a relevant domain of public policy, it is also appropriate to facilitate access to the debates on language policy for the general public. This is, after all, a requirement of democracy – an issue discussed in Chapter 8, and this book hopes to make a relevant contribution in this area as well.

Preparing a fully-fledged national policy plan for the implementation of the European Charter for Regional or Minority Languages (and also, at a previous stage, in the drafting of a ratification instrument) is, undoubtedly, a major undertaking. Commenting on governmental proposals in this field can be equally demanding. Such tasks requires those who perform them to move between five levels, namely the text of the Charter itself; the legal approach to the implementation of such instruments; the organising concepts usually developed by political scientists and sociologists; a number of core sociolinguistic issues (in particular, those related to minority language promotion); and some basic principles of policy analysis. Building bridges between these levels, or combining them, certainly is a prerequisite for the design of 'good policies'. This book aims at helping readers devise their own combination, before applying it to the particular case or cases of concern to them.

Structure

This book is organised in four parts and 10 chapters.

This introductory chapter, together with Chapter 2, constitutes the first part of the book. Chapter 2 addresses the question of what *language policy* is. I start out from the idea that, contrary to what is often assumed, language policy is certainly about language, but that many of the fundamental questions it raises, particularly the modalities of intervention, must be grounded not so much in the language disciplines as in policy analysis.

Part II contains Chapters 3 and 4 and is devoted to the *European Charter for Regional or Minority Languages*. Chapter 3 presents the history and main features of the Charter. The Charter does not only represent the practical context within which we wish to address language policy issues; it also constitutes, in its own right, a remarkably interesting instrument, and a significant step forward in the logic underpinning standard-setting.[16]

Chapter 4 addresses a range of practical problems, including some that authorities intending to sign the Charter are likely to encounter already before the text is ratified by their country. How can consensus between different actors be built? How can different ministries (many of which will, at some stage, need to get involved in the implementation of new policy measures resulting from the adoption of the Charter) co-operate efficiently? How should information circulate between various *tiers* of governments (national, regional, local)? How can authorities and NGOs collaborate? This chapter also discusses the practical questions arising in the monitoring mechanism required by the Charter. What are the goals pursued by this monitoring? How does it make the Charter different from other instruments? What precise requirements in terms of information gathering and sharing does it entail? How can all these tasks be co-ordinated efficiently? The answers to these points will be illustrated by elements of experience acquired in recent years.[17]

Part III, which moves on to applications, makes up most of the rest of the book. Chapter 5 discusses the nature of *policy*, as distinct from both *political* issues (in which political debate results in some political choices being made) and *legal* issues (which emphasise the codification of norms and their compatibility with other norms). Policy is, in a sense, more focused on technical questions and is concerned with the practical results of the measures adopted. This paves the way for a critical discussion of the notion of 'good policy' (or 'good practice', or 'best practice', etc.), and to the selection of criteria that can give substance to such worthy goals. Although the criteria adopted here do not exhaust the list of those that can be applied, there are strong grounds for seeing them as particularly relevant: they are 'effectiveness', 'cost-effectiveness' and 'democracy'.

Chapters 6 through 8 are devoted to a closer examination of these criteria, as well as to an introduction to the issue of cost identification and measurement in language policies. In both chapters, the issues are illustrated by examples for expository clarity. Chapter 6 presents the notion of effectiveness, and its application to language policies, building on the analytical framework of Chapter 2. Chapter 7 examines costs and cost-effectiveness, addressing some more technical points of identification and measurement – occasionally using hypothetical figures for the sake of the example. Chapter 8 is much shorter, and is devoted to a brief – yet, in my opinion, essential – discussion of the role of democracy, particularly participatory democracy, in policy choice. Finally, Chapter 9 is entirely devoted to a 'walk-through' example of language policy evaluation, providing, as it were, a check-list of issues that language planners will usually need to address. The type of policy examined in this chapter deals with the teaching of (or in) a regional or minority language.

Part IV contains only one chapter (Chapter 10). It offers a general conclusion, recalling the essentials of this book and raising several related issues, such as the function of language planning bodies.

It is followed by an Appendix with some useful background material, in particular the text of the Charter and corresponding 'Explanatory Notes', and a list of relevant internet resources.

It is my hope that this book may constitute a useful tool for those, in national, regional, or local administrations, non-governmental organisations, international organisations, as well as in some specialised research or advisory bodies, who are interested in the protection and promotion of regional or minority languages in Europe.

Notes

1. This is not be confused with the legal notion of 'positive law', which implies that a particular rule derives its existence from an act of creation which took place in history, by competent authorities, and may be perceived objectively (*Encyclopaedia of Public International Law*: 1073). The implied concept of 'positivity' is therefore deeply different from that derived from the epistemology of the social sciences which I use in this chapter.
2. Welfare theory is associated with many of the most prestigious names in economics. It is often criticised by non-economists who confuse it with 'utilitarianism' – actually, with a narrow version of utilitarianism that does not reflect the true import of the theory. Presentations of welfare theory can be found in public economics textbooks (e.g. Zajac, 1995; Cullis and Jones, 1998); for a non-technical introduction to the basic concepts, see e.g. Simonnot (1998).
3. Early calls for a structured evaluation of interventions on language can be found in Rubin and Jernudd (1971), Jernudd (1983) or Rubin (1983); this is echoed in the more recent literature on language policy; see for example Cooper (1989, 87 ff.), Falcon (1995), Ó Riagáin (1995) or Kaplan and Baldauf (1997: Chaps 4 and 6).
4. On the *Framework Convention*, see e.g. Estébanez and Gál (1999) or Benoît-Rohmer (1999).

5. In a 1999 report, the HCNM defines his involvement in 'linguistic-related issues as part of his conflict-prevention mandate' (HCNM, 1999). In the same way, the explanatory note of the *Hague Recommendations Regarding the Education Rights of National Minorities* (1996), indicates that '[...] the issue of inter-group/inter-ethnic cohabitation and harmony is also of vital importance to their internal stability. Such cohabitation and harmony is also an important factor in the preservation of regional peace and security'; see also the HCNM's *Oslo Recommendations Regarding the Linguistic Rights of National Minorities* (1998), and the *Lund Recommendations on the Effective Participation of National Minorities in Public Life* (1999). The Hague and Oslo recommendations were elaborated under the auspices of the Foundation for Inter-Ethnic Relations, which at the time served as the analysis unit of the Office of the HCNM.

6. Grin (2003).

7. At most, the *Explanatory Report* of the Charter presents provisions on 'trans-frontier exchanges' (Art. 14) as a factor of mutual understanding.

8. On the differences between the Charter and the Framework Convention, see e.g. Albanese (1999) or Dunbar (2001).

9. As a minimal requirement under 8.1.a.iii, where there is a request for this. If the state has no direct competence in this area, it undertakes to favour and/or encourage the provision of pre-school education in the regional or minority languages concerned.

10. See Council of Europe (1998a, 1999); what I have referred to above as the 'core social science' perspective remains, however, relatively absent from the debate specifically focusing the Charter.

11. On (minority) language rights, see e.g. Edwards (1994a), Blumentwitz (1996), de Varennes (1996), Henrard (2000) or May (2000, 2001); Ó Riagáin (1998) contains a selection of the most important international legal texts in this area.

12. See e.g. Taylor (1992); Kymlicka (1995a,b); Benhabib (1996); Patten (2002).

13. For an overview of regional and minority languages in Europe, see e.g. Sanguin (1993), Nelde, Strubell and Williams (1995), Baggioni (1997) or Breathnach (1998).

14. References in these latter two areas of research are provided in the next chapter.

15. At the time of writing, this is precisely the logic adopted by France, according to declarations by its Minister of Education (see *Libération*, Thursday 26 April 2001, p. 18).

16. This chapter was contributed by Dónall Ó Riagáin, former Secretary General of the European Bureau for Lesser Used Languages.

17. This chapter was contributed by Regina Jensdóttir, Administrator at Directorate General I (Legal Affairs) of the Council of Europe.

2
Language Policy

A note on terminology

Policies for the promotion of regional or minority languages are highly complex. Most of the time, they also raise delicate political issues. For both reasons, it is important to clarify at the outset a few points of terminology. Further terminological points will be addressed later on, as the core analytical concepts are introduced progressively.

Language, minority, territory

The first point has to do with the type of languages to which we are referring. The scholarly literature generally refers to 'minority languages'. However, there is nothing automatic about the concept of minority; rather, the notion of minority is socially constructed, just as the ascription to any given group to the status of 'minority', is a political process. Language is undoubtedly one of those traits with respect to which a person may be 'in the majority' or 'in a minority', but whether this trait matters or not, the extent to which it actually shapes a person's perception of himself or the way in which he is perceived by others is a distinct question. This book therefore adopts, a *constructionist* (as opposed to *essentialist*) view of 'minority', and of the 'ethnicity' that may be used as its defining feature.[1]

However, much of the scholarly and political debate over what a minority actually is revolves around more elusive concepts than language, in particular 'ethnicity' or 'culture', and despite the complexity of 'language', it is a reasonably identifiable aspect of human experience. Therefore, specialists in language policy interested in a linguistic minority can by and large apply most variants of the standard definition of 'minority'. The latter is often derived from the definition developed in 1979 by Francesco Capotorti for the United Nations:

> A group numerically inferior to the rest of the population of a State, in a non-dominant position, whose members – being nationals of the State – possess ethnic, religious, or linguistic characteristics differing from those of the rest of the population and show, if only implicitly, a sense of solidarity, directed towards preserving their culture, traditions, religion or language (Capotorti, 1991).

Some of the literature avoids the word 'minority', and hence the expression 'minority language'. Preference is given instead to the adjective 'regional', which matches categories normally used in the political debate (for example in the French case). Clearly, this choice of terms harks back to the debate over the more or less 'essential' nature of traits that can be used to define a group: referring to a 'region' stresses a geographical association, yet defuses a cultural, possibly more essentialist one. Other expressions are also used in the European political arena. The term 'lesser-used languages' has been coined in the context of the institutions of the European Union, chiefly in order to avoid the term 'minority', which would not have been to the liking of member states that recognise no minorities, autochthonous or otherwise, among their citizens; the term 'regional', however, would not have been adequate to take account of non-regional languages, such as Yiddish or Romani.

Because this book is mainly concerned with the implementation of the Charter, I shall henceforth use the terminology of the latter, and refer to *regional or minority languages*, occasionally abbreviated to 'RMLs' for the sake of brevity. The definition of such languages is provided in Article 1 of the Charter, reproduced below:

a 'regional or minority languages' means languages that are:

i traditionally used within a given territory of a State by nationals of that State who form a group numerically smaller than the rest of the State's population; and

ii different from the official language(s) of that State;

it does not include either dialects of the official language(s) of the State or the languages of migrants;

The notion of territory, which is centrally important in the Charter, is then defined as follows in the second part of Article 1:

b 'territory in which the regional or minority language is used' means the geographical area in which the said language is the mode of expression of a number of people justifying the adoption of the various protective and promotional measures provided for in this Charter;

This allows for the following definition of 'non-territorial languages', found in the third part of Article 1:

c 'non-territorial languages' means languages used by nationals of the State which differ from the language or languages used by the rest of the State's population but which, although traditionally used within the territory of the State, cannot be identified with a particular area thereof.

The same definitions and criteria will apply hereafter, and for the purposes of this text, the expression of 'regional or minority languages' will include non-territorial languages.

Policy

Some ambiguities often surround the meaning of the term policy; to some extent, these ambiguities can be traced back to the fact that the usual meaning of the term varies from one discipline to another. For some, a 'policy' refers to the intentions of the state (or other actor), and therefore directly reflects its ideological choices. For example, a state may have a *policy* to assimilate immigrants linguistically and culturally, while another state may have a *policy* to encourage communities to cultivate their specific character; another example is a state's 'foreign policy'.

In this book, 'policy' is used in a narrower, more technical sense, and it is distinct from the notion of 'politics' (although, of course, any policy reflects political options), and much closer to the notion of 'measures'. For example, *after* a political choice has been made to fund a minority-language television channel, 'policy *A*' could be to set up a fully state-run authority to provide this service, while 'policy *B*' could be to entrust provision of the service to a private company (following a call for tender imposing certain specifications). Further distinctions can be made: for example, within a broad 'policy *A*', 'policy *A1*' could imply full state financing through an annual grant, whereas 'policy *A2*' could imply a smaller grant but allow the television channel to generate revenue through advertising or re-selling of previously aired programmes, etc. Hence, the word 'policy' as used here chiefly refers to the *way* in which a particular goal is being pursued, rather than to the goal itself.

The notion of 'policy' as defined here need not imply a purely mechanistic or technocratic process. Such a process would be one in which a 'problem' is duly sanitised and processed through the following stages: the issue is somehow abstracted from its context, then recast in terms of 'rational goals' and 'objective constraints'; a set of policy options is formulated; the 'best' one is chosen, and the corresponding legal texts and administrative procedures adopted. In actual practice, the preconceptions, motivations and interests of various groups of actors, including the state, exert a determining influence on the policy process. As I define it here, the function of policy analysis, in a democratic setting, is not chiefly to provide an account of this complex web of factors, but to focus on more technical questions which arise quite independently of those factors. The function of policy analysis, therefore, it first and foremost to provide analysis and information that contributes to the public debate, while bringing a certain degree of transparency and analytical rigour into it, particularly in spelling out the precise implications of different policy options. This book was written with this function in mind. I shall return in greater detail to the notions of 'public policy' and 'policy analysis' in Chapter 2.

Positive v. normative

The adjective 'normative' has already been used on several occasions in the introduction. It is therefore useful to recall that the distinction between 'positive' and 'normative', which is a time-honoured one in the social sciences. It has often come under attack, for a number of epistemological reasons, largely because the demarcation between what is 'positive' and what is 'normative' is not an absolute, and therefore not a fully dependable one. However, despite the limitations of this distinction, it is still a convenient one for reflecting on the discourse, theory and practice of language policy.

A *normative* analysis is chiefly concerned with what *should be*. A typical theme for normative discourse is social justice: for example, a greater or lesser extent of income redistribution can be considered 'more just' than another, as a result of moral and political preferences. Legal standards are an example of an inherently normative discourse, because they formulate 'what should be' – as a result of the preferences of a particular society at a particular point in time. Normative discourse, in fact, can take different forms. In a standard form of normative discourse, specific norms are accepted as such – for example, an absolute right to use one's language with the authorities, irrespective of the size of the language group to which one belongs. These norms are then taken as a starting point to evaluate a real situation, such as the extent to which the language rights enjoyed by a particular group are adequate, or to identify aspects of reality (such as patent violations of rights) that require correction. The 'linguistic human rights' perspective exemplifies this approach, and claims that certain language-related rights should be included in the list of universal human rights.[2]

A *positive* analysis, by contrast, does not ask whether one option is philosophically or morally superior to another, or for what reasons; its aim, rather, is to keep moral issues at bay and to understand *how* processes actually operate. To a large extent, positive analysis will endeavour to clarify how X affects Y, and if the influence of X on Y is predicated on a set of particular conditions C_1, C_2 and C_3. Clearly, positive analysis is a prerequisite for effective intervention on social reality, where the goals of such intervention reflect normative choices. Positive analysis can then be used to rank-order policy options by elucidating their outcomes – the desirability of the latter remaining, however, a normative question. This can help to establish that some are 'better' than others, but *only* in terms of their capacity to achieve goals set exogenously – that is, outside of the policy analysis process.

The divides between positive and normative discourse are not always clear. For example, it is perfectly possible to enter a positive debate over competing normative judgements. This type of linkage is provided by normative political theory (or political philosophy), where the emphasis is on the critical examination of the criteria on the basis of which certain norms can be considered valid, or superior to others, producing a positive analysis of normative principles.[3] It must also be pointed out that all positive analyses take place in a context defined by the analyst's more or less conscious normative choices. This also applies to this book, which is why my preferences must be stated clearly.

The ideological view running through this volume is that the long-term preservation of regional or minority languages is a good thing in itself. Therefore, I endorse the protection and promotion of regional or minority languages as an appropriate social and political goal. This personal view fully converges with the philosophy exposed in the Preamble of the Charter (see below).

This being clear, this book attempts to identify and clarify the *positive* criteria which can be called upon to conclude that some measures are better able to reach certain goals under certain conditions. The choice of criteria itself is not, of course, a strictly technical question, and is therefore not devoid of ideology. The very fact that it cannot be lies at the root of some of the criticism addressed at the distinction between 'positive' and 'normative'. Yet once some criteria are agreed upon, positive analysis can take precedence over normative analysis. For example, let us *assume* that cost-effectiveness has been acknowledged as one appropriate criterion (among others), meaning that all other things being equal, it is better to achieve a certain goal by spending a small amount than by spending a large amount of money. The evaluation of the amounts spent under policy *A* and under policy *B*, if both deliver more or less the same result, is a *positive* question.

Language maintenance: why bother?

The question is often raised of why anybody (or society as a whole, for that matter) should be concerned with the maintenance of regional or minority languages. This is a perfectly valid question, and one which must lie at the root of any public policy perspective on language revitalisation. In this context, the question 'why bother?' was used, somewhat provocatively, as the title of a paper discussing aboriginal languages in Australia.[4]

Although this question is not central to us here, it is useful, before moving on to evaluative considerations, to discuss it briefly in order to clarify the role and position of this book with respect to leading questions in language policy. Clearly, the types of justifications for language maintenance are linked to the distinction between the positive and the normative just discussed. However, this distinction captures only some aspects of the issue.

Several responses can be offered to the question 'why bother?' and it is convenient to arrange them in three categories: those based on moral considerations, those based on welfare considerations, and a third category that bridges the preceding two. Of course, the various types of justification can be arranged in a different way. The break-down proposed here, however, converges with comparable delimitations between families of academic discourse, as well as with the motivations expressed by political actors, whether as grassroots activists, as officers of international organisations, or members of the civil service.

Both the moral and the welfare-based perspectives harbour two types of arguments. The standard legal discourse falls under this category, in the sense that it essentially amounts to an interpretative commentary on norms – which happen to be enshrined in international legal instruments and in national or regional legislation. In this case, engaging in minority language protection and promotion will generally be justified by the notion there exists a right (which may be realised in different ways) to 'live' in one's own language. The extent of those rights is a matter for debate, and the subjects of those rights are the members of the community who traditionally used this language. The 'linguistic human rights' discourse mentioned earlier simply asserts that this right is very far-reaching (more far-reaching, at any rate, than is usually conceded by commentators using strictly legal arguments), and that it ought to be recognised as a basic human right.

The welfare-based argument, by contrast, does not assign any greater moral worth to a course of action with respect to another. As already pointed out in the very first section of this book, what matters in a welfare-based argument is whether a certain policy promises to deliver more 'welfare' to society as a whole. Putting it differently, the emphasis of the welfare-based argument is not on whether something is morally 'good' or 'bad', but on whether resources are appropriately allocated. The test of an 'appropriate' allocation of resources is whether society is better off as a result of a policy. In theory, the allocation of resources is satisfactory if and only if there is no way to improve the lot of one person in society without, at the same time, making another member of society worse off.[5]

Of course, all policies, in that they modify reality, create winners and losers. The winners are those who benefit from the policy measures (like museum goers in the case of public financing of the fine arts, or minority language speakers in the case of public financing of minority language protection). The losers may be those who actually dislike art or resent the existence, let alone the vitality, of minority languages. Let us put aside the question of the extent to which such dislikes ought to be factored in as relevant elements of policy evaluation. Many people would agree that, for example, racial prejudice should not be recognised as a legitimate dimension of the evaluation of an urban development policy that aims to reduce racial segregation. A more common realisation of the situation of loser is simply that of a taxpayer who has to contribute to the financing of a public service that she does not use. This is the case for taxpayers without dependent children, whose tax bill contributes to the financing of education, or for taxpayers who never go to the opera, although the opera receives state subsidies. In a welfare-based argument, the question is whether the winners, who stand to gain from a policy, can compensate the losers and still be better off. This point remains very under-researched in language policy.

In a welfare-based argument, the protection and promotion of minority language maintenance will then be justified on the grounds that it improves society's lot (taking account, at least in theory, of compensations paid by winners to losers), very much as society may be better off if it devotes some resources to other public policies in fields as diverse as education, transport, or the environment. In other words, if one questions the appropriateness of minority language promotion, one should also, in the same terms, question the appropriateness of devoting social resources to various forms of regulation affecting, say, urban development, or to publicly-maintained commodities such as art museums or opera houses.

Consequently, whether minority languages should be protected and promoted is, in a welfare-based perspective, an empirical question. At this time, there is no empirical evidence to the effect that society's welfare is higher or lower, all other things being equal, when minority languages are protected and promoted or not. In fact, given the extraordinary complexity of the issues at hand, it is doubtful that a general proof could be provided either way, and it is more reasonable to cobble together a coherent view of the matter by combining various strands of evidence. These strands of evidence, in turn, are based on the evaluation of various aspects of linguistic diversity. What can be said, at this time, is that converging circumstantial evidence suggests that individuals derive considerable market and non-market value from speaking many languages (that is, from being multilingual). It does not automatically follow, however, that multilingual societies are better off, since value estimated at the individual level (particularly the market component of this value) usually rests on the premise that the societies they live in are multilingual in the first place. However, the existence of non-market values alone points to a strong parallel between linguistic diversity on the one hand, and biophysical diversity on the other hand, not in terms of their intrinsic nature, but in terms of their contribution to welfare.

Putting it more simply, diversity seems to be positively, rather than negatively, correlated with welfare: people seem to enjoy diversity, at least as long as the costs associated with it do not become excessive. On this count, available evidence indicates that the monetary costs of maintaining diversity are remarkably modest.[6] The 'peace and security' type of argument briefly mentioned earlier is also relevant in this context: devoting resources to the protection and promotion of minority cultures may help to stave off political crises whose cost would be considerably higher than that of the policies considered.

Therefore, there are strong grounds to suppose that protecting and promoting regional or minority languages is a sound idea from a welfare standpoint, not even taking into consideration any moral argument. This being said, this question is not a central one for this book. The reason for this is that we are placing ourselves in the context of the Charter, and focusing on its implementation. The very fact that the Charter has been adopted by a given country as the result of a political process, and that attention can now turn to its implementation, logically presupposes that the conclusion has been reached earlier that, *for whatever reasons*, protecting and promoting regional or minority languages was a good thing. It is not the function of a book such as this to call this political choice into question. We shall now proceed on this assumption and move on to the analysis of a core concept for the implementation of the Charter, namely, language policy.

What is language policy?

Language policy, or language planning, is the field of theoretical and empirical knowledge that combines the most directly useful tools for the implementation of the Charter. Let us therefore begin by discussing its nature and scope. As a field of inquiry and academic specialisation, language policy or planning has progressively acquired an identity of its own over a long period of time. Although it would be futile to look for a precise date for its birth,[7] it is a reasonable approximation to say that it emerged around the early 1970s. The recognition of language planning as a type of public policy, with the corresponding methodological requirements, is, however, an aspect that has remained in the background since then, because much of the work of language planning specialists has focused on the linguistic or sociolinguistics dimensions of policy intervention, rather than on the macro-level issues of policy choice. To the extent that it places the emphasis on this latter type of question, this book addresses a relatively less explored side of language policy and planning.

A fully-fledged account of language policy and planning, however, would take us too far. Only selected aspects of the field will be discussed here, and recast in accordance with the aims of this book. Those looking for an in-depth treatment of language policy will find suggestions for further reading in the notes.

Language politics, policy or planning?

A distinction is often made between 'language policy' and 'language planning'. This distinction exists not just in English, but also in, for example, German and French,[8] even if the semantic differences between terms are not necessarily the same in each of these languages – or even between authors.

Generally (although this is a very long way from being an absolute rule), 'language policy' tends to be somewhat broader than 'language planning' and to be located at a more general or macro level. Relatedly, 'language planning' tends to emphasise intervention on a language itself (for example, spelling reform and terminological development). By contrast, 'language policy' tends to emphasise intervention regarding the position of a language *vis-à-vis* other languages (for example, the choice of a certain language, or of a set of languages, as official languages, or as languages that can be used to offer or to access public services). However, there is considerable overlap between those terms, which means that the actual importance of the distinction between them should not be overestimated. In what follows, I will normally use the expression 'language policy', which is used by many as a more broadly encompassing term, to denote all forms of intervention on language. A formal definition will be provided momentarily.

Nonetheless, it remains useful to have the vocabulary for distinguishing between different levels of intervention, particularly if the difference has a generally clear substantive interpretation. A convenient distinction, credited to Kloss (1969), is one often made between 'language corpus' and 'language status', and we shall use it here as well. Language corpus refers to the language itself (including for example the choice of a writing system, or spelling reform), while status refers to the relative position of a language (for example, which language or set of languages may be used in which situation). Of course, the boundary between corpus and status planning is often blurred, as when decisions have to be made regarding a choice of standard among competing dialectal variants of what is generally considered one and the same language.[9] A variant of this problem is reflected in the fact that the scope of the real-world processes referred to by either term can vary. For example, status planning is often equated with the problem of choosing a language (for example, in the case of a newly independent country in a process of decolonisation) and then making sure that the choice sticks.

It is helpful, therefore, to take the notion of 'status' in a broad sense, and to use it to refer not only to the strictly legal position of a language, but also to its social, political and economical position. The reason for taking this broad view of language status is that the legal recognition of a language denotes only a small part of the real position of a language – and often not the most important part. Consider for example the case of Irish: although it is 'as the national language ... the first official language' of the Republic, according to Article 8 of the 1937 Constitution, its decline has continued unabated since the establishment of the

Irish state, and for well over 60 years afterwards; it is only with recent initiatives addressing its social and economic role that the actual vitality and visibility of the language have shown genuine signs of improvement.[10]

Policy intervention can therefore equally well target the corpus of a language or its status *vis-à-vis* other languages. However, there is little doubt that many, or even most forms of corpus intervention are only a means towards status improvement. Adopting a writing system is a precondition for using the language in writing, and writing the language seriously enhances its vitality and hence its long-term survival prospects.[11]

Much more refined distinctions between types of intervention on language can be found in the literature. However, for the most part, they are derived from the case-specific description of various settings. For example, distinctions can be made between 'lexical modernisation', 'language standardisation', 'terminological unification', and so on. The resulting categories are therefore relevant with respect to the linguistic techniques that have to be used to implement the policy, but somewhat less from a policy analysis standpoint, and they need not be discussed further here.[12]

Another distinction worth discussing (and which has already been addressed in the preceding chapter) is between 'policy' and 'politics'.

Language matters are, of course, eminently political, in the sense that they raise issues of power, and the conflicting interests of different social actors often crystallise around language issues. This book, however, is not about the *politics* of language. There is no doubt that these political dimensions have crucial importance and enjoy given considerable visibility through the political process. This occurs in parliamentary debates over the status to be accorded to minority languages in the national legislation of certain states,[13] or over the decision to ratify the Charter – or not.[14] Issues of language politics and the role of ideology in policy discussions have also given rise to a considerable amount of literature.[15] My focus, however, is clearly on the evaluation of policy measures 'downstream' from the political debate.

The evaluation of policy measures is relevant to three types of situations.

1. The first occurs when major orientations have already been adopted in the political debate 'upstream', and attention must then be shifted to the implementation of those orientations through specific measures.

2. The second situation arises when social actors (including various interest groups, parliamentarians, and of course the authorities) seek to assess beforehand the respective advantages and drawbacks of policy alternatives that could be adopted if (for example) the Charter were signed and ratified. They would normally wish to use this type of knowledge to define their own political position on language matters, or win over other actors to their position. In both of the situations just described, policies are analysed *ex ante*, because they have not been put into place or implemented yet.

3. However, it often necessary to examine them *ex post*, that is, to examine the effects of existing policies; this is the third case in which policy evaluation is useful. We shall return later to the distinction between *ex ante* and *ex post* evaluations.

A definition of language policy

A formal and sociolinguistically based definition of language policy can of course be derived from the observation of various forms of language policy across time and space, or from a more analytical review of the functions of language in society. There is no need to reopen this discussion, which has already been extensively covered by others in primers on language policy or planning,[16] in a growing number of scholarly journals,[17] or in an expanding range of edited volumes, or monographs adopting a more specific angle on language planning issues.[18] Without further ado, I shall therefore adopt the following definition of language policy, which stresses is public policy character:

> Language policy is a systematic, rational, theory-based effort at the societal level to modify the linguistic environment with a view to increasing aggregate welfare. It is typically conducted by official bodies or their surrogates and aimed at part or all of the population living under their jurisdiction.[19]

This definition is broader than what is often found in the sociolinguistic literature. Let us briefly clarify the key notions used in it.

1. 'Systematic' means that language policy ought to be organised with respect to a certain method, aiming at clearly defined goals. 'Rational' refers to the logical links between means and ends, and implies that the former are judiciously applied to achieve the latter. It follows that policy recommendations must be based on reasoned arguments.

'Theory-based' suggests that language policy must rest on a scientific analysis of reality and of the causal relationships through which reality can be modified by policy.

2. This definition points out that language policy takes place 'at the societal level'. This serves to place a clear emphasis on language policy as a form of public policy under the responsibility of the state. It is therefore distinct from, say 'corporate language policy', which refers to choices made by organisations such as a multinational company – for example, to use language X or Y for internal communication; however, the state may take measures requiring firms to use certain languages or providing them with incentives to do so, as in the well-known case of Quebec.

3. According to this definition, language policy is intended to modify our 'linguistic environment'. The underlying idea is that all language policy measures contribute, in a big or a small way, to modify the status of the various languages in society, and therefore influence essential features of the environment in which we live. Within limits, a parallel can be made with physical and biological features (such as climate, the degree of pollution, the type and extent of urban development, etc.). Taken together, these features characterise our bio-physical environment. In the same way, the relative position (status) of different languages characterises our *linguistic environment* – the latter is therefore the object of language policy, through interventions in fields as diverse as education, media, and so on. The concept of linguistic environment implies no biologising parallel, and in fact steers clear away from it. The parallels arise not between the intrinsic nature of these two broad dimensions of our environment, but between the rationale for intervention in both.[20]

4. The goal of language policy as defined here is to 'increase welfare'. This notion requires commentary at two distinct levels. First, it reflects an important methodological and ideological choice, which is shared by the overwhelming majority of the policy analysis literature. It is encapsulated in the notion that no societal objective – apart from the most general one of 'welfare' is intrinsically superior than any other, and that there is no *a priori* list of the elements that should be considered as conducive to welfare. Even if policy measures cannot increase welfare directly, they can create, maintain and develop conditions necessary for welfare to be higher than it would have been in the absence of those measures. A corollary of this principle is that it is not the role of the policy-makers to impose preferences on the members of their constituency. If nothing can be said to be good or

bad in the absolute, it is up to the political process to allow for the expression of personal preferences, and to derive policy choices from the aggregation of these preferences. This perspective is, of course, in fundamental agreement with the principles of liberal political philosophy.[21]

5. Using the concept of welfare as a goal and evaluation criterion for policy interventions is also fully in keeping with the spirit of the Charter. Whereas numerous interventions in the area of minorities are inspired by a concern for human rights or minority rights, this is not the prime objective of the Charter. The Charter does recognise, in its Preamble, a 'right to use a regional or minority language in private and public life'. However, the concept of 'rights' is not central to the Charter, whose main goal is to preserve and develop regional and minority languages in order to guarantee Europe's linguistic diversity in the long run. This, of course, raises the question of why such a goal is worth subscribing to, apart from considerations of human rights or minority rights. The answer, quite simply, is that well-being (or 'welfare') is likely to be higher if Europe remains linguistically diverse than if it becomes linguistically uniform – or, to use a notion just introduced, that a higher quality of life obtains if a diverse linguistic environment is preserved, instead of being eroded and replaced by a monolithic, unilingual one.[22,23]

6. Finally, the definition above stresses the role of 'official bodies'. This harks back to the specific responsibility of the state, which is discussed in the following section, and then again, from a different angle, in Chapter 8.

It is important to clarify two points regarding the status of 'ideology' in this representation of language policy. My focus on the workings of language policy *after* political decisions have been made implies that ideology is also taken as a contextual question. Ideology is an ingredient in the political debate, and through the latter, in language policy; as such, it is located 'upstream' from the latter. Although I focus on technical questions that generally arise independently of the ideologies that have inspired or at least influenced policy orientations, I am not assuming that there is an unequivocal relationship between ideologies and policies. In fact, opposing ideologies can give rise to converging policy orientations, just like one ideology can result in contrasted policy recommendations.[24]

The approach to language policy adopted here, therefore, in no way denies the role of power relationships at the various stages of selection, design, and implementation. They are in fact crucial to the understanding of what is done, and to the identification of what can be done, in a given context, for the protection and promotion of a regional or minority language. It is important to point out, however, that the fact that the elucidation of such power relationships is not the topic of this book does not imply that they are forgotten.[25]

A word must also be said of the related issue of the historical dimension of language planning.[26] My emphasis on intentionality, on the links between cause and effect, and on the relationship between resources and costs does not imply any kind of 'a-historical' perspective on language policy. Quite the contrary, it should be clear that it is not possible to develop good policies without a sound understanding of historical circumstances. However, historical circumstances are, by nature, case-specific, or even idiosyncratic. It follows that in a general treatment of language policy we must eschew these questions, while bearing in mind that they take paramount importance in actual application.[27]

Attempts have been made to systematise the way in which case-specific (often 'historical') circumstances can be accounted for in the *ex post* analysis of the success or failure of language policies. The corresponding construct is that that of 'success conditions', which can be derived from the observation of existing policy interventions. Owing to the intrinsically inferential character of these conditions, they are not suited to an analysis that aims at a higher level of generality, and will not be discussed further in this book.[28]

Language policy and the role of the state

It is generally accepted that it is incumbent on states, which are responsible for maintaining the rule of law, to guarantee certain standards in terms of minority rights. Hence, if my argument were cast in the logic of language rights, this question would not need to be raised. However, this book focuses on the implementation of the Charter, and the Charter's main concern, rather than language rights or human rights, is the preservation of linguistic diversity as a source of welfare. This raises afresh the question of why the state should be involved.

One could indeed argue, following a standard 'laisser-faire' ideology, that government should not regulate language matters at all. In a public policy perspective, such an approach would, however, require the assumption that maximum welfare will proceed from the uncoordinated actions of people, whether these are individuals, firms, or third-sector organisations. Consequently, the 'production' of diversity would be left over to market mechanisms. The crucial question, then, is whether the unregulated interplay of these mechanisms (or, turning the terminology around, 'market regulation') will actually ensure that the 'right' amount of diversity is 'produced'.

Although such a view is marginal among specialists, there is no lack, among politicians or media pundits, of persons who advocate allowing market mechanisms to regulate the 'production' of diversity. The actual motivations behind such a stance are probably more complex than their advocates let on. However, strong resistance to the notion that the state should intervene on behalf of regional and minority languages is often expressed, not only on the grounds that language use is a private matter, but also on the grounds that taxpayers' money (out of general tax revenue levied on the *entire* population) should not be spent on minority language promotion (which is assumed to benefit to a small subset of the population).[29] This view is probably mistaken, and there are strong analytical reasons for state intervention – unless one were to argue that linguistic diversity is a bad thing in itself.

Let us recall, as a starting point, that in the spirit of the Charter, the preservation of diversity, including of minority languages as key elements of diversity, is regarded as a worthwhile goal. As noted earlier, such goal-setting takes place in the political arena; therefore, it is not the role of the policy-maker to dispute the goals set as the result of a democratic political process. The question, rather, is *how* these goals can be achieved. If the free market could be seen as an appropriate mechanism whereby all of society's goals could always be reached and maximum aggregate welfare delivered, there would be no grounds for state intervention. Everything should be left to private initiative; this is the stance of extreme libertarians, often associated with the names of Nozick in political philosophy, or Friedman in economics. The underlying adjustment mechanism, based on the neo-classical economic model of behaviour, runs as follows: if 'not enough' of something is produced, its price rises. Producers will then have an incentive to respond by increasing output to the desired level, while the rise in price simultaneously discourages some consumers. Conversely, if 'too much' of something is being produced, its price will drop, meaning that more of the good will be absorbed by consumers, while some producers will simply turn away from a production line that no longer generates sufficient profits.

The neo-classical market model is a fairly credible line of argument for 'simple' goods such as tomatoes, television sets or car tyres. However, its relevance is dubious (or at least severely limited) in the case of more complex commodities such as education, health, the environment – and, of course, languages as components of our linguistic environment.

Even mainstream economics acknowledges that there are some cases where the market is not enough. These cases are known as 'market failure'. When there is 'market failure', the unregulated interplay of supply and demand results in an inappropriate level of production of some commodity, where 'inappropriate' can mean 'too little' or 'too much'. In theory, there are essentially six sources of market failure:[30]

1. insufficient information, which prevents economic agents (producers and consumers) from making the right decisions in terms of output, purchases, lending and borrowing;
2. high transaction costs, which move agents *not* to do something that would eventually have been economically beneficial;
3. the fact that some markets cannot exist (for example, yet-unborn generations cannot be present on today's oil market to express their valuation of this non-renewable resource);
4. the existence of 'market structure imperfections' such as monopolies and oligopolies;
5. the presence of 'externalities', that is, of a situation where the behaviour of one agent affects (positively or negatively) the position of another agent, without the gain or loss so created giving rise to a corresponding compensation;
6. the existence of so-called 'public goods', which have (in the 'pure' textbook case) two main characteristics described below: non-rival consumption and impossibility of exclusion.

Therefore, if linguistic diversity is a good, and if 'market failure' occurs in its production, then state intervention is justified in terms of economic theory, more specifically in terms of its application in public policy.

In the case of linguistic diversity, market failure certainly emerges through more than one of these six channels. In fact, a strong case can be made that all six sources of market failure are present. Furthermore, these manifestations of market failure are often inter-connected: public goods are typically under-supplied by market forces, because they give rise to externalities. Hence, if languages present some of the characteristics of public goods, then at least two types of market failure arise in the case of linguistic diversity, namely types (5) and (6). In fact, what may be analytically the most fundamental characteristic of diversity (and of the languages that make up this diversity), is precisely the fact that it presents the decisive characteristics of a 'public good'.

Linguistic diversity has many features in common with biodiversity, which is generally recognised as type of public good. A parallel can be drawn without engaging in debatable biological metaphors; instead, the same analytical reasons that justify intervention to preserve and maintain our natural environment (which, for the analytical reasons presented above, *cannot* be left over to market forces) also apply to *linguistic environments* – a concept that was introduced as part of the definition of language policy. Just like other amenities that surround us, such as street lighting or the quality of air and water, languages, as well as the greater or lesser diversity of these languages, constitute an environment which presents the two core characteristics of 'public goods'.

The first of these core characteristics is 'non-rival consumption'. There is 'non-rival consumption' when use of a commodity by one person does not reduce the amount of the commodity available for use by another person. Street lighting is the usual textbook example. This clearly applies to language, since the fact that one person speaks a language does not limit the 'amount' of that language that another person can use – in fact, quite the contrary. This point is made throughout much of the language economics literature.[31]

The second of these core characteristics is 'impossibility of exclusion', which denotes the fact that there is no practical mechanism (particularly no price-dependent one) for preventing a person from using the commodity in question. Street lighting, once again, is a standard example because it is difficult to think of a device that would keep a person from experiencing the diversity of a linguistic environment.

Since linguistic diversity presents the two decisive features of public goods, there is absolutely no guarantee that the free market (that is, decentralised decisions made by social actors) will induce the behaviour that will result in an *appropriate* degree of diversity, and in an *adequate* presence, use, learning, and so on, of minority languages in our environment.

It may be that some dimensions of the linguistic environment can be left to private initiative. This is the case, for example, for the occurrence of second language skills in the population, when one considers only the learning of languages of wider communication. The reason why the occurrence of those skills may be adequate is that private actors are likely to find a directly marketable interest in it, in addition to non-pecuniary motives. Hence, people will normally invest in language learning in proportion with the market and non-market benefits they derive from it; in other words, there will be a demand for second language instruction, so that people can acquire those skills. Reciprocally, the language teaching (supply) required can be provided and paid for as a result of this demand. This does not mean that the state should retreat from regulating the supply and demand of skills in languages of wider communication, because the social reasons for teaching them often go beyond the range of motivations that guide the action of private persons. The point made here is that in theory, not all the dimensions of our linguistic environment *require* state intervention.

This, however, does not hold for several dimensions of this linguistic environment, such as the visibility or presence of regional or minority languages. Because the symbolic and financial returns on minority languages skills are low, not to mention the fact that using them may actually carry a social stigma, people will be discouraged from learning, maintaining and passing on these languages. This perfectly understandable behaviour ultimately results in the erosion of diversity. To the extent that the preservation of diversity has been, at the outset, recognised as a 'good', it follows that only the state (or its surrogates) can be counted on to take the measures that will result in an appropriate presence and visibility of regional or minority languages in our linguistic environment.

Before concluding this discussion on the necessity of state intervention, two points need to be highlighted.

First, the above shows that the case for state support to regional or minority languages may very well rest not on moral or political arguments, or on an appeal to human rights or minority rights, but on economic theory, by taking account of some specific features of diverse linguistic environments as a valuable commodity.

Second, the fact that private actors 'under-invest' in regional or minority languages cannot simply be shrugged off as 'rational behaviour' responding to 'market realities'. The low rates of market and non-market return on RML skills are usually the result of the social, political and economic marginalisation of these languages, which in turn are the product of deliberate action – or, more explicitly, oppression. Dominant powers have gone to considerable lengths to eradicate these languages, and some have a horrific record of violence against children, aiming, quite literally, at beating the language out of them. Among many other examples, it is a tribute to the resilience of languages such as Gaelic, Welsh and Breton that they have survived those campaigns amounting to what May (2001) calls 'evisceration'. The aim of this reminder, however, is not to engage in a renewed indictment of various manifestations of colonialism or imperialism,[32] but to draw the reader's attention to an often overlooked fact. Small languages are not *intrinsically* less profitable, in market or non-market terms, than large dominant languages; their current, often unenviable position is generally not the result of some 'natural' evolution, but of deliberate action by wielders of power, who have resorted to decidedly *non-market* instruments to achieve their ends. Therefore, the often-heard argument that RML promotion efforts are ill-advised *because* of they are allegedly contrary to market forces only has very limited analytical value.

The policy analysis perspective

The preceding considerations place language policy squarely in the realm of *public* policy. Hence, language policy ought to be approached in the same way as health, education, transport or energy policy. This does not mean, of course, that all policies are the same. What it means, however, is that the choices that societies have to make in these various areas have a number of analytical traits in common, and that some of the questions to be answered are similar. Identifying these questions and processing them appropriately presupposes the application of a certain methodology, and of the corresponding concepts.

Policy analysis makes considerable use of the notion of *rationality*, and this book proposes to do the same for preparing language policy plans. However, it does not advocate a mechanistic application of rational choice theory. I am not making the assumption that government operates as 'a single rational and disinterested mind, [who] analyses the situation, develops ... optimal policy options, chooses between them, embodies parts of them in the law, embodies others in administrative mechanisms, and closes the cycle by monitoring results'.[33] Rather, 'the political function of policy analysis is to contribute to the continuous debate between coalitions ...',[34] to work out the details and to contribute appropriate methods and analytical rigour to the weighing of the advantages and drawbacks of policy options. People's ideology and values necessarily influence, consciously or not, the process of policy analysis and subsequent recommendations; personal preferences characterise the work of policy analysts too. However, 'to say that policy formation is a social process in which an intellectual process is embedded does not mean that the relative effectiveness of the intellectual process cannot be increased, or that the social process cannot be "improved" '.[35] Hence, once those limitations are clear, public policy analysis remains a useful discipline to draw on.

It would be beyond the scope of this book to venture into a crash course in public policy analysis, but interested readers can find ample material on it in a number of textbooks.[36] Rather than reviewing concepts and methods, I shall attempt, in this section, to highlight some essential features of the policy inquiry process, drawing principally on Dunn (1994).[37] In the next section, I shall look at the general framework of policy analysis, as it can be adapted to the needs of policies addressing regional or minority languages.

1. Policy analysis aims at creating knowledge about the consequences and performance of possible (*ex ante*) or existing (*ex post*) public policies – in our case, those that affect the position of regional or minority languages. The methodology used in this enterprise consists of a system of standards, rules and procedures for creating, critically assessing, and communicating knowledge.[38] Although applying the methodology to possible policies would normally require hypothetical figures – which can be generated by simulation – *ex ante* analysis can be informed by *ex post* analysis of existing policies, particularly by evaluations carried out on very similar policies.

2. Policy analysis is partly *descriptive*, in the sense that is seeks knowledge about the causes and consequences of public policies. Nevertheless, it can serve *normative goals*, in the sense that the knowledge acquired is used to achieve goals which reflects values that have flown into political decisions – in our case, the idea that linguistic diversity is worth preserving.

3. Policy analysis examines public action in highly complex settings, making it virtually impossible, in practice, not only to produce exhaustive comparisons of policy alternatives, but also to be certain that policy *A* will yield better results than policy *B*. In order to gain knowledge about the effects of policies *A* and *B*, it is desirable to employ multiple perspectives, disciplines, methods, measurements and data sources, which generate mutually complementary perspectives on a policy problem.

4. Given the impossibility to provide iron-clad proof that '*A* is preferable to *B*' (or the reverse), it is perfectly acceptable to use the *plausibility* of desirable results from a policy (rather than *certainty* of such results) as a criterion for comparing them. Plausibility, which is inferred from the combination of approaches (hence the term 'inductive plausibility'), is not, however, confined to enumerating arguments that support certain conclusions, but also requires identifying, evaluating, eliminating and synthesising rival theories, including some which challenge the analyst's conclusions. In a sense, this is precisely what has been done in the preceding section, where we have presented the 'laisser-faire' argument and explained why it is not valid in the case of minority language policies.

5. The relevance of policy analysis can be further enhanced by using multivariate models, that is, to take the role of multiple variables into account. In doing so, it is useful to pay attention to the interpretive frameworks and perspectives of different stakeholders (for example, members of majority and minority communities; members of different professional groups such as teachers, businesspeople, etc.).

6. Since the role of policy analysis is to generate knowledge to be used by actors in a democratic debate, such knowledge must be appropriately disseminated. This implies that a variety of media must be used to reach stakeholders, and give them the opportunity to react and comment on the knowledge already acquired.[39]

7. Policy analysis is useful throughout the successive stages of policy-making, which can be characterised as a chain as follows: *problem structuring ⇒ formulation of policy proposals ⇒ debate and adoption of policy recommendations ⇒ policy implementation ⇒ monitoring of policy results ⇒ ex-post evaluation of policy.*

This brief overview captures little more than the basic features of a public policy approach, but it indicates how this book's perspective on the implementation of the Charter is related to the discipline of policy analysis.

At the same time, it is important to point out that in the policy analysis literature, language issues are generally not considered at all. This may be due to the fact that language issues, though *politically* central in the domestic or sometimes international action of states, remains a very minor field in *policy* terms; in any event, the amount of resources devoted by states to language matters remains much less than what is spent on transport, defence, or education. Consequently, policy-makers or other actors concerned with language policy are unlikely to directly applicable models in the policy analysis literature. The implication is straightforward: for the purposes of this book, we shall have to build our own. Let us therefore turn to an analytical representation of language policy.

A framework for language policy

Defining outcomes

Language policy is supposed to achieve certain results, which we shall call 'outcomes'. This simple idea has far-reaching implications, which have to do with the links between policy decisions and outcomes. More precisely, which are the outcomes that we actually expect from a policy decision, and how do we know that a policy *will* give rise to the outcomes desired? To address this point, it is useful to develop a general representation of the language policy process, connecting the policy decision with the outcome; we shall, however, work our way backwards, starting from the desired outcomes.

As stated in the Explanatory Report to the Charter (see Appendix), 'the Charter is designed to protect and promote regional or minority languages as a threatened aspect of Europe's cultural heritage' (Paragraph 10). It follows that the desired outcome of the policy measures to be adopted under the Charter ought to be the continuing vitality of those languages, meaning that they ought to be known – and used.

The precise extent of the vitality that those languages should display, in order to remain living elements of Europe's linguistic diversity, is a complex question in itself. A frame of reference can be found in Fishman's *graded intergenerational disruption scale* (GIDS) (1991). The GIDS contains eight stages on a scale of the 'threatenedness' of a language, where stage 8 represents the highest, and 1 the lowest degree of threat.

- Stage 8 represents the lowest rung of the ladder of language vitality. It describes the situation of a language that only has vestigial speakers, and often no written standard.
- Stage 7 represents the case where speakers of the regional or minority language are socially integrated, but are mostly past child-bearing age. This means that 'they can no longer contribute to the number of [minority-language] users demographically'.
- In stage 6, there is reappearance of the intergenerational family functioning in the minority or threatened language. This is a strategically key stage, because, as Fishman puts it, 'the lion's share of the world's intergenerationally continuous languages are at this very stage and they continue to survive and, in most cases, even to thrive, without going on to subsequent ("higher") stages' (1991: 92). Stage 6 is crucial to 'home-family-neighbourhood-community' reinforcement, a cluster that Fishman considers to be the core of language revitalisation.
- Stage 5 includes regional or minority language literacy in the home, school and community, but such literacy remains restricted to the confines of the community, that is, it enjoys virtually no official recognition and support. Reaching stage 5 allows a minority language to remain intergenerationally secure.[40]
- Stage 4 represents a major break, because it is the stage in language revitalisation where the regional or minority language gains some official recognition and moves into mainstream formal education.

- In stage 3, use of the regional or minority language is present (and hence relegitimised) in the 'lower work sphere', thereby recovering one more domain.[41]
- Stage 2 represents the case where the minority language is used in lower governmental services and the mass media, though not in the higher spheres of either. It clearly represents an important step towards full recognition in formal domains.
- At stage 1, the regional or minority language is used in higher education and in the higher reaches of government, media and professional life. It does not mean that language revitalisation is complete and that language policy is no longer necessary. Nevertheless, reaching stage 1 ensures that language revitalisation has by and large succeeded in recreating a natural, living language community, in which the use of the regional or minority language is *normal*.[42]

Even though the order of succession in which a language 'loses' or 'recovers' particular domains may not always be the same and its applicability may vary, the GIDS provides a powerful frame of reference, on its own as well as in combination with others. In particular, locating a regional or minority language with respect to the GIDS can help to identify appropriately the needs of a given language community, and to formulate the priorities for language protection and promotion. Fishman's GIDS assigns a key role to language group *reproduction* in the process of language revitalisation. This indicates significant overlap between his analysis and that developed in the *Euromosaic* report on 'the production and reproduction of the minority languages groups in the European Union'.[43]

The desired outcome of policy measures can therefore be defined as *a general movement towards stage 1 of the GIDS*. It may not be possible for all regional or minority languages to reach 'GIDS 1' (if only for simple demographic reasons); furthermore, even nearing stages *below* GIDS 1 would constitute, for many languages, such a dramatic improvement from their current position that it may difficult, for political reasons and in certain contexts, to adopt and implement policies professing such an ambitious goal. Nonetheless, policies should generally aim at *improving* the position of regional or minority languages on the GIDS scale. Such improvement, however, should seek to achieve at least some minimum results. Since the Charter's aim is to safeguard the existence of languages in the long run, this minimum can be defined as *restoring and maintaining a self-priming mechanism of language reproduction*. This coincides with (though it is not necessarily *identical* to) stage 5 of the GIDS.

Capacity, opportunity and desire: three conditions for language use

The definition of the type of outcome presented above makes one thing clear, namely, that its realisation depends on people's behaviour. Even the most comprehensive system of language teaching throughout the education system will fail to guarantee the long-term survival of the language if people do not *use* it. Hence, the outcome must be analysed as a *result* of actors' behaviour.

It does not follow, however, that people (in particular, members of a language minority) bear the sole responsibility, through their behaviour, for the destiny of their language. Three conditions must be met for them to use their language – and hence for the language to be, in accordance with the aims of the Charter, a living element of linguistic diversity.

1. The first condition is the *capacity* to use the language. This simply means that members of language community (and perhaps persons who do not necessarily identify with that community) must know the language, and if they do not know it, or only to an inadequate degree of competence, they should be given the opportunity to learn it. 'Capacity' therefore implies an adequate degree of linguistic competence.[44] The degree of competence required for 'capacity' to play its role as a necessary condition of language survival is a relatively little-explored aspect, but circumstantial evidence suggests that it probably implies fluency, and the ability to use the language in question at least as well as any other language. Obvious as it may seem, it bears repeating that 'capacity' is an absolute requirement.
2. The second condition reflects the plain fact that even if speakers are *capable* of using their minority language and have the *desire* (or *willingness*) to do it, they also need *opportunities* to use it. To some extent, these opportunities are a purely private matter. In all but the most orwellian societies, individual actors determine what language they speak in the privacy of their homes. However, genuine language vitality goes well beyond strictly private use, and encompasses the public use of a language. This is where the state often has a crucial role to play through its language policies. By creating opportunities for people to use their language outside of the strictly private sphere, authorities contribute to the *supply* of a linguistic environment.
3. The third condition points most directly to people's behaviour. Members of a linguistic minority will only use their language if they

have a *desire* (or *willingness*) to do so. Typically, minority language speakers are bilingual. This implies that in principle, they have a choice to carry out their various activities through the medium of the majority language *or* of the minority language. If there is a choice, one of the conditions for the choice to be made in favour of 'doing things through the medium of the minority language' is therefore people's *desire* (or *willingness*) to do so.

In short, languages need three things to thrive: capacity, opportunity and desire (or willingness). Each of them can be seen as a necessary, though not a sufficient condition for language use. The three of them taken together constitute a necessary and sufficient set of conditions for language use.[45] These conditions, which apply to all languages, manifest themselves differently depending on the status of the languages considered (where the word 'status' is used in a broad sense), and to the resulting linguistic environment – as defined in this chapter. Capturing the conditions for language use with these three conditions must not be interpreted as insulating language dynamics from their broader context. Quite the contrary, these three conditions are expressions of this very context, making the approach proposed here compatible with most of the central tenets of the 'language ecology' paradigm, which stresses the interrelations between a language and the context in which it is embedded.[46]

I am concerned here with the case of regional or minority languages, where people are, to a larger extent than for dominant languages, *dependent* on the state for those conditions to be present. The role of language policy is therefore to ensure that all three are.

The policy-to-outcome path

In the preceding paragraphs, we have established, albeit succinctly, what amounts to a causal chain that can now help us give a more explicit substance to our framework for language policy. Working backwards from the desired outcomes, I have first noted that those result from people's language behaviour. I have then noted that the type of behaviour ensuring that a regional or minority language keeps being used will obtain if three conditions are met: capacity, opportunity and desire (or willingness). It follows that policy measures must focus on guaranteeing people's capacity to use their language, providing them with opportunities to use it, and encouraging their inclination, or desire to use it.

These concerns are apparent in the text of the Charter, even if they are not identified in the Charter under these same labels.

Capacity is mainly developed through the *education system*. Teaching the regional or minority language concerned to all those who want to learn it is therefore a logical necessity. This is also why the Charter recognises the crucial importance of education, by requiring states ratifying the Charter to choose at least three paragraphs from Article 8, which concerns education.

The opportunity to use a regional or minority language is provided not just by people themselves (for example, when friends or work colleagues get together and use the language in conversation, supplying each other with interlocutors), or by organisations which depend on people's own decisions (for example, by setting up a cultural association operating through the medium of that language, or attending religious services and ceremonies in which that language is used). Many of the opportunities that people need are provided by the state. Education is obviously one of them, and presumably the most important one,[47] but others are also important, such as courts (to which Art. 9 of the Charter is devoted), administration and public services (Art. 10), and the media (Art. 11). The state can also have a major influence on language use in cultural activities and can significantly contribute to the position of a regional or minority language by supporting cultural facilities where this language is used (Art. 12).

Finally, desire, or willingness, largely reflects people's *attitudes* towards different languages. Language attitudes constitute an important variable in sociolinguistic research.[48] For our purposes, it will suffice it to say that attitudes are complex constructs drawing on the individual as well as on the collective: people's willingness to use a language is not merely a function of their personal dispositions; such dispositions are also a function of the environment in which they live. For example, speakers of a regional or minority language are more likely to want to use it if the language is not the object of negative judgement (or ridicule, let alone overt or covert repression) in society at large. Hence, state policies in favour of a regional or minority language can also contribute to the social legitimisation and symbolic prestige of that language. This type of effect can be expected from most measures proposed in the Charter, including in particular those in Article 13 about 'economic and social life'.

What the Charter requires from states acceding to it (spelled out in Art. 2 'Undertakings') therefore coincides with the logical necessity to ensure 'capacity, opportunity and desire', by enjoining parties to apply paragraphs chosen in *each* of Articles 8 through 13.

Of course, measures with different logical targets cross-fertilise each other. Creating opportunities to use a regional or minority language, for example by expanding the offer of television programmes in it or using it in the provision of public services also stimulates people's desire to use the language, because it re-legitimises the language and gives it a social acceptability that it did not have before. These cross-fertilisation effects can be modelled formally, but they are little-known empirically. In what follows, I shall therefore focus on 'direct' effects, and keep assuming that a certain type of measures *mainly* affects capacity, *or* opportunity, *or* desire, it being clear that the full effect of a policy normally goes beyond the direct effects.

Readers will observe that our discussion so far has made no mention of Article 14 of the Charter, which refers to 'transfrontier exchanges'. The importance of transfrontier exchanges rests less with the fact that they open up another range of protection and promotion measures than with the fact that they allow for useful co-operation (and financially attractive economies of scale) with others in the implementation of Articles 8 through 13 (for example, sharing of the cost of developing educational materials or media programmes). In addition, the Charter's reference to transfrontier exchanges has a particular political meaning. On the one hand, in the spirit of the Charter, such exchanges, particularly in the cultural sphere, can enhance mutual understanding. On the other hand, the issue of 'cross-border minorities' is a matter of geopolitical concern for some states. Addressing the issue in a simple and straightforward manner, as the Charter does, is a way of suggesting that such concerns are not ignored, but need not be exaggerated.

The policy-to-outcome path can be represented as a 'flow-chart' (Figure 2.1). Figure 2.1 summarises, in large part, the analytical framework of this book. I shall keep referring to it as I progressively introduce a set of criteria for policy evaluation. The logical structure of the policy-to-outcome path is straightforward, and readers should have no difficulty in rapidly acquiring the ability to 'locate' on this flow chart most of the questions they are confronted with in matters of policy selection, design, and implementation.

Before moving on to the next stage of the argument, let us briefly survey the ground covered so far.

I have first explained the role of this book as one of bridge-building between various approaches to minority language issues, arguing that a policy analysis perspective provides an appropriate integrative tool in which the contributions of law, sociolinguistics and 'core social sciences' can be conveniently positioned with respect to one another. The core idea of this book is to approach language policy, in particular policies in favour or regional or minority languages, as an issue of social choice.

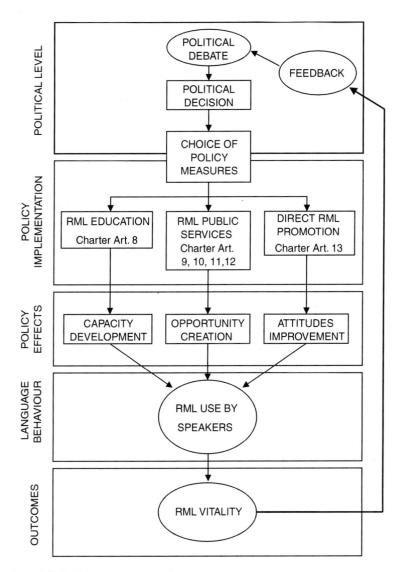

Figure 2.1 Policy-to-outcome path

I have then clarified some core terminology, discussing in particular the notions of 'minority' language, of 'policy' (as opposed to 'politics'), and proposing a definition of 'language policy' as a form of public policy, stressing the logical necessity of state intervention. I have then characterised the policy analysis perspective, before using it to formulate a general analytical framework summarised by the policy-to-outcome path.

All this lays the groundwork for our study of the selection, design and evaluation of language policies. We shall, however, return to these questions in Part III. Let us now take a closer look to the Charter itself, to which Part II is devoted.

Notes

1. For a detailed discussion of the relationship between language and ethnicity, see May (2000, 2001), who usefully positions them with respects to theories of nationalism (Anderson, 1991; Kellas, 1991). For a robust definition of ethnicity that has weathered the test of time, see Fishman (1977).
2. This approach is found, for example, in Skutnabb-Kangas (e.g. 2000).
3. Examples can be found in the writings of Kymlicka (e.g. 1995a,b) or Patten (2002).
4. Thieberger (1990).
5. Further considerations on this question are proposed in Chapter 5.
6. Various aspects of this issue are studied in Grin (1994, 1997, 2000c, 2001b) and Grin and Vaillancourt (1997).
7. Historical accounts of the development of language policy or planning can be found in Ricento (2000b) and Jernudd (2001). Fishman (1993), under the general notion of the 'first congress' phenomenon, reviews the emergence of organised (i.e., planned) intervention on behalf of a variety of languages, showing that a professed concern for language corpus usually veils (thinly) a more fundamental concern with language status.
8. E.g. 'Sprachpolitik' and 'Sprachplanung' in German; 'politique linguistique' and 'aménagement linguistique' in French (where the expressions 'planification linguistique' or even 'glottopolitique' are sometimes used), etc.
9. A formal decision was, for example, made in the case of the Basque language, where *batua* (from Basque 'bat', 'one') was adopted as the unified standard for some 500,000 speakers. In the case of Romansch in Eastern Switzerland, where a little over 30,000 speakers use any one of five different written standards (Sursilvan, Sutsilvan, Surmiran, Vallader, and Puter), one additional standard was coined in the early 1980s, under the name of 'Rumantsch Grischun'. Its function is not to replace any of the existing forms of the language, but to ensure the presence of Romansch in those cases where fragmentation would have had, as a consequence, the omission of the language altogether.
10. Coimisiún na Gaeltachta (2002).
11. This case is cogently made in Durand (2001: 11 ff.).
12. See e.g. Kaplan and Baldauf (1997, Chs 2 and 3).
13. For an in-depth discussion of an exemplary case, see e.g. Daftary and Gál (2002) on Hungarian in Slovakia.
14. National circumstances are of course specific and have given rise to an extensive literature. For example on the French case, see e.g. Moutouh

(1999), and corresponding cultural-historical background in Schiffman (1996, Ch. 4).

15. See e.g. Tollefson (1991); Phillipson (1992); Schiffman (1996); Ricento (2000a); Schmid (2001).

16. E.g. Lapierre (1988); Cooper (1989); Calvet (1996); Kaplan and Baldauf (1997).

17. For example *Language Problems and Language Planning; Language Policy; the International Journal of the Sociology of Language; Current Issues in Language Planning;* etc. as well as several other journals in the field of 'language-in-society', in which policy questions are often addressed.

18. Important edited volumes addressing the case of various minority languages include, for example, Maurais (1987a); Weber (1999); Fishman (2001) or Nelde and Rindler-Schjerve (2001). For a core sociolinguistic perspective, see e.g. Fishman (1989); on the spatial dimensions in geolinguistic perspective, see e.g. essays collected by Williams (1988, 1991); for an emphasis on the political and geopolitical dimensions of language planning, Laponce (1992) or De Swaan (2001). Jernudd (2001) proposes a historical account of the development of different strands of research in language planning.

19. Grin (1996: 31), combining definitions presented in Cooper (1989).

20. See e.g. Grin (2000c); the term 'linguistic environment' is also found in other authors such as Calvet, albeit with a near-exclusive emphasis on the *visibility* of a language (e.g. Calvet 1996: Ch. 3).

21. A relevant question at this juncture is that of the distance between 'overt' and 'covert' policies, which has been extensively studied by Schiffman (1996). Given that this book focuses on the implementation of the Charter, my goal here is to analyse the corresponding policies, which comes down to assuming that the commitment of signatories is a sincere one. However, it should be obvious that taking states at their word (and possibly, in some cases, exposing their ambivalence or even calling their bluff) does not require a naïve belief that governments' attitudes towards minority languages and communities is always unequivocal.

22. The specification of 'aggregate' welfare is a mostly technical one. It means that overall, total welfare (and therefore *average* welfare) will be higher, independently of possible increases or decreases of welfare affecting specific sub-groups in society.

23. Respect for human rights, however, certainly enhances welfare, which means that these two rationales converge, even if they are inspired by epistemologically different considerations.

24. This point is explained e.g. by Sonntag (2000) with reference to the role of English in North India.

25. For an integrative, yet concise discussion on language and power, see e.g. Wright (2001).

26. See in particular Tollefson (1991), Ch. 2.

27. The importance of history in language policy is particularly manifest in the case of Switzerland, which enjoys the flattering, but not entirely deserved reputation of a 'model' in the management of linguistic diversity; see Schoch (1999) or Grin (2002a).

28. Seven success conditions have been identified in the evaluations of the cost-effectiveness of some language policies: 'avant-garde', 'redistribution',

'normalcy', 'technical effectiveness', 'shadow price', 'individual language maintenance', and 'strict preference'. See Grin and Vaillancourt (1999, Ch. 6) for details, and Grin, Moring *et al.* (2002) for an application to a wider range of cases.

29. For an extreme statement of this view, see Jones (2000).
30. For a detailed treatment of market failure, see e.g. Cornes and Sandler (1996).
31. Grin and Vaillancourt (1997). The fact that the usefulness of a language can actually increase with the number of its users places it in the very unusual category of 'super-collective' or 'hypercollective' goods (de Swaan, 2001). This, however, does not automatically translate into higher economic value, and the increasing frequency of skills in a given language may ultimately drive down the return on those skills (Grin, 1999b).
32. These questions have recently been revisited by Skutnabb-Kangas (2000).
33. Wimberley (2000).
34. Ibid.
35. Bauer, quoted in Dunn (1994: 1).
36. E.g. Stokey and Zeckhauser (1978); Dunn (1994); Scharpf (1997).
37. This list of features emphasises 'problem-oriented policy research', as distinct from 'interaction-oriented policy research'. The latter focuses on the behaviour of political and social actors (using, for example, game theory) to explain why some courses of action (including policy proposals) are adopted instead of others – this type of question, of course, puts 'policy' issues back into the 'political' arena, in terms of the distinction made earlier. For the most part, I am concerned with the former kind of policy research (that is, 'problem-oriented').
38. The 'standards' referred to here are *methodological*, not legal.
39. 'Only when knowledge *of* the policy-making process is communicated *in* that process can policy stakeholders use knowledge to improve public policies' (Dunn, 1994: 28).
40. Fishman indicates, however, that this 'security' obtains only if there is sufficient ethnocultural 'separation' from the dominant/majority culture and the pull it may represent. In my view, such separation is not intrinsically desirable; it follows that, in order for the language to be secure *without* needing this separation from dominant or majority culture, language policies should aim at reaching a stage *beyond* GIDS 5.
41. 'Domain' is an important construct in sociolinguistics, defined by Fishman as a 'prototypical cluster of interactions' that can be characterised in terms of the language used; language use in a given domain depends on participants, setting and topic. For a more extensive presentation, see e.g. Holmes (1992), pp. 23–31. In this book, I use the concept of domain without necessarily referring to the various aspects into which it can be parsed.
42. Readers will recognise here the concept of *normalització*, used for example in Catalan language policy. It essentially refers to the recreating of a context (or 'linguistic environment') in which it is *normal* to use the language concerned; I return to this notion in Chapter 10.
43. In the *Euromosaic* report, 55 language communities from the 15-member European Union are distributed over five 'clusters', which reflect their position in terms of a number of demolinguistic and institutional indicators. Membership of a cluster is therefore an indicator of 'strength'. There is a high degree of co-variation between the *Euromosaic* ranking of language communities over the clusters and their GIDS score. The high number of

communities taken into account in the *Euromosaic* report reflects the fact that a distinction was systematically made between any two communities who, though they speak the same language (e.g. Basque) live in two different countries (e.g., France and Spain) (Nelde, Strubell and Williams, 1996).

44. 'Linguistic competence' is used here in a broad sense. The reader may think of it as language skills, plus the confidence to use them. The word 'competence' implies no particular reference to Chomskyan generative grammar.

45. This representation of language use in based a formal model of language use by bilinguals, first proposed by in a one-period model (Grin, 1990), then in a dynamic model (Grin, 1992). The model has subsequently been adapted to evaluations of minority language policies in Grin and Vaillancourt (1998) and Grin, Moring *et al.* (2002). For a formalised presentation, see the Appendix in Grin and Vaillancourt (ibid.).

46. On language ecology, see Mühlhäusler (2000).

47. However, the provision of minority language education is, by itself, *not* sufficient to guarantee the long-term vitality of regional or minority languages (Fishman, 1991; Edwards, 1994b).

48. On the concept of language attitudes, see e.g. Baker (1992) or Holmes (1992).

Part II

The European Charter for Regional or Minority Languages

Summary of Part II

Part II contains two chapters, both devoted to the *Charter for Regional or Minority Languages*. Chapter 3 presents the history behind the Charter, and then describes its contents (the full text of the Charter, however, is provided in the Appendix). It stresses the originality of the Charter in comparison with most international legal instruments on minority rights, language rights, and so on. Chapter 4 presents some organisational aspects linked to the preparation of a ratification instrument and to the setting up of the monitoring mechanism by parties to the Charter.

3
The Charter: an Overview[1]

A brief history of the drafting and adoption of the Charter

The European Charter for Regional or Minority Languages should be viewed in the context of the evolution of European legal and political thinking on the treatment of minorities in the second half of the twentieth century. Post Second World War Europe did not offer a friendly environment to minorities, their languages, their cultures or their political aspirations. The continent had been ravaged, millions were dead and unemployed and the polarisation between the liberal democratic world of Western Europe and that of communist Eastern Europe was becoming all too evident.

Memories were still very much alive of how Hitler had used the presence of German minorities outside of the Reich as an excuse for interfering in the internal affairs of other states and in some instances (e.g. Czechoslovakia) invading them. There was also the impression, in many instances grossly exaggerated, that disgruntled minorities had collaborated with the invading Nazis (e.g. in Flanders and in Brittany) and that the best way forward for Western Europe was to keep such groups firmly in check. Even if the western powers did not like Stalin or Tito, they at least offered an element of stability which so many sought.

In 1948, the United Nations' Universal Declaration of Human Rights was adopted.[2] The Universal Declaration of Human Rights had nothing to say about the rights of linguistic minorities. However, Article 2 of the Declaration does contain an important reference to language:

Article 2.

Everyone is entitled to all the rights and freedoms set out in this Declaration, without distinction of any kind, such as race, colour, sex, language, religion, political or other opinion, national or social origin, property, birth or other status.

Furthermore, no distinction shall be made on the basis of the political, jurisdictional or international status of the country or territory to which a person belongs, whether it be independent, trust, non-self-governing or under any other limitation of sovereignty.

We see here established the principle that language cannot be used as a basis for denying the fundamental human rights, outlined in the Declaration, to any person.

Two years later, the Council of Europe adopted its Convention for the Protection of Human Rights and Fundamental Freedoms that carried an almost identical provision in Article 14.

The UN and its associated bodies, UNESCO and the ILO, made modest but important advances in this field. Special mention should be made of the International Covenant on Civil and Political Rights.[3] The Covenant saw the prohibition on language-based discrimination being extended into areas such as the administration of justice, the treatment of children and the uninhibited use of language.

European institutions tended to be more timid, probably because of the aforementioned fears and reservations, but evidence of new thinking can be found both in the Galway[4] and Bordeaux Declarations.[5] The first breakthrough of substance came from the Parliamentary Assembly of the Council of Europe with the adoption of Recommendation 928 (1981) on the Educational and Cultural Problems of Minority Languages and Dialects in Europe.[6] The rapporteur was a Catalan Socialist, Cirici Pellicer, and the Recommendation was adopted by a landslide majority. This Recommendation might be deemed to be the precursor of the Charter. What is also of interest is that only nine days later, the European Parliament, meeting the same hemicycle in Strasbourg, adopted the now famous Arfé Resolution.[7]

Another interesting feature of both documents is that they sidestepped the thorny issues of recognising national/ethnic minorities, self-determination, autonomy, and so on. Instead they focused on matters of language and culture. This allayed the fears of governments, who would have reacted negatively to anything seen as posing a threat to national unity or the territorial integrity of the state, but which were more open to accepting the existence of cultural and linguistic diversity on their territories. The Charter and indeed subsequent resolutions adopted by the European Parliament continued in this tradition.

The next major initiative came from another body of the Council of Europe, the Standing Conference of Local and Regional Authorities of Europe, now known as the Congress of Local and Regional Authorities, which convened a public hearing, entitled *Towards a Charter of European regional and minority languages*. Its intentions were clear from the start. In a letter, dated 16 February 1984, from Rinaldo Locatelli, the Executive Secretary of the Conference, the opening paragraph states:

> The Standing Conference of Local and Regional Authorities of Europe, made up of local and regional elected representatives from the member states of the Council of Europe, has embarked upon a study of the problems relating to regional and minority languages in Europe. The Conference's Committee on Cultural and Social Affairs, and more particularly its rapporteur Mr. Herbert Kohn (Fed. Rep. Of Germany), are preparing a report, the ultimate aim of which is to propose a Charter of European regional and minority languages.

The recipients of this letter were invited to a public hearing in Strasbourg on 15–16 May 1984. The consultants to research the situation of the languages had circulated a data sheet around Europe and much information was gleaned from the completed forms, and prepared a document entitled 'Regional and Minority Languages in Europe – Summary of the information gathered',[8] which was made available to participants, along with a 'Collection of fundamental texts on the protection of the rights of ethnic and linguistic minorities'.[9]

The public hearing was attended by over 250 representatives of small linguistic communities and can only be described as an eminent success. The rapporteur and his supporters received a resounding endorsement for their initiative. Following on the public hearing a small team of expert consultants was assembled and charged with drafting the text of the Charter. When the work of this group had advanced to a certain point further experts were called in, and by the middle of the following year the final draft text had been prepared. A preliminary discussion took place at the Standing Conference's autumn session in 1987 but no vote was taken. Amendments, proposed in the course of the discussion, were incorporated and an amended text was tabled at the spring 1988 Session of the Standing Conference. It was carried on 16 March 1988 and then sent to the Parliamentary Assembly for an opinion. A favourable opinion was delivered in October of the same year. The draft Charter then faced its greatest challenge to date – adoption by the

Committee of Ministers of the Council of Europe, that is, the Foreign Ministers of the member states or their representatives.

The text, as it stood, was not acceptable to the Committee but a total rejection was avoided by the establishment of another expert committee, comprising representatives of the member states, to rework and revise the text. The group became known as CAHLR (Comité ad hoc langues régionales). It worked assiduously for three years (1989–92) under the chairmanship of Sigve Gramstaed (Norway). Although the views of the delegates were often widely divergent, a kind of understanding and camaraderie developed and many delicate and thorny issues were discussed and resolved informally. Another interesting feature of the term of office of CAHLR was the crumbling of the Iron Curtain. The new democracies of Central Europe started to join the Council of Europe – first Hungary, followed by Poland and then Czechoslovakia. These delegations were invariably positive on the question of language rights.

The contributions and expertise of the Council of Europe staff were invaluable, especially those of Ferdinando Albanese and Philip Blair. Compromises had to be made. If the Charter were to be accepted, it would have to obtain a two-thirds majority in favour (abstentions counting as 'no' votes). The choice facing those who passionately wanted a really strong document was that of an excellent Charter, which would be doomed to rejection, or a good one, which stood a chance of being accepted. They wisely opted for the latter. However, not all changes were dilutions: weaknesses and inconsistencies were addressed and vague formulations tightened up.

The draft Charter was adopted by CAHLR in spring 1992 and forwarded to the Committee of Ministers, who adopted the Charter on 23 June 1992 and accorded it the legal form of a Convention. Of the then 28 member states of the Council of Europe, none opposed the Charter. Only five abstained – Cyprus, France, Greece, Turkey, and the United Kingdom.[10]

On 5 November 1992 the Charter was opened for signature. After a gestation period of over eight years, the first ever international legal instrument for the protection of lesser used languages had become a reality.

The document[11]

After much deliberation and heart-searching it was agreed to use the term *regional or minority* in the title of the Charter. The authors were only too conscious that this choice of words was not entirely appropriate in all cases and that it could even give rise to problems in some instances.

However, in the absence of a more attractive formulation, it was agreed to accept *regional or minority* and to clarify the meaning in the text of the document – see Article 1 a. and Article 3.1.

The European Charter for Regional or Minority Languages comprises a preamble and five parts:

Preamble
Part I – General provisions
Part II – Objectives and principles
Part III – Measures to promote the use of regional or minority languages in public life
Part IV – Application of the Charter
Part V – Final provisions

The Charter is also accompanied by an Explanatory Report, which, although not legally binding, is very useful in gaining a clear understanding of what is entailed in the various provisions.

Preamble

The philosophical and legal concepts on which the Charter is based can be found in the Preamble.

It starts by recalling that the aim of the Council of Europe is to achieve a greater unity between its members, particularly for the purpose of safeguarding and realising the ideals and principles which are their common heritage. It goes on to state that the protection of the historical regional or minority languages or Europe, some of which are in danger of eventual extinction, contributes to the maintenance and development of Europe's cultural wealth and traditions. So we have here the issue of regional or minority language firmly placed in the context of European unity and the conservation of its cultural wealth.

The Preamble then turns to legal issues and states that the right to use a regional or minority language is an inalienable right conforming to the principles embodied in the UN International Covenant on Civil and Political Rights, and according to the spirit of the Council of Europe Convention for the Protection of Human Rights and Fundamental Freedoms. It also alludes to the work of the OSCE and refers in particular to the Helsinki Final Act of 1975 and the Document of the Copenhagen Meeting of 1990.

Returning then to more ideological or philosophical considerations, it stresses that the protection and encouragement of regional or minority languages should not be to the detriment of the official languages or the need to learn them.

It finishes by recalling the specific conditions and historical traditions in the different regions and by declaring that the protection and promotion of regional or minority languages in the different countries and regions of Europe represents an important contribution to the building of a Europe based on the principles of democracy and cultural diversity within the framework of national sovereignty and territorial integrity.

In short, the Charter is based on broad principles of international law and on the perception of linguistic diversity, including regional or minority languages, as being a cultural asset that should be conserved and developed. No reference is made to ethnic groups or collective rights. Rather, the Charter explicitly respects national sovereignty, the territorial integrity of the Council of Europe member states and the importance of official languages.

Part I – General provisions

This part is given up to definitions, undertakings, practical arrangements and existing regimes of protection.

'Regional or minority languages' are defined as being languages traditionally used within a given territory of a state by nationals of the state who form a group numerically smaller than the rest of the state's population, which are different from the official language(s) of the state, and which are not dialects of the official language(s) or the languages of immigrants. So the languages of recent immigrants are out as are dialects.

The Charter does not contain any list of regional or minority languages, nor does it offer any set of criteria for defining the difference between a 'language' and a 'dialect'. As the Explanatory Report puts it:

> [a]lthough the States Parties are not free to grant or refuse a regional or minority language the status it is guaranteed under Part II of the Charter, they are responsible, as authorities for the application of the Charter, for deciding whether the form of expression used in a particular area of their territory or by a particular group of their nations constitutes a regional or minority language within the meaning of the Charter.

This implies a not inconsiderable degree of discretion on the part of states. However, it is clear that should a contracting state exclude a language on spurious grounds, such as 'that is not really a language', it would be in violation of the Charter. The self-perception of the community that uses a particular form of expression would certainly have to be taken into account. As the Explanatory Report says, '...this question depends not only on strictly linguistic considerations, but also on psycho-sociological and political phenomena which may produce a different answer in each case'.

Sign languages are not mentioned. While there is certainly scope for asking whether or not these languages are eligible to be covered by the Charter, it is clear that applying parts of the Charter, particularly certain provisions in Part III that refer explicitly to the written and spoken forms of the language, would be very difficult, if not completely impossible, in the case of sign languages. It should also be said that CAHLR, the committee that drafted the final version of the Charter, did not envisage it being applied to sign languages.

Another phrase, which may lead to some confusion, is the expression 'according to the situation of each language'. Those who drafted the Charter were obliged to face and accept the great variety of language situations which obtain across Europe. The issue of stating a percentage of language users was addressed and it was agreed that mentioning a precise figure could give rise to more problems than it would solve. A certain number of language users, residing in a fairly compact area, could reasonably expect certain services in their own language from the authorities. However, if the same community were scattered over a much wider area it could prove to be extremely difficult and prohibitively costly to offer the same services.

'Non-territorial languages' are also covered by Part II. These are languages, which, although traditionally used within the territory of the state, cannot be identified with a particular area thereof. In practice, these are almost invariably Gypsy or historical languages of the Jewish community.[12]

A contracting state must apply the provisions of Part II to all regional or minority languages within its territory. At the time of ratification, it must also specify what languages are being covered by Part III and which paragraphs or sub-paragraphs, chosen from among the provisions of Part III, will be applied. It must also state on what territory or territories these measures will be applied. Interestingly, the provisions may be applied, not only to 'regional or minority languages' as defined, but also to official languages, '... less widely used on the whole or part of its territory ...'. This is very important as some 'official' or 'national' languages (such as Irish in the Republic of Ireland) are not in a majority position and can benefit from the provisions of the Charter just as much as languages which do not enjoy the same degree of official recognition. Other regional or minority languages, not covered by Part III, but which have to be covered by Part II, must also be listed.

A very important provision of the Charter is that in Article 3.1 which states that:

> [a]ny Party may, at any subsequent time, notify the Secretary General that it accepts the obligations arising out of the provisions of the Charter not already specified in its instrument of ratification, acceptance or approval, or that it will apply paragraph 1 of Article 3 to other regional or minority languages, or to other official languages which are less widely used on the whole or part of its national territory.

This, in fact, ensures that the Charter is a living and flexible instrument for supporting regional or minority languages. Its scope can be expanded, the provisions of an instrument of ratification can be broadened and, *ipso facto*, its usefulness and impact enhanced. Of course, a ratifying state may specify in its instrument of ratification only those measures, which are already in place. The Charter is not, and should not be mistaken for being, a manifesto for action or less still, a wish list. However, a government or language community can set as its objective the enhancement of the instrument of ratification in question, as soon as additional provisions are in place. Used intelligently, the Charter can thus become a practical and acceptable tool for language planning.

Other points worth noting are that the Charter cannot be construed as limiting or derogating from the European Convention on Human Rights, nor can its provisions affect any more favourable provisions concerning the status or regional or minority languages or the legal regime of persons belonging to a minority. As already noted, some lesser used languages enjoy official status. This latter provision should allay any fears that the Charter might be misused to undermine their status.

The counterpoint of this is the provision that nothing in the Charter can be interpreted as implying any right to act in contravention of the UN Charter or impinge on the sovereignty or national integrity of the state.

Finally, Part I requires that authorities, organisations and persons be informed of their rights and duties under the Charter.

Part II – Objectives and principles

There is only one article in this Part – Article 7 – but a very important one, which merits study and reflection. For it is here that the central *credo* of the Charter is to be found. All contracting states must accept Part II, even if the provisions of Part III cannot be applied to a particular language. The key elements are:

1. Recognition of regional or minority language as an expression of cultural wealth;
2. Respect for the geographical area of each regional or minority language;
3. The need for resolute action to promote such languages;
4. The facilitation and/or encouragement of the use of such languages, in speech and writing, in public and private life;
5. The provision of appropriate forms and means for the teaching and study of such languages at all appropriate stages, including the provision of facilities enabling non-speakers to learn them;
6. The promotion of study and research on regional or minority languages at universities or equivalent institutions;
7. The promotion of relevant transnational exchanges.

In the second paragraph of Article 7 contracting states are required to eliminate any unjustified exclusion, restriction or preference, relating to the use of a regional or minority language and intended to discourage or endanger its maintenance or development. The adoption of special measures in favour of regional or minority language, aimed at promoting equality between the users of these languages and the rest of the population (i.e. positive discrimination), cannot be considered to be act of discrimination.

Paragraph 3 requires states, by appropriate measures, to promote mutual understanding, especially respect and tolerance, between all linguistic groups in the state. The inclusive and non-threatening nature of the Charter is clearly evidenced here.

Paragraph 4 is important in that it requires states to take into consideration the needs and wishes expressed by the groups, which use regional or minority languages. They are furthermore encouraged to establish bodies, if necessary, for the purpose of advising the authorities on all matters pertaining to regional or minority languages.

In the final paragraph of this Article, the states undertake to apply, *mutatis mutandis* the principles contained in the Article, to non-territorial (i.e. Gypsy and Jewish) languages.

Part III – Measures to promote regional or minority languages

It is in Part III that much of the substance of the Charter can be found, that is, in concrete measures to promote the use of the languages.

Part III, with its uncompromisingly concrete approach, distinguishes the Charter from other international conventions, such as the Framework Convention for the Protection of National Minorities. There are seven Articles in this part, each one dealing with a specific domain of language use:

Article 8 – Education
Article 9 – Judicial authorities
Article 10 – Administrative authorities and public services
Article 11 – Media
Article 12 – Cultural activities and facilities
Article 13 – Economic and social life
Article 14 – Transfrontier exchanges

No fewer than 68 concrete undertakings are listed here and, as already stated, a contracting state must chose a minimum of 35 of these. A minimum of three each must be chosen from Articles 8 and 12 and one each from Articles 9, 10, 11 and 13. Critics of Part III, who describe it as being *à la carte*, might better describe it as resembling a *table d'hôte* menu, where one is expected to chose something from each course. A less flexible formula would not work because of the greatly differing language situations obtaining in Europe.

The 'menu' system requires particular attention to be paid to the inner consistency of choices made. When a ratifying state chooses a particular measure in a paragraph, in which there are a number of options, the weaker options automatically become redundant and cannot be counted among the required 35 paragraphs or sub-paragraphs. For instance, if a state were to choose sub-paragraph b.i from Article 8 (Education – 'to make available primary education in the relevant regional or minority language') it could not then choose sub-paragraph b.ii from the same article ('to make available a substantial part of primary education in the relevant regional or minority language') because clearly sub-paragraph b.i leaves b.ii redundant.

Article 8 [Education] breaks Education down into five categories – primary, secondary, technical and vocational, university (tertiary) and adult and continuing education. A number of options are offered in most of these categories – using the regional or minority language as a medium of instruction, making substantial use of it as a medium of instruction (as well as the dominant state language), having it taught only as a subject, and finally applying one or other of the above options only in case where students or their families, in 'a number considered sufficient' so wish.

Likewise, Article 9 [Judicial Authorities] breaks the administration of justice down into three main areas – criminal proceedings, civil proceedings and administrative matters. Options are again offered – to hear the proceedings in the regional or minority language, to guarantee the right of the person in question to use his/her regional or minority language, to provide that evidence will not be deemed to be inadmissible solely because it is presented in a regional or minority language, and finally to provide documents in the regional or minority language, if necessary by using an interpreter or translator, and to do that without any extra cost to the person in question. Because this article is probably the most difficult to accept for some states, a soft option was included in order to ensure that the Charter could be adopted and come into force. This relates to the making available in the regional or minority languages of the most important statutory texts and those relating particularly to users of these languages, unless otherwise provided.

Article 10 [Administrative Authorities and Public Services] addresses oral communications, written communications and the provision of texts and form. Among the options we find are ensuring that officers in contact with the public use the regional or minority language, ensuring that users of these languages may submit written or oral applications in their languages and receive a reply in these languages, and simply that applications can be made in these languages (although presumably the reply may be in the major state language). The article also deals with use of regional or minority languages in the assemblies and the making available of interpretation facilities, the use of the correct and traditional forms of place-names and the recruitment and appointment of employees competent to use the regional or minority language.

Article 11 [Media] deals with radio, television and the printed media. Options include the provision of a complete service (e.g. a radio station broadcasting solely in the regional or minority language) or the use of the language in a service which also uses the majority language. The use of the words 'encourage' and 'facilitate' recur in this article, because in some countries, governments are forbidden by law to become directly involved in the media.

Article 12 [Cultural Activities and Facilities] covers various forms of cultural expression and promotes equitable treatment, in the form of financial support and the provision of facilities, for expression in regional or minority languages. As in the previous article, the concept of encouraging and fostering cultural expression is strongly in evidence. Users of the regional or minority language should be treated equally with those expressing themselves in the major language. Various aspects of cultural development are touched upon, including the development of terminology and the pursuance of cultural activities outside the state, such as exhibitions abroad.

Article 13 [Economic and Social Life] endeavours to ensure that any measures that prohibit the use of regional or minority languages in this domain are discontinued. It adopts a broad interpretation of social life and specifically addresses the question of the delivery of medical and social services. This domain is largely in the private sector, so the emphasis is on the prohibition of any legal impediments to the use of regional or minority languages, rather than on the obligation to use them. Banking, the provision of information to the public, and the making available of safety instructions are the main areas touched upon.

As many regional or minority languages are spoken in more than one country, the issue of transfrontier cooperation is a critical one. Article 14 [Transfrontier Exchanges] deals not only with formal bilateral or multilateral agreements, but also with promotion of transfrontier cooperation.

Part IV – Application of the Charter

At the end of a year after the coming into force of the Charter with respect to a contracting state, that state must provide a written report on their policy pursued in accordance with Part II and on the measures taken in applying those provisions of Part III which they have accepted. Similar reports have then to be supplied thereafter at three-yearly intervals. The reports must be made public.

A committee of experts, appointed by the Committee of Ministers from a list of individuals 'of the highest integrity and recognised competence in the matters dealt with in the Charter' – one per contracting state – is established. This committee examines the reports submitted by the states.

Bodies or associations, legally established in a contracting state, may draw the attention of the committee to matters relating to the undertakings entered into under Part III. After consulting with the contracting state, the committee may take into account this information when preparing the report it eventually makes to the Committee of Ministers. In short, if a state is felt not to be honouring its commitments, a complaint can be lodged with the committee of experts. While the experts are at liberty to ignore ill-founded or vexatious complaints, they are equally at liberty to investigate ones that seem credible and discuss them with the state authorities.

The report made to the Committee of Ministers by the experts is accompanied by comments made both by the state authorities and the public and must also contain the experts' proposals in relation to these. The Committee of Ministers may publish these reports. In any event the Secretary General makes a two-yearly detailed report to the Parliamentary Assembly on the application of the Charter. This monitoring is open, transparent and would appear to be effective.

Part V – Final provisions

This part is of a merely technical nature, specifying how the Charter must be signed and ratified. A country may sign and ratify on the same day but this rarely happens. A signature is an indication of a moral and political engagement on the part of the state although the putting in place of the necessary legal and administrative measures, which make ratification possible, can take even some years. The Charter is open to non-Council of Europe countries for signing and ratification.

The Charter is unique in that it is the only international legal instrument whose primary aim is the protection and promotion of regional or minority languages. It is also interesting in that it is pro-active and displays an internal dynamic. Unlike many conventions, which once domestic law is brought into line with their provisions, become somewhat static, the Charter requires ongoing active measures in order that a ratifying state remains in compliance. It also offers many opportunities for ratifying states to strengthen their support for regional or minority languages by 'upgrading' the applicable paragraphs or sub-paragraphs from Part III.

Since it was opened for signature in November 1992, the Charter has slowly but steadily attracted signatures and instruments of ratification. By the end of 2000, 23 countries had signed the Charter and of these 11 had already ratified it. The fact that the number of states ratifying it is lower than those ratifying other conventions (such as the Framework Convention for the Protection of National Minorities) simply underscores the fact that ratifying the Charter is no mere declaration of adherence to general principles, but rather a serious commitment which entails specific and measurable undertakings.

It has earned the almost universal approval of lesser-used language proponents throughout Europe and is likely to remain the definitive yardstick for decades to come.

Notes

1. I am grateful to Dónall Ó Riagáin for the original version of this chapter.
2. Adopted by the General Assembly of the United Nations on 10 December 1948.
3. Adopted by the General Assembly of the United Nations on 16 December 1966 and entered into force on 23 March 1976.
4. Unanimously adopted by the first convention of Regional authorities from the periphery of Europe – 16 October 1975.
5. Adopted by the Council of Europe Convention on the problems of regionalisation, held in Bordeaux, 30 January–1 February 1978.
6. Adopted by the Parliamentary Assembly on 7 October 1981.
7. Resolution on a Community Charter of Regional Languages and cultures and on a Charter of Rights of Ethnic Minorities, prepared by Gaetano Arfé MEP, and adopted by the European Parliament on 16 October 1981 [A1-965/80] 16.10.81 OJ C 287 p.57.
8. Doc. No. CPL/Cult (18) 21.
9. Doc. No. CPL/Cult (18) 28.
10. By 1999, three of these, Cyprus, France and the United Kingdom, had signed the Charter.
11. The chief aim of this book is to assist users in the *implementation* of the Charter, rather than to provide a detailed presentation or commentary of the text itself. Hence, this section is kept relatively short; but the reader can turn to the Appendix for the full text of the Charter and the accompanying *Explanatory Report*.
12. These are Yiddish and Judeo-Spanish. For further information, see e.g. Weinstock *et al.* (1997).

4
Implementing the Charter: Organisational Issues[1]

The pre-ratification stage

General principles: consultation and communication

Important elements in a democratic society are transparency and consultation of those that are affected by policy-making of governmental authorities. Transparency is essential for those affected by a given policy to be informed of action to be taken, and consultation matters because it is considered to be an important way of guaranteeing endorsement of the policy by those who will be affected by it – also in terms of peaceful cohabitation between the various groups affected in different ways.

Once a decision has been taken to sign and ratify the Charter, several factors must be taken into consideration by the state:

1. the existing state language policy must be evaluated in the light of the Charter's provisions;
2. the need of protection and promotion of the regional or minority languages has to be evaluated and how the Charter can contribute to its improvement;
3. a consultation with those that are affected by the adopted policy has to take place.

When a state decides to initiate this ratification procedure it thereby acknowledges its willingness to adopt a certain language policy or to develop existing policy within that state. Clearly, language policy cannot be homogeneous (that is, it cannot be the same everywhere), because the political, social or economic situation can vary greatly from state to state. This unavoidable diversity of measures also reflects the fact that the situations of the regional or minority languages concerned are very different, whether in terms of the number of users of the languages, the demolinguistic concentration of users in certain territories, and so on.

The Charter has already taken these differences into consideration by prescribing a 'flexible solution' whereby a choice must be made of paragraphs and sub-paragraphs that are to be implemented in relation to the various languages to which Part III applies. It is up to the relevant state to make the decision of which paragraphs and sub-paragraphs of Part III should be chosen for each language. This, however, requires a number of actions to be taken by the state *before* the Charter is ratified.

Accordingly, the contracting parties are required to prepare their instrument of ratification very thoroughly, for it is this instrument which confirms the concrete obligations applicable to the languages covered under Part III of the Charter. It should be noted here that Part II of the Charter applies to *all* the regional or minority languages in the state, without the state being required to formulate any specifications in the instrument of ratification. This process, which takes place during the pre-ratification stage, consists of collecting and evaluating information of two types: first, the nature and extent of existing protection and promotion; second, the needs of the regional or minority languages. On the basis of a comparison between needs and existing protection and promotion, states can clarify how the Charter can be used in the most effective manner in establishing a regional or minority language policy. This work should be done in close cooperation with the responsible authorities (at national, regional or local level) and in consultation with the users of the languages in question, in particular with the organisations representing them and directly knowledgeable about their needs and concerns. By applying these cooperation and consultation principles throughout the process, the state not only keeps its decision-making more transparent, but also secures higher success during the implementation stage that follows ratification.

As regards the authorities, experience has already shown that the establishment of an inter-ministerial commission, for example, has the positive effect of bringing together all the ministries and other authorities responsible for the application of the Charter after it has been ratified, and encouraging them to cooperate in looking for the most suitable set of policy measures for the various languages. This kind of cooperation between authorities also is particularly helpful in providing information as to what kind of obligations states can, in theory and practice, undertake – and actually fulfil. The ministries in question are, in principle, those responsible for the same fields as those mentioned in the Charter (education, justice, etc.), for it is the central (national) authorities that have an overview of the existing laws and regulations applying in the state in the respective field.

Authorities which are, however, often 'forgotten' in this process are local and regional authorities. Nonetheless, local and regional authorities are essential partners in the implementation of the Charter, because they are more likely to use the regional or minority languages on a daily basis within those parts of the national territory where the languages are used. It has sometimes been observed that central authorities have taken the decision to ratify the Charter, but that the resulting obligations have not been discussed in consultation with the local or regional authorities that will largely be responsible for implementing those obligations. In some cases, these obligations have not been communicated adequately to the local and regional authorities. The result of this is that the regional or minority language is not used within the given local or regional administrative unit in accordance with the international obligations that the state has undertaken.

In the light of the experience acquired by the present contracting parties since the Charter came into force in 1998, it has become clear that the consultation and evaluation process may take a long time, which explains why it may take a state party a significant amount of time to ratify this treaty. This should, however, be seen as asset, because if the instrument of ratification has been well prepared, the monitoring procedure for the Charter works more efficiently – and, more generally, the chances of success of the policy measures adopted under the Charter will be increased. The obligations regarding each language, in each territory in the state, are therefore clear and detailed, leaving no doubt as to how the language(s) is (are) to be used.

Organisation of the pre-ratification process

This consultation process should result in decisions being taken concerning the languages to be covered and the paragraphs and sub-paragraphs chosen.

In practice, the very first step that the authorities have to take in this process is to identify which languages are to be considered as regional or minority languages within the state. Article 1 of the Charter provides a definition that guides the state in its choice, whereby the following criteria must be borne in mind:

1. The languages must be traditionally used by nationals of the state, that is to say, they must be historical regional or minority languages,

spoken over a long period of time, in the State in question. Therefore, the languages of migrants are not included in the protection and promotion mechanism of the Charter.

2. The languages must be clearly distinct from the official language of the state; hence, the definition excludes the dialects of the official language.[2]

3. The languages must be traditionally used within a given territory or region of the state, in conformity with the principle of territoriality underlying the Charter. For example, in the Netherlands, the Frisian language is traditionally spoken in the Province of Frysland, and receives protection and promotion according to the Charter within that Province: this has been clearly identified by the Netherlands in its instrument of ratification.

At the same time, the state must decide which languages have a territorial base and are used by a sufficient number of speakers to justify granting protection and promotion under Part III of the Charter. At this stage, the work of a cooperative body of the authorities, such as a special inter-ministerial commission that examines the situation, can be very helpful, because it is apt to identify which undertakings can in practice be fulfilled.

Other regional or minority languages which cannot qualify for protection and promotion under Part III, because of the low number of speakers or because the language lacks a substantial territorial base, are covered under Part II of the Charter, but this part contains general objectives and principles that must guide each state in the protection and promotion of all regional or minority languages used on the state's territory in public and private life (see Chapter 3).

A special duty is imposed on the ratifying states to consult the speakers of regional or minority languages on the *manner* in which they wish their languages to be protected and promoted, and thereby to involve them in the actual policy-making. This is quite unusual in an international treaty such as the Charter, but it is considered important that the users of the languages have the opportunity to be involved from the beginning in consulting with the authorities as to how their languages should be protected and promoted. In Sweden, for example, the authorities organised a series of seminars with the various language groups, at which they discussed and assessed the actual situation of the languages and took note of the needs expressed by the representatives of the users of the languages concerned. The discussion was open and democratic, with the participation of experts in the field of regional or minority languages, both from the national and the international level. The obligations deriving from the Charter were explained and the protection and promotion to be granted was discussed. This procedure can be considered democratic and creates an atmosphere of consensus and cooperation between the authorities and the representatives of the users of the languages.

Let us briefly recall the two main reasons why it is important to have a strong and detailed instrument of ratification: first, this goal matters because the obligations of the states are then clear. They are clear to the authorities who will be responsible for implementing them, and they to the users of the languages that will benefit from protection and promotion. Second, the effectiveness of the monitoring mechanism of the Charter will be jeopardised if the obligations undertaken are not clear or do not correspond to the actual situation within the state. This will be further analysed in the next section.

The different undertakings of both Parts II and III could appear as resulting in a costly and difficult operation for a state where several languages are to be considered. But in fact, it does not have to be so. The Explanatory Report of the Charter (see Appendix II) takes into consideration the costs entailed by many of the provisions and the varying administrative and financial capacity of the European states. Therefore, the state has the option to add to its commitments at a later stage, as its legal situation develops or its financial circumstances allow. The fact that the state may amend the instrument of ratification shows the continuing impact of the Charter, because as the situation in the state changes for the better, the instrument of ratification may be improved with the aim of achieving increased protection and promotion. If the state cannot, owing to its economic situation, subscribe to certain provisions, there is a possibility that this may be done at a later stage. This underlines the 'living element' in this convention: its flexibility is embodied into its structure from the initial stages by the 'menu system' and continues after ratification with the possibility of improvement of the ratification instrument. This paves a solid path for the protection and promotion system established for each language in each state. To achieve this, however, it is important to be able to count on the good faith of the contracting parties.

Setting up the monitoring

The authors of the Charter and the member states of the Council of Europe provided for a control mechanism consisting of an examination of states' reports by an independent body of experts. Part IV (Articles 15–17) of the Charter deals with the main aspects of this mechanism.

Every signatory state to the Charter is obliged to provide periodical reports on its policy pursued in accordance with Part II of this Charter (objectives and principles) and on the measures taken in application of those provisions of Part III which they have accepted (measures in public life). The first report must be presented within one year of the date when the Charter enters into force for the state concerned. This report is intended to describe the situation of the regional and minority languages at that moment. The subsequent reports must be presented at three-yearly intervals after the first report. According to the Charter, the reports have to be made public by the parties.

The initial periodical report provided by the contracting party is divided into three parts. Part I gives general information on the existing legislation concerning the languages, both territorial and non-territorial, in that country and the number of speakers of those languages. States are also asked to list bodies or organisations that promote the languages, and to state whether these bodies have been consulted in preparing the report. Part II refers to languages defined under Article 7 of the Charter, while Part III requires parties to give detailed answers for each regional or minority language specified in the ratification instrument, taking each language separately. This part of the report will give a detailed listing of the measures that exist for the protection and promotion of each language.

Article 17 of the Charter determines that the independent committee of experts shall be composed of one member per state party to the Charter. Each party is entitled to nominate a list of individuals 'of the highest integrity and recognised competence' in the matters dealt with in the Charter. The Committee of Ministers then appoints one person from the list for a period of six years. They are eligible for re-appointment. The emphasis is on the independence of such experts. Even though they are nominated by their respective states, they do not represent those states, but rather they represent themselves and contribute their knowledge and are elected because of their professional experience.

The Committee examines the reports presented by the parties to the Secretary General of the Council of Europe under Article 15 of the Charter. The examination of the reports consists of assessing that the measures taken by each party correspond to their actual undertakings and that the report corresponds to the real situation of regional or minority languages in the respective State party. On the basis of the evaluation of the Committee of Experts, the latter adopts its own report and suggestions for recommendations to be addressed to the Committee of Ministers of the Council of Europe. The adoption of such Recommendations will therefore encourage the parties to gradually reach a higher level of commitment in accordance with the Charter, a factor that underlines the dynamic nature of this treaty.

In reviewing the reports, the Committee can be approached by bodies or associations legally established in the respective State party and wishing to supply additional information or to give their views on specific situations relating to the application of the Charter. The Charter itself does not pose any limitations as to the nature of these associations, other than the requirement that they have to be established in the State concerned in accordance with national legislation. Accordingly, they can be associations of a cultural, political, or any other character which have an interest in the situation of regional or minority languages in their country. Their comments and input may be received by the secretariat before or after the publication of the periodical reports. It has been observed that in those states where the publication of the initial periodical report has been well organised by the State, the participation of these organisations with the Committee of Experts is more efficient. It therefore gives a clear indication to the Committee as to how well the authorities have encouraged their participation and how well the reports have been made public. The Committee of Experts may verify any information submitted by the states concerned and must call on them for further explanations, where necessary, in order to ascertain the exact situation.

As to the concrete method of examining the periodical reports, the Committee has at present initiated the actual examination of the reports that it has received. This approach rests mainly on the analysis of the information contained in the reports, and on a comparison of this information both with the information that it receives from the outside and with the actual undertakings of the respective party. It is safe to say at this stage that the special system of the Charter, which consists of choosing the exact paragraphs and sub-paragraphs to be applied, facilitates this analysis. The reason is that the undertakings in respect of each party are very clear, and therefore the work of the Committee is clear in the sense that they only need to find out if and how these specific undertakings are being fulfilled in legal terms and in actual practice. The options chosen by a State for the languages in Part III may be looked upon as the 'goals' of regional or minority language policy, and one observes that when the instrument of ratification is detailed, as for instance in the instrument provided by Finland, the work of the Committee of Experts is quite targeted and precise. This instrument details separately the paragraphs and sub-paragraphs relating to Swedish, which is the less widely used official language in Finland, and to the Sámi language. This is logical, since one cannot view the situation of the Swedish language as similar in any way to that of the Sámi language in the North of Finland. The needs of these two languages are different, the number of speakers is not the same, the cultures of the two language communities are very diverse and their separate needs are, accordingly, specific.

Another important element in the monitoring mechanism is the possibility for the Committee to undertake so-called 'on-the-spot visits'. In this case, a delegation of the Committee travels to the respective state to gather information, consult with the government and meet bodies and associations concerned by the situation of regional or minority languages in that state. This method permits the Committee to gain a better insight into the results of the concrete policies and measures taken by states for the real protection and promotion of the languages in question. These visits give the speakers of the regional or minority languages and the authorities in the state the opportunity to express their satisfaction or discontent as to various policy measures, and to try to find common grounds for reaching an appropriate and peaceful solution to what often turns out to be a very practical and simple matter. The Charter, in this sense, has very often raised the level of awareness of the need to open the discussion on how language policy could be improved.

The Committee is not a judicial body. It is not authorised to issue judgements on state parties. It is authorised, however, to monitor the implementation of the Charter and receive information to that end. Naturally, it is entitled to form an opinion on the situation of the various languages in a particular state party.

On the basis of these procedures, the Committee will finally be in a position to prepare its report to the Committee of Ministers of the Council of Europe, which will be based, as indicated above, on the report, the comments from bodies and associations in the state, and the conclusions of the 'on the spot visits'. The findings of the Committee take the form of a report, addressed to the Committee of Ministers, and containing suggestions for recommendations to be addressed to the relevant contracting party.

The last element in the monitoring process is the unusual role given to the Parliamentary Assembly of the Council of Europe. The Charter has a unique provision that requires the Secretary General of the Council of Europe to present a biennial detailed report on the application of the Charter to the Parliamentary Assembly. This is a very unusual provision in a Council of Europe treaty, which underlines the importance of involving parliamentarians of the member states of the Council of Europe in the protection and promotion of regional or minority languages. This review mechanism specific to the Charter must be evaluated differently for each state. As the regional or minority languages are different in each state, and are confronted with specific needs and challenges, the case of each state is different. Time and practice will show us how this cooperation of European states in subscribing to common legal standards for the benefit of the languages traditionally used on their territory will contribute to the safeguarding of an essential element of the cultural heritage of Europe.

Notes

1. I am grateful to Regina Jensdóttir for the original version of this chapter. The views expressed in this chapter are those of its author in her capacity as an expert, and are not intended to represent the official views of the Council of Europe as the organisation under whose authority the Charter was developed and is being monitored.
2. However, as pointed out in the preceding chapter, the protection afforded by the Charter also extends to official languages which are less widely used on the whole or part of the territory of a state.

Part III
Application

Summary of Part III

Part III contains five chapters and is the most substantial of this book. Chapter 5 describes the general logic with which we can move from legal texts to practical measures, introducing the key concepts of 'effectiveness', 'cost-effectiveness' and 'democracy' as principles of what is often called 'good policy', 'best practice' or similar expressions. The following chapters focus on language policy, examining how we can assess their effectiveness (Chapter 6), their costs and cost-effectiveness (Chapter 7) and their more or less 'democratic' character – where the operative notion is that of 'participatory democracy'. Concepts are presented analytically and illustrated with examples. They are then applied in a walk-through example devoted to education (Chapter 9). Education has been chosen because it is arguably the key element of policies in favour of regional or minority languages. Throughout Part III, the emphasis is on the links between, on the one hand, theoretical principles and methodology and, on the other hand, their practical application. The aim of this exercise is not to provide ready-made solutions to the problems encountered on the terrain since, given the variability of real-world situations, this would be an unrealistic goal. The goals pursued in these chapters are to help users structure their own policy analysis approach to the practical problems with which they are confronted.

5
From Legal Texts to 'Good Policy'

Negative rights, positive rights and results

The originality of the European Charter for Regional or Minority Languages is in large part the result of its concern for linguistic diversity as a feature worth preserving. Nevertheless, it is useful, in keeping with the bridge-building logic of this book, to position the Charter with respect to key aspects of the legal and political discourse about rights. This discussion will help us to fully grasp the specificity of the Charter.[1]

Most of the important legal developments took place after the Second World War, although some instruments for minority protection were initiated after the First World War by the League of Nations. Lists of relevant legal documents often start with the Universal Declaration of Human Rights (1948), followed the Convention for the Protection of Human Rights and Fundamental Freedoms (1950) and the International Covenant on Civil and Political Rights (1966). These instruments

> ... provide for the classic liberal civil and political rights such as the right to life, the freedom from torture, the right to liberty and security of the person, the freedom from arbitrary detention, the right to a fair trial, the right to freedom of thought, conscience and religion, the freedom of expression, the freedom of assembly and association with others, and so on, as well as the fundamental principle of freedom from discrimination.[2]

However, such rights are primarily 'negative' as opposed to 'positive' rights, in the sense that states must *abstain* from acting in certain ways; this emphasis on protecting individuals from the state was a clear reaction to the atrocities of national-socialism. Nonetheless, essential as they are, negative rights may not prove sufficient.

Let us first consider this point from a 'language-in-society' perspective. Some rights can only be exercised by individuals in interaction with others, and much of this interaction takes place in the public domain. This is largely the case for language rights. Using a language requires interlocutors, and the viability of a language in the long run requires that it must be possible to use it in as many different contexts as possible – this to avoid that some registers of language fall into disuse, and that a language be de-legitimised and excluded from certain functions or 'domains'. It follows that the full exercise of language rights requires the language to be considered appropriate for pleading in a court of law, arguing with a policeman in the street, retrieving information about current affairs in the media, or sealing a business deal. Clearly, many of the 'domains' concerned are influenced by the action of the state, or may even be said to be within the state's competence. Consequently, the state must also safeguard some *positive* rights, in the sense that the state must take certain actions, such as ensuring that a regional or minority language can be used in court or heard on the airwaves.

This 'language-in-society' reading of the necessities of minority language maintenance is echoed by recent developments on the legal plane. The drafting and adoption of a growing range of international instruments over the past decade reflect an increasing recognition of the fact that negative rights must be supplemented by positive rights, which require states not only to abstain from certain actions (for example, abstaining from practising discrimination against members of linguistic minorities), but also actually to engage in action (for example, taking appropriate steps for the maintenance of regional or minority languages). This results in a two-pillar system comprising both negative and positive rights. From a legal perspective, the need for positive rights is rooted in the principle of substantive equality. In order to enjoy the same conditions as members of the majority, members of the minority must be given particular protection, which is aimed at creating or maintaining the conditions that are practically necessary for those conditions to be realised for them as well (and not just for members of the majority).

Put differently, the principle of substantive equality implies that in order for a true equality of conditions to be achieved, a differential treatment for people facing different circumstances is justified.[3] This principle is not new, and it can be observed in jurisprudence issued by the Permanent Court of International Justice in the 1930s.[4] However, it has become more manifest in recent years. Even if it can be observed across international organisations,[5] this evolution seems most visible in instruments developed under the auspices of the Council of Europe. The key document in this respect is not the often-quoted Framework Convention for the Protection of National Minorities adopted by the Council of Europe in 1994, and which came into force in 1998, but, of course, the Charter.

Before returning to the Charter in relation to the notion of 'pillars' of minority protection, it is important to address the question of the link between negative and positive rights on the one hand, and individual and group rights on the other hand. Some commentators of certain ongoing language policy debates (for example, in the case of language minorities in Canada) set great store by the notion of group rights. The underlying analytical concepts, whether from the perspective of law or from that of political philosophy, are complex, and it would far exceed the scope of this book to venture into an account of this debate.[6] However, it is useful to note that the invocation of collective or group rights is not a necessity for language policy, to the extent that positive rights can be derived from the notion of individual rights alone. This point is also important in order to establish unequivocally the full congruence of language policies in favour of regional or minority languages with the principles of liberalism – a term to be understood here as an analytical category in political philosophy. I shall attempt to make this point clear on the basis of a 'non-legal' approach.

Let us first recall that in a liberal perspective, the fundamental entity of human society is the individual. Rights are therefore vested in the individual, and are thus 'individual rights'. Any invocation of 'collective' rights presupposes that collective entities like 'groups' are legally instituted, which raises delicate and potentially worrisome questions of democracy; in particular, how are the possibly opposing interests of individuals within the group safeguarded? How can decisions made 'by the group' guarantee internal democracy within it? For this reason, collective rights are often viewed with understandable suspicion.

However, this raises a difficulty regarding the nature of the rights invoked to justify language policies. For example, one might object that when a minority community demands public services in its own language, this claim is based on a collective right. Consequently, many forms of much-needed support for regional or minority languages can be excluded on such grounds. It is true that some advocates of minority languages have (perhaps imprudently) invoked the notions of collective rights, as if it were generally unproblematic, and as if the implied logical requirements, such as the necessity of *identifying* the group granted those rights were unproblematic too. This notion of collective rights has been called upon by some to establish the legitimacy of Quebec's language policies.[7] However, the right to receive public services in one's language, even if it is not the majority (or, at a given moment, official) language of the state, need not rely on some concept of 'collective' or 'group' right. The point is that certain individual rights can only be exercised socially, in interaction with other individuals. The 'social' or 'collective' provision of such rights must therefore be seen as a logical condition for the full exercise of individual rights, but the collective nature of the rights so created is, at most, derivative. These rights can admittedly be put in a special category,[8] but it seems sufficient to view them as rights 'belonging to some people individually, but in their capacity of member of a certain group'.[9]

These group-differentiated rights (or 'community rights') can be broken up into three main forms ('self-government rights'; 'polyethnic rights'; 'special-representation rights')[10] to accommodate the specific needs characteristic of members of specific groups of people. However, they all serve to ensure that individuals who belong to a minority have access to the same rights as if they belonged to the majority. This principle is embodied in the notion of a 'context of choice' to which individuals must have access. This point has been expressed by Habermas as follows: 'a correctly understood theory of [citizenship] rights requires a politics of recognition that protects the individual in the life contexts in which his or her identity is formed'.[11] Following Kymlicka, a distinction can further be made between potentially illiberal 'internal restrictions' through which the autonomy of putative minority members would be restricted, and 'external protections' which serve to guarantee this 'context of choice' and enable individuals to maintain their distinctive language and culture, if they choose to do so. Such external protections promote fairness, in that they reduce the disparities between the range of choices offered to members of the majority and members of the minority, and are perfectly in keeping with liberal political theory. It follows that minority rights do not require a communitarian political philosophy, and are fully compatible with a liberal perspective.[12]

The Charter, however, goes beyond positive rights; in a sense, it proposes to build a 'third pillar' to complement the first (negative rights, in particular non-discrimination) and the second (positive rights, *possibly* interpreted as a particular form of 'group-specific' rights whose necessity is derived from the application of the principle of substantive equality). Yet this 'third pillar' cannot be understood strictly in terms of rights.

Let us start out from the observation that the existence of positive rights enjoins the state to act (instead of abstaining from certain actions). This, however, may imply relatively little in terms of actual results, because even well-intentioned action can prove unsuccessful. The chink in the armour is, evidently, located at the level of the actual outcomes of policies adopted on the basis of an array of rights. Let us briefly refer to the Framework Convention as an example. Its Article 5 (paragraph 1) provides that '[t]he Parties undertake to promote the conditions necessary for persons belonging to national minorities to maintain and develop their culture, and to preserve the essential elements of their identity, namely their religion, language, traditions and cultural heritage.' Apart from the very general character of this provision, we should note that it leaves much of the burden of language maintenance on people themselves. Suppose for example that in compliance with this measure, a state decides to support the printing of literary works in a regional or minority language. The fact that a large number of titles are published every year does not necessarily mean that those books will be bought, that they will be interesting or relevant enough to be read, and that this measure will be *effective* in terms of securing an increase in actual language use. Returning to the concepts introduced in Chapter 2, such a measure increases opportunity, but not (or only very indirectly) capacity and desire. Putting it differently, the success of such a measure remains, to a large extent, dependent on people's behaviour, which will depend in turn on their capacity to read those books and on their willingness to buy and read them. Merely requiring the state to offer opportunity (for example, by subsidising the publication of minority language books) practically exempts the state from responsibility for the fate of the language concerned.

There is no doubt that the behaviour of actual or potential language users is crucial for the success of any policy measure. Language use cannot be mandated, and there are many examples of well-intentioned revitalisation policies that have failed to produce any results, because of their top-down perspective, which ignored the role of actors.[13] This does not mean that the authorities must substitute themselves to the individuals and make language decisions in their place. However, should we not expect the state to select measures in such a way that they actually engage actual and potential users, and result in effective minority language use? This idea is reflected in the triple necessity of 'capacity, opportunity and desire', and it is also present in the Charter. Because it insists, for example in Article 7, on 'the need for resolute action to promote regional or minority languages *in order to safeguard them*' (Paragraph 1c, my italics), and on 'the facilitation and/or encouragement of the use of regional or minority languages' (Paragraph 1d), the Charter goes beyond positive rights, and calls for actual results.

In this sense, as pointed out earlier, the Charter represents the vanguard of a trend in legal instruments, because it shifts the emphasis towards the effectiveness of the policies to be adopted. This notion is not absent from the legal literature, particularly in the field of human rights and minority rights, where reference to the 'effectiveness of rights' is increasingly made.[14] Yet it also raises a new range of questions that can be summed up as follows: how do we know that some policies are effective, or that some are more effective than others? The analytical framework for effective language policies, represented by Figure 2.1 in Chapter 2, focuses precisely on this question, that is, how a particular policy is related to 'outcomes' (or results). Clearly, effectiveness should be a feature of 'good policies'. This requires a closer examination of the meaning of 'good policies'.

Defining 'good policy'

The structure of decision-making

In the field of policy analysis, whose basic principles have been presented in Chapter 2, a number of methods have been developed to assist in decision-making. Directly or indirectly, they rest on welfare theory, which sits astride economics and political science.

Much of welfare theory rests on fairly traditional concepts, such as 'Pareto optimality' – so named after Vilfredo Pareto, who at the beginning of the twentieth century made fundamental contributions to economic theory. Pareto optimality characterises a situation such that it is not possible to make one person better off (that is, increase his or her welfare) without at the same time making another person worse off (that is, decreasing that other person's welfare).[15] In other words, the best possible situation would be achieved. This notion of optimality is, of course, highly abstract. Besides, it says nothing about the distribution of welfare between members of society.[16] The Pareto optimality criterion is therefore a purely allocative concept, in the sense that it focuses on the efficient allocation of scarce resources, leaving out distributive considerations. However, it may be expanded: if the set of goals is broadened so as to include 'equality', 'equity' or some other notion of social justice, the characteristics of an optimum can take the latter into account. While the Pareto criterion remains an important frame of reference in theoretical analysis, it is of limited use in practical policy analysis.[17]

Typically, policy analysts are confronted with narrower choices, such as the choice between a limited number of policy alternatives. Therefore, they can proceed on the assumption that one of them is better than all the others or, if more than one is in top position, that a particular choice is 'at least as good' as any other.

A policy analysis exercise first requires a thorough examination of goals. More specifically, the three following steps must be undertaken:

1. Formulating explicitly and precisely the goals to be reached. This normally requires more than the enunciation of general principles, like 'preserving a regional or minority language'. This book suggests, as a further but not final step in goal determination, to aim at restoring and maintaining a *self-priming mechanism* for regional or minority language reproduction. Specific paragraphs in the Charter can then be applied with a view to achieving this goal.
2. Detailing the general goal into more specific objectives, and then setting up a sequential hierarchy between objectives. For example, if the general goal is to 'restore the self-priming mechanism', achieving this goal will depend on a well-designed, probably step-wise approach, which will avoid putting the cart before the horses. For example, an objective such as opening tertiary (university-level) minority language education streams makes little sense if some effort has not first gone into a more basic objective, such as teaching the language to a sufficiently high number of people at an adequate level of competence. This requirement, which points to the importance of logical consistency, also implies that mutually incompatible goals must be avoided.
3. Analysing the interdependency between goals; some are reachable only if other goals have been met first (again, the education example of the preceding paragraph may be quoted).

Once goals are clearly set and understood, it is possible to focus on the measures themselves and on the evaluation of alternatives. In its most elementary form, this evaluation requires the following steps, which form the core of cost–benefit analysis, whose textbook principles can be summarised as follows:

1. A set of alternative measures for reaching the goal is identified and formulated in detail;
2. all the impacts, both favourable and unfavourable, present and future, on all of society are determined, for each of the policy measures considered;
3. values, usually (but not necessarily) in monetary units, are assigned to these impacts. Favourable impacts will be registered as benefits, unfavourable one as costs;
4. the net benefit (total benefit minus total cost) is calculated for each policy measure;
5. a choice is made to pursue one policy measure (instead of the others).

If the policy analysis exercise aims not at selecting and implementing a policy, but at preparing information for debate about them, step 5 may take the form of a simple recommendation that one particular measure be given particular consideration.

In practice, many policy problems cannot be sorted out in such a straightforward manner. For example, policies often imply a complex sequence of interrelated decisions that depend on factors (such as reactions by the general public) about which policy analysts cannot make reliable predictions – and over which, of course, they have no control. In such cases, the likely effects of policies can be represented in the form of a decision tree, in which uncertain future events are given a probability, yielding conditional evaluations of the effects of policies.

The entire procedure can of course be dismissed as 'reductionist' – a criticism which usually amounts to saying that the procedure does not pay adequate attention to the complexity of the issues at hand and shoehorns them into an unduly rigid framework. This warning is unquestionably a useful one. However, the question is whether there exist manifestly superior ways of comparing courses of actions and preparing decisions. The fact remains that ultimately, most decisions are made in this way, including by the most righteous critics of cost–benefit analysis; the main point of this type of procedure is to make the decision-making process as transparent as possible. An honest, well-designed approach using a cost–benefit (or, more generally, a 'drawback v. advantage') rationale will generally force analysts to think hard about the logical merits of the statements that they make, and to formulate arguments transparent to themselves as well as to others. Let us also remember the proviso made earlier: in this book, the public policy perspective is seen strictly as an instrument in clarifying the options at hand, not as tool for dictating choices.

An in-depth technical treatment of the evaluation of benefits and costs would take us too far, and in any event, the actual estimation of the benefits and costs of alternatives in language policy is, of course, eminently case-dependent.[18] In the following chapters, I shall therefore focus on generally applicable principles, and to illustrate them with examples related to the application of specific articles in the Charter.

Devising shortcuts

Even when a full-fledged, formal evaluation of the benefits and costs of a policy is impracticable (usually because only a part of the necessary data is available, or simply because there is not enough time to carry out an extensive evaluation), it is necessary to refer to explicit principles for choosing between alternatives.

This concern presumably lies behind frequent invocations of 'good policy', 'good practice', 'best policy' and 'best practice'. Unfortunately, most of the time, only the most fleeting attention is paid to the actual meaning of those terms.[19] This raises the problem of what is 'good', what is 'better' and what is 'best', and of the criteria on the basis of which these labels can be assigned to a particular 'policy' or 'practice'.

A review of the use of those terms in the materials produced by international organisations, government agencies or non-governmental organisations (for example the OECD or the World Bank), whether in printed form or on the internet, indicates that a number of characteristics are normally associated with 'good' or 'best' 'policy' or 'practice'. These are, in particular, 'improvement', 'effectiveness', 'efficiency', 'equity', 'better services', 'better quality', 'reduction of expenditure', 'performance', 'accountability', 'citizens' satisfaction', 'more responsive government' and 'sustainability'. Conversely, it seems that 'good policy' requires avoiding 'inconsistency', 'incoherence', 'major failure in implementation', 'corruption', 'wastefulness', 'opacity', 'any action that generates tension between groups', and so on. On those grounds, an acceptable alternative to formal policy analysis may be to compare a set of alternative measures and to rank-order them in terms of these desirable and undesirable characteristics. However, applying this technique to clarify the meaning of 'good/best' 'policy/practice' in the case of *language* policies is made more difficult by the lack of policy experience documented *in those terms*. More precisely, policy discussions found in the literature, including reports published by the major organisations that refer to 'good/best' 'policy/practice' typically focus on other (that is, non-language) policy issues, such as public finance management, economic and social development, the performance of education systems, income distribution, agriculture, energy, and so on. This once again confirms that an application of those principles to language policies probably is a novel enterprise.

However, in the discourse of governments, international organisations, and non-governmental organisations about 'good/best' 'policy/practice', three notions emerge with regularity: the *effectiveness* of policies; their *cost-effectiveness*; and the *democratic* character of the procedures for the selection, design and evaluation of policies. Moreover, many of the more specific characteristics often mentioned can be subsumed under those three notions. These notions, which were, for the first time, placed at the centre of a conference on minority language policies in 2000,[20] will also guide us in the following chapters of this book.

Before moving on to a discussion of these notions, however, it is important to recall the reasons for their strategic usefulness in the context of the Charter.

The Charter requires states to identify the regional or minority languages to which particular provisions will apply, as well as the parts of the territory under their jurisdiction where they will apply, in addition to selecting a set of measures proper, in accordance with the requirements laid out in Articles 2 and 3. This implies multiple levels of variability. Countries are different from one another in terms of their legal and political structure, history, economic resources, and so on; even within a particular state, different regional or minority languages are confronted with completely different situations. Therefore, it is practically impossible to claim that 'good practice' requires, for all languages, that a particular measure be adopted.

Consider for example the issue of language use in the packaging of consumer goods: feasibility will depend on social, political and economic context, as well as on the state of development of a language itself. In the case of a highly fragmented language with several written standards (for example Ladin in the Dolomites of Italy, Sámi in northern Scandinavia, or Romansch in eastern Switzerland), encouraging the use of the language on labels and packaging will raise different questions (including that of using, or not, a unified standard if one has been developed) than in those cases, such as Swedish in Finland or Catalan, where the problem of language fragmentation does not arise. In the same way, defining the educational level up to which it is advisable to provide teaching through the medium of a regional or minority language will, among other things, depend on demolinguistic figures. What is feasible for a regional or minority language with more than half a million speakers like Euskera (such as offering a range of subjects in Euskera at university level) is likely to be considerably more difficult in the case of the much smaller Sorab community in Germany, with its approximately 50,000 speakers. Furthermore, the relative urgency of different measures (whether in the perspective of objective probabilities of language survival, or in terms of the priorities of the members of the language communities concerned) will vary. Some communities may, for historical and institutional reasons, set great store by the official recognition of their language and its use in formal situations (such as the judiciary), while others will prefer a focus on educational measures.

For all these reasons, it should be clear that it would not make sense, in this book, to recommend specific measures. Rather, the emphasis will be placed on the way in which policy alternatives are evaluated and on the criteria for such an evaluation, a question to which I now turn.

Three basic principles of good policy: a preview

Though fairly clear in general and theoretical terms, the notions of effectiveness, cost-effectiveness and democracy have not often been applied explicitly to practical problems of minority language policy. Furthermore, as soon as we move away from theory and edge towards application, clear-cut meanings are sometimes blurred – hence also the relative vagueness of notions of 'good/best policy/practice', as shown in the preceding section. Effectiveness, cost-effectiveness and democracy are viewed here as three principles of good policy. They will be examined in detail, along with their application to language policies, in the following chapters. In this section, I shall introduce their essential aspects, deliberately avoiding some potentially difficult ones, and focusing instead on transposing the theoretical notions to the sphere of practical questions.

Effectiveness

The terminology of effectiveness is far from stable and is actually liable to vary from one author to the next. Nonetheless, the underlying concepts remain very much the same, making the issue one of terminology, rather than one of contents. Therefore, what we need is to agree on a set of definitions, knowing full well that other authors might have preferred other conventions.

As a general starting point, we can say that what is 'effective' is 'something that works relatively well', or at least not worse than some alternative we care to consider. To take a very simple example, when learning a foreign language by oneself, two hours of study every day will normally, all other things being equal, produce more effect (and be *more effective*) than only half an hour of study every day. Generally, measures that are more effective than others also tend to cost more (in the example just given, the extra cost can be measured in time), but cost is not the issue right now (it will be addressed below).[21]

Even in this simplest of representations, it is not always easy to assess the effectiveness of an option. The problem largely rests with the identification of the ultimate goal of a policy, and of the links between the policy measure and the ultimate goal. For example, suppose that a government programme is introduced, offering optional minority language courses to civil servants in order to raise their language skills, which will better enable them to serve the public in the minority language concerned. How is the effectiveness of such a programme to be evaluated? One tempting option would be to count how many members of the civil service have actually taken this course, or completed it successfully.

But unless the programme is very unattractive or poorly designed, we would quite naturally expect the number of civil servants with some knowledge of the minority language to increase as a result of such a programme. A much better criterion may well be the extent to which, as a result of this programme, the number of people who do use the minority language in their dealings with civil servants actually increases (or, alternatively, if the people who normally attempted to can now do so with higher frequency). Ultimately, the success of a promotional policy in favour of minority languages can only be evaluated by the public (in particular language users), and their perception of the effects of the policy are more likely to depend on whether they can use the minority language than on whether civil servants have taken a language course.

To evaluate policies, the first thing to do is therefore to identify a goal, or an outcome, that makes sense from the standpoint of the 'users' of the policy (that is, ultimately, the members of the minority groups, or even society as a whole), and to clarify this desired outcome in detail, as explained earlier in the chapter. One convenient language convention, in this respect, is to keep the word 'output' to denote the direct effects of a policy, and the word 'outcome' to denote its effects in terms of the ultimate goal pursued. In the case of language policies, and more specifically the implementation of the Charter, we already have a starting point in terms of goal-setting. We have seen in Chapter 2 why the goal to be pursued, in the spirit of the Charter, should imply recreating and securing a 'self-priming mechanism for language reproduction', which corresponds to stage 5 in the 'Graded intergenerational disruption scale'. Looking at it from another angle, we have noted that this goal is more likely to be achieved if three conditions are present among actual or potential language users: the capacity, the opportunity, and the desire (or willingness) to use the regional or minority language.[22]

Hence, the crux of effectiveness evaluation is to ascertain, referring to the 'policy-to-outcome path' presented in Chapter 2, the chain of events that links a policy measure to *actual* increases in language use. This question, of course, arises with respect to any of the policies that can be considered for the implementation of the Charter, whether they pertain to education (Article 8), judicial authorities (Article 9), administrative authorities and public services (Article 10), the media (Article 11), cultural activities and facilities (Article 12), economic and social life (Article 13), or transfrontier exchanges (Article 14).

One of the most important dimensions of effectiveness evaluation is that of the choice of units of measurement. It is impossible to assess effectiveness unless these are clearly defined. While this requirement is primarily a general one of conceptual consistency, it becomes indispensable for comparing the effectiveness of two policies. For example, when considering two different approaches to language teaching, with the aim of developing capacity (one of the three necessary conditions of actual language use), one sensible unit of measurement of the results is learners' proficiency at the end of the programme. One might therefore start with a pilot phase to assess the effectiveness of both policies, and test the language competence of three groups of learners at the end of their studies (one having been taught under policy *A*, another under policy *B*, and a third as a control group). The results provide a set of indicators of the respective effectiveness of the policies considered.

Costs and cost-effectiveness

The concept of effectiveness presented above is only a starting point; and as a general rule, policies endowed with more resources will have more noticeable effects. However, as we have seen before, it is also important to take cost into account. Even the most effective policy does not necessarily represent the best policy, if it is extremely expensive. This is why it is useful to move on to a second step, and to examine cost-effectiveness (which is also sometimes referred to as 'efficiency', as explained in note 21 of this chapter).

In order to examine cost-effectiveness, one must first evaluate the costs of a policy. Costs must not be confused with expenditure. Expenditure is a direct money outlay related to a policy (for example, subsidies paid out to minority-language publishers or radio stations). Cost, however, goes beyond direct expenditure. It also includes, for example, the value of the time spent by civil servants in the central government on administering the subsidy programme. Costs therefore hark back to the output, with which a set of heterogeneous elements of expenditure can be associated. Many such costs are difficult to assess, and expenditure on a subset of actual cost is, most of the time, considered an acceptable approximation of actual cost.

In general terms, a production process or a policy can be considered cost-effective if, given a certain amount of resources, the results are as good as possible, or if, given a certain goal, it is achieved at the lowest possible cost.

Assessing cost-effectiveness in this absolute sense requires immense knowledge, because it implies that we *know* that given a certain cost, it would not be possible to achieve more – or that, given that a certain result is achieved, it would not be possible to save and achieve the same goal at lower cost. In practice, it is almost impossible to be certain, and the problem is normally tackled in a slightly different way, using the principle of comparison.

Suppose that we are comparing two policies, *A* and *B*, both of which promote the use of a regional or minority language by civil servants interacting with the public. It is unclear if either of them is cost-effective in the absolute sense, for the reasons just mentioned. However, it is very likely that one is more cost-effective than the other. To assess this point, we would first express the results of policies *A* and *B* in similar units of measurement. This may have occurred already at the early stage of effectiveness evaluation, where we might compare, as a possible indicator, the frequency of minority language use in the provision of social services under both policies – as revealed, for example, by survey data or by office records (or as can be estimated with a theoretical model). Suppose that under policy *A*, the actual or expected increase is 1,000 clients served every year in the regional or minority language, and that under policy *B*, the actual or expected increase is 1,400 such clients a year. Policy *B* is therefore 40 per cent more effective; but it does not mean that is more cost-effective.

Suppose now that policy *A* requires the training of a certain number of bilingual staff, at the cost of €10,000 spent once and for all, and that civil servants' bilingual skills will remain active and relevant for a ten-year period, after which retraining would become necessary. Let us assume that policy *B*, which includes further cultural awareness training, would entail a once-and-for-all outlay of €21,000. The per-year expenditure, over the ten-year period considered, is €1,000 under policy *A*, and €2,100 under policy *B*. What are the per-client and per-year policy costs?

In the case of policy *A*, the ratio of cost per client served is 1,000/1,000, that is, €1 per client and per year (counting the additional clients served in the regional or minority language). In the case of policy *B*, the ratio is 2,100/1,400, that is, €1.5 per client and per year. Even if policy *B* is more effective, it is also, in this example, less cost-effective. Of course, it may be that some important benefits of policy *B* have not been taken into account. For example, since policy *B* includes not only language training, but also cultural awareness training for the civil servants, not just the quantity, but also the quality of the interaction would be improved. If so, the measurement of the effects of policy *B* needs to be adjusted upwards, and *B* can, after all, turn out to be not only more effective, but also more cost-effective. Again, no mode of measurement can claim to be perfect or superior to any other, but some can be shown to be more coherent or more complete than others.

The evaluation of cost-effectiveness gives rise to a new set of indicators. We shall take a closer look at them in Chapter 7, when we return to the questions of cost and cost-effectiveness. All this may look like a needlessly tedious discussion, both too obvious and too complicated. However, there is ample reason to think that cost-effectiveness matters and deserves close attention, for at least two reasons. The first is a simple one of public finance: an expensive policy is likely to be unsustainable in the long run; besides, the state has other goals to achieve and other policies to finance, in the fields of education, health, security, or transport, to name but a few. The second is one of acceptability in majority opinion: typically, majorities are not always inclined to look genially on expenditure for minority language promotion; they may dismiss it as an unnecessary indulgence (coming in the way of more urgent government tasks) or as pandering to special interests. The acceptability of policy measures in favour of minority languages can be greatly enhanced if the authorities or institutions advocating them are able to show that these measures are cost-effective.

Democracy

Even if a policy is effective and cost-effective, it does not mean that it should be adopted. Two distinct problems need to be identified.

The first is that among all the cost-effective policies, not all are necessarily equally good. Though an *a priori* desirable feature, cost-effectiveness taken on its own can be a somewhat blind criterion. Most likely, some cost-effective solutions are absurd, while some are better than others – and one may be preferable to any other. Selecting one policy among the cost-effective policies is, in final analysis, a political process. Lest the message of this book be misconstrued, let this be repeated once more: the role of this political process is fully acknowledged in our policy analysis framework, and represented as the box at the very top of Figure 2.1. However, as explained then, the workings of this political process are beyond the scope of our discussion, and the service this book is intended to render is not to review these political issues, amply discussed in the sociolinguistics and language planning literature, but to focus on more mundane evaluation issues that arise 'downstream' from the political debate.

Even from an economic standpoint, the choice of one Pareto-optimal solution among the infinity of such solutions is ultimately deemed to be a political, not an economic question. For the purposes of theoretical analysis, economists will often assume the existence of a 'collective utility function', representing the preferences of society as a whole.

However, such a function cannot be derived from the individual preferences of members of society,[23] even if those preferences were fully known. It follows that choices made by society lie outside the analytical realm of economics, and should be assigned to a democratic political process offering appropriate safeguards for minority rights.

In theory, democratic institutions and majority rule, coupled with appropriate safeguards for minorities, constitutes a procedure more reliable than others for selecting and approaching the policies that citizens prefer out of a set of alternatives. However, this theoretical vision is not sufficient. Apart from the possible unreliability of majority voting revealed by Arrow's impossibility theorem (see note 23), or the question (not addressed here) of whether non-citizens should also have a say in such matters, there is one frequently overlooked problem in the approach to effectiveness and cost-effectiveness sketched out above. This problem is that of 'technocracy'. The vetting process whereby policies can be labelled as more or less 'effective' or 'cost-effective' is one that could be approached in purely technical terms, but a purely technical approach to this process may embody a technocratic ideology, which may well be at variance with the implementation of democratic procedures.

Hence, depending on the notion of democracy adhered to, it may not be deemed sufficient merely look into the formal institutional set-ups whereby people (including members of linguistic minorities) can participate in the language policy process. It is important, at all stages of this process, to remember the autonomy of social actors and to allow for constant feedback from civil society and its organisations onto the political process. This point is taken into account in the Charter (albeit in rather general terms) and exemplified by the explicit mention of the role of non-governmental organisations in the monitoring mechanism (see Chapter 4). These issues, however, have remained under-researched in the field of language policy although actors' responses to language revitalisation policies have been studied, and we shall return to them later.

Notes

1. For a specialist presentation of language rights in legal perspective, see e.g. Dunbar (2001), de Varennes (1999b) and Henrard (2000).
2. Dunbar (1999: 1).
3. See e.g. De Witte (1992). One should note, however, that the principle of substantive equality can already be invoked in relation with the 'negative' right to non-discrimination; as pointed out by de Varennes (1996: 119):
   'what non-discrimination requires from a government is not special privileges for some because they are members of a minority group. Non-discrimination calls instead for the following: if the states provides to some of its inhabitants

a service of benefit, such as education in their primary language, then it must do so in a non-discriminatory way. ... if the state or government has no obligation to do anything, but if it chooses to provide any benefit or service, it must do so without discrimination'.

4. In a 1935 ruling, the Court formulates the aim of minority protection as including the possibility to preserve 'the characteristics which distinguish them from the majority, and [satisfy] the ensuing special needs.' The Court further states that: '... nationals belonging to racial, religious or linguistic minorities shall be placed in every respect on a footing of perfect equality with other nationals of the State', and that minority elements need 'suitable means for the preservation of their racial peculiarities, their traditions and their national characteristics' (see Henrard, 2001). The opinion of the Court strikes the reader as remarkably modern, apart from some notions that no longer have currency, like 'racial peculiarities'.

5. A similar evolution can be observed in OSCE documents, particularly the Document of the Copenhagen Meeting of the Conference on the Human Dimension of the CSCE (1990), the Hague Recommendations Regarding the Education Rights of National Minorities (1996), and the Oslo Recommendations Regarding the Linguistic Rights of National Minorities (1998).

6. It appears that the domain of language law is regarded as quite separate from other strands of legal expertise, in the view of lawyers themselves; for example, the legal expert de Witte (1989: 89) observes that 'language law is characterised by a high degree of conceptual autonomy with respect to other branches of law'.

7. This notion of collective rights is arguably present in the very Preamble of the 1977 Charter of the French Language.

8. Henrard (2000), following Kymlicka (1989), identifies the category of 'minority rights', which the latter (1989: 90) describes as 'an important part of a recognizable liberal theory of equality'.

9. Henrard (2000: 153, n. 549); another lawyer, Benoît-Rohmer, commenting on the Framework Convention for the Protection of Persons belonging to National Minorities, notes that 'certain rights can be exercised only if several persons agree to use together this right [sic] which belongs to each of them' (1999: 16; my translation).

10. See e.g. May's discussion (2001: 116 ff.) of Kymlicka's concept of 'multicultural citizenship' (Kymlicka, 1995a).

11. Habermas (1994: 116), quoted by May (2000: 376).

12. See e.g. Kymlicka (1995a,b). I am therefore in general agreement with de Varennes, who notes that 'European and international documents all agree as to the individual nature of those rights' (1999a: 131), and that they 'clearly are [carrément] individual rights' (1999a: 129).

13. For example, on the experience of Irish language policy following independence, see Tovey, Hannan and Abramson (1989).

14. See e.g. Henrard (2000: 131 ff.) or the OSCE's *Lund Recommendations on the Effective Participation of National Minorities in Public Life* (Foundation for Inter-Ethnic Relations, 1999).

15. Neo-classical economic theory predicts that in a world characterised by perfect information and competitive markets, and in which there are none of the externalities typically associated with 'public goods', free markets result in a set of equilibrium prices and outputs of goods and services which

amount to a Pareto-optimal situation. We have already seen, in Chapter 2, that there are cases of *market failure* associated with public goods, and that a diverse linguistic environment can be seen as a public good. Hence, a Pareto optimum does not obtain in the real world, and a pure free-market equilibrium can be considered 'optimal' only in the context of theoretical analysis.

16. However, the relatively little-known redistributive impacts of language policies are eliciting rising interest, particularly in the economic approach to language policy; see Pool (1991a), Grin and Vaillancourt (2000) or Van Parijs (2002).

17. On the Pareto criterion and Pareto optimality, see e.g. Zajac (1995, Ch. 2) or Cullis and Jones (1998: Ch. 1).

18. For example, choosing between a mandatory or a voluntary scheme of bilingual packaging of goods carries benefits and costs which are dependent on local political context, on the general dispositions of firms, possibly on the distribution of firm ownership over members of the majority and minority communities, etc.

19. See e.g. documents published by the OSCE with a generous use of such terms without any definition, also when calling for an ombudsman to 'develop standards of good practice' (e.g. under http://www.osce.org/adihr/docs/).

20. 'Evaluating policy measures for minority languages in Europe: towards effective, cost-effective and democratic implementation', European Centre for Minority Issues, Flensburg (Germany), 23–24 June 2000. For a report of this conference, see Grin (2000b).

21. There is some ambiguity in the terminology used by the economic and policy analysis literature. The meaning of the underlying concepts, however, is stable, so that the issue is only one of vocabulary. Let us simply point out that the term 'effectiveness' is used by some authors to denote not just 'the effects' (as I do), but 'the effect per amount of resources used' (which I call 'cost-effectiveness'). What I refer to as 'cost-effectiveness' in this book is called by some authors 'economic efficiency' or 'technical efficiency' – sometimes simply 'efficiency'. However, this latter expression, in economic theory, is also used to describe a much more complex conjunction of characteristics (efficient production, efficient consumption, and efficient product-mix). The choice of terminology made in this book offers the advantage, in my opinion, of minimising the overlap of terms and the possible ensuing confusion; for a discussion of the respective meaning of these terms with an application to language education, see Grin (2001); on the full-blown concept of economic efficiency, see Zajac (1995) or Cullis and Jones (1998).

22. This objective is echoed for example in the mission statement of the Welsh Language Board, whose aim is 'to enable the Welsh language to become self-sustaining and secure as a medium of communication in Wales'. This requires, according to the Board, meeting four main challenges, namely: (i) increasing the number of people who are able to speak Welsh; (ii) providing opportunities to use the language; (iii) changing habits of language use, and encouraging people to take advantage of the opportunities provided; (iv) strengthening Welsh as a community language (see http://www.bwrdd-yr-iaith.org.uk/).

23. More precisely, Arrow's 'impossibility theorem' shows that 'there is no constitutional [decision] rule that will simultaneously satisfy what might be considered to be a list of "reasonable" conditions' (see Cullis and Jones, 1998: 76–7).

6
Effectiveness

In light of the preceding discussion, effectiveness evaluation is the first and most fundamental question to consider when preparing a language policy plan. We have seen that this requires in particular going through the following steps, which, *mutatis mutandis*, apply equally to *ex ante* and *ex post* analysis:

1. the in-depth examination of the goals to be achieved;
2. the analysis of the logical cause-and-effect links connecting the proposed policy, or policies, with the goals aimed at (the 'policy-to-outcome' path);
3. the choice of a unit of measurement of the outcome of different policy alternatives aiming at the same goal, making it possible to define indicators of effectiveness;
4. when very different policies have to be compared, the computation of a common unit of measurement;
5. to the extent possible, the assessment of the effects specifically due to the policy.

These questions are examined at closer range in this chapter.

Examination of goals

Let us assume, for reasons explained previously, that the overarching policy goal is the recreation and maintenance of a 'self-priming mechanism of language reproduction'. Although this is already more specific than 'the revitalisation of a regional or minority language' (let alone something even broader like 'implementing the Charter'), and therefore represents a step in the right direction, further detail is needed.

All of the measures proposed in the text of the Charter share this common goal, and measures are proposed in the seven major areas corresponding to Articles 8 through 14. The general goal can therefore be reformulated as follows: 'restoring and maintaining a self-priming mechanism of language reproduction through measures in the field of ... ', where the 'fields' correspond to those defined by articles in the Charter. We have also seen that the achievement of language policy goals is a process that ought to be parsed. This parsing can, for example, be summarised by the policy-to-outcome path, stressing the role of three conditions (capacity, opportunity and desire) for language use to occur.

Combining these notions, we can clarify the goals associated with the measures under each article in Table 6.1.

Table 6.1 only mentions, for each category of measures, the main condition targeted out of the three necessary conditions we have identified. There are, of course, many 'cross-effects'. For example, measures that increase the visibility of the language in commercial life or introduce its

Table 6.1 Goal specification

Art.	Area	Main condition targeted	Specification of objectives
8	Education	Capacity	Measures in the domain concerned must prioritise the increase in the *number* of users (quantity) and the development of their *skills* (quality).
9	Judicial system	Opportunity	Measures in the domains concerned must prioritise the *number, frequency* and *duration* of opportunities to use the language in dealings with the authorities.
10	Administration and public services	Opportunity	
11	Media	Opportunity	Measures in the domains concerned must prioritise the *number, frequency* and *duration* of opportunities to use the language in information, entertainment, cultural activities, and business and commerce.
12	Culture	Opportunity	The choice of measures must also prioritise those that will have the most beneficial influence on the *image* and *legitimacy* of the language, both in the eyes of users and non-users.
13	Economic and social life	Opportunity/ Desire	

use in official forms do not only provide opportunities to use the language; they also relegitimise the language and increase its prestige. In this way, they are likely to affect people's attitudes, which is, in turn, a reflection of their preferences regarding languages. In other words, offering opportunity will generally encourage willingness to use the language, and contribute to at least two of the three necessary conditions.

Existing research on the effectiveness of minority language policies sometimes defines willingness-enhancing measures as 'direct language promotion'. Such measures could be a seen as form of direct language marketing, which attempts not only to encourage speakers to use the language more, but also to foster positive attitudes among non-speakers of the language. However, the type of measures included in the Charter target mostly (in terms of direct effects) capacity and opportunity, rather than willingness or 'desire', which is why this latter condition is featured only once, as a complement to 'opportunity', in the column on 'main condition targeted' of Table 6.1. There is nothing in the Charter, however, to stop governments from engaging in direct language promotion.[1]

Readers will notice that Article 14 on transfrontier exchanges is not included in Table 6.1. The reason for this is that provisions regarding transfrontier exchanges are of a different logical standing than the preceding ones. Whereas Articles 8 through 13 concerns areas of human activity (whether directly linked to the operations of the state system, like Articles 8, 9 and 10, or less directly so – and to varying degrees – like Articles 11, 12 and 13), transfrontier exchange can be envisaged in any of those areas. For example, national authorities on both sides of an international border can sign an agreement to pool resources for the development of teaching materials or the financing of television programmes in a regional or minority language. Consequently, transfrontier exchange is not directly about creating 'capacity, opportunity and desire (or willingness)', but about facilitating the provision of such conditions.[2] We can therefore view transfrontier exchange as a complementary, rather than as a primary type of measure. In what follows, the emphasis will therefore be placed on measures adopted in application of Articles 8 through 13.

Analysing cause-and-effect relationships

In order to be certain (or at least reasonably confident) that a particular measure will generate the desired results, it is necessary to take a closer look at the links occurring at two different stages. Even though they are difficult to tease apart in practice, they are analytically distinct.

The first set of links connects the policy measures with the direct, or first-line objectives indicated in Table 6.1: for example, can we be certain that the introduction of a new syllabus will really increase learners' command of the language? Or could the programme place, for example, too much emphasis on literature and not enough on everyday communication skills, thereby discouraging students of the language? Will the airing of a new television series in the regional or minority language targeting young viewers really create viewing opportunities for them? Or would it be aired in the early afternoon, when young people are generally at school? Checking these aspects, depending on the type of measure, may require basic common sense, or a fully-fledged study of the likely effects of the measures considered. This requires, of course, drawing on area-specific expertise, in terms of analytical tools, empirical methods, or expertise acquired in other cases. The extent of recorded expertise, however, is very uneven. The workings and measures in the field of education are the object of an abundant literature, whether general and theoretical, or applied to specific cases.[3] Research results can be accessed in a number of specialised journals on language and education. There is, however, far less information about the effects of language policy measures in other domains.[4]

The second set of links is essential to the evaluation of the success of a policy. Once we are confident that a policy enhances capacity (for example, if a language teaching programme is well-designed), or that it creates opportunities (for example, if a new television series is aired at a convenient time), or that it encourages people's willingness to use a language (for example, by effectively improving the prestige of a hitherto marginalised language), we can say that language policy-makers have done most of their job, with respect to the particular policy measure concerned. However, success is not necessarily assured. The criterion of success is not the direct output of a policy; it is its ultimate outcome, in terms of whether people do use their language more in the various activities of their life; and this, as I have pointed out in the analytical framework of Chapter 2, crucially depends on the joint presence of the three conditions discussed before. This can be tested in different ways.

Arguably the best way (but also the most demanding in terms of organisation, know-how and resources) is to carry out surveys of language competence and language use in the population on a representative sample at regular intervals. Such surveys serve to monitor patterns of language use in the population as a whole or in selected subgroups of the population. At the same time, data must be collected about actors' exposure to the policy measures whose effect is being investigated – for example, whether they can in practice tune in to a new minority language television channel. A less integrated, and less demanding, approach is also possible, by separately collecting data on a range of language skills and language use variables. These may include enrolment in selected minority language education streams, television audiences for minority language programmes, sales of books and magazines in minority languages, and so on. The evolution of indicators of language use then needs to be analysed in relation with the introduction of different policies, in order to establish whether positive changes in indicators of language use can be credited to the policies implemented (see Assessment of policy-specific effects, below).

In the absence of purposeful data gathering, however, analysts will need to rely on plausibility, rather than hard evidence, as a criterion for establishing the effectiveness of policy measures. For example, the Welsh language board has been targeting young mothers, giving all of them, just before the birth of a child, an information package on Welsh-medium education, including kindergartens. The evolution of enrolment figures in those kindergartens is an indirect test of the effectiveness of the scheme. Similarly, enrolment figures in minority language medium higher education is presumably a function of the linguistic confidence acquired by learners at *earlier* stages of their schooling, and can therefore be an indication of the effectiveness of competence-increasing language programmes.

However, this method is applicable only in the case of *ex-post* policy evaluation. For *ex-ante* evaluations, analysts will have to rely on projections based on reasonable assumptions, on simulations (which are nothing but a more formalised version of the same), or to draw analogies with comparable language policies in place elsewhere.

In any event, effectiveness evaluation requires a relentless emphasis on the policy-to-outcome path. Although the methodology will be different in *ex-ante* and *ex-post* evaluation, it serves to remind analysts and decision-makers to verify a set of general conditions. These are:

1. that the policy implemented (or considered) does (or will) objectively contribute to at least one of the three core conditions of capacity, opportunity and willingness;
2. that other necessary conditions not targeted by a given measure are (will be) met also, whether because they already exist or because they are (will be) pursued in parallel through other measures;
3. and that once progress on those conditions has demonstrably been achieved (can demonstrably be expected), the policy programmes implemented (considered) do (will) result in actual and positive changes in language behaviour.

The joint operation of policy measures can be modelled formally, but formalised analysis mainly serves to provide a check of analytical rigour and internal consistency. It needs to be complemented by empirical evidence, even if the latter is circumstantial and does not fully coincide with the formal model.

Output and outcome measurement: basic indicators

An indicator is often seen as an item of information collected at regular intervals to track the performance of a system.[5] However, we shall use the term here in a slightly less restrictive sense, to denote *the measurement of a variable which is relevant in the policy-influenced causal relationship*.

The measurement of outcomes constitutes one of the most difficult parts of policy evaluation, particularly when its object is as multi-faceted as language. It is also much more resistant to general treatment, since the way to measure outcomes is obviously a function of the domain in which a policy operates.

The problem of outcome measurement will therefore be approached in two steps. In the first step, I shall propose a range of case-specific measurements that are usually sufficient for comparing policies within an area of application, such as 'education' or 'media'. In a second step, I shall examine how they can be expressed in terms of a common unit of measurement across all policy measures, and this common unit of measurement will normally correspond to the ultimate outcome targeted by the policy.

As shown before, effectiveness obtains if the policy measures do affect language use via one or more of the three core conditions for language use. What needs to be measured can therefore be formulated with respect to those conditions, as suggested in Table 6.2. The problem, of course, is to obtain reliable information on these indicators. To my knowledge, nowhere in the world is such extensive information available on any regional or minority language. Some language planning authorities have started many years ago to constitute a data bank of indicators on the relative position of languages in their area of jurisdiction. One such example is the *Office de la langue française* (French Language Office – OLF) in Montréal, because although French is a demolinguistically dominant language in the province of Québec, it is a minority language in Canada – or, more to the point, on the North American continent. The OLF regularly publishes 'language indicators' (*indicateurs linguistiques*), where information is organised in 11 categories: demolinguistics; language and labour statistics; language and ownership of and decision-making power in business; language-based earnings differentials; language use at work;

Table 6.2 Policy indicators

Art.	Area	Main condition targeted*	Indicators
8	Education	Capacity	81 – Number and percentage of RML users at different levels of competence, in different age groups 82 – Competence levels of RML learners at different stages in the education system
9	Judicial system	Opportunity	91 – Number and percentage of court cases handled in all or in part in RMLs 92 – Amount of translation into RML of court proceedings requested and supplied
10	Administration and public services	Opportunity	101 – Number and percentage of RML oral (face-to-face and telephone) interactions 102 – Number and percentage of RML written (mail, e-mail, etc.) interactions 103 – Percentage of official forms available in RMLs 104 – Time spent by RML-users interacting with officials in the RML 105 – Percentage of civil servants fluent in RML 106 – Average competence level of civil servants in RML 107 – Percentage of RML signs and information displays in public administration premises
11	Media (audiovisual)	Opportunity	111 – Total number of RML radio and TV programming, differentiated by genre as well as between new programmes and replays 112 – In case of bilingual stations: relative share of RML programming in prime time 113 – Audiences of RML radio and TV programmes, differentiated by genre of programme and by viewer profile (age, sex, etc.)
12	Culture	Opportunity	121 – Total number of RML books published per year 122 – Sales figures of RML books (c) Number of RML periodicals (dailies, weeklies, monthlies, etc.) 123 – Circulation figures of RML periodicals

Table 6.2 (continued)

Art.	Area	Main condition targeted*	Indicators
			124 – Reader profile of RML materials
			125 – Amount and distribution of state subsidies to RML publishing and distribution
			126 – Total number of RML live arts productions per year
			127 – Number of RML films showed (usually majority language works with dubbed in RML or with RML subtitles)
			128 – Attendance figures for RML live arts and cinema shows, with audience profile
			129 – Amount and distribution of state subsidies to RML live arts, film production, dubbing or subtitling
13	Economic and social life	Opportunity/ (Desire)	131 – Percentage of RML and/or bilingual commercial signs visible from the street
			132 – Percentage of RML and/or bilingual signs visible inside shops and other commercial establishments (restaurants, etc.)
			133 – Percentage of consumer goods with RML or bilingual packaging and labelling
			134 – Percentage of consumer goods with RML safety instructions (e.g. electrical appliances and drugs)
			135 – Share of RML or bilingual advertisements in written and audiovisual media
			136 – Type of goods and services advertised in RML or bilingually
			137 – Frequency of RML use on the workplace, by economic sector, position held and language of owners or managers
			138 – Ownership of firms by language group
			139 – Usefulness of RML skills for access to employment
			140 – Amount of wage premia for bilingual workers

RML: 'Regional or minority language'
* *See comment on direct and cross effects in preceding section*

'certification' of business firms; language use in high-tech contexts; 'certification' in the civil service; language and education; language and immigration; language and cultural activities.[6] Some of the OLF's indicators can be interpreted as direct outputs of language policy, while others (for example, sociolinguistic figures on actual language use) are closer to a concept of final outcome.

Catalonia is another instance where considerable experience has been acquired on the monitoring of language policies and the structured collection and storage of data, many of which have the form of indicators. This experience is reflected not only in the specialist journal *Llengua i ús* mentioned in a preceding footnote, but also in the on-line review *Noves SL* (also supported by the Directorate General of Language Policy), devoted to sociolinguistics and general topics. Particularly relevant to the concerns of all language policy specialists is the work of the *Consorci per a la Normalització Lingüística* (Consortium for Linguistic Normalisation), which brings together the regional Catalan government, town councils and local authorities throughout the region. Its aim is 'to promote the process of recovery of Catalan in society in a coordinated manner'. It supports the *OFERCAT* project, which focuses on the development of numerical indicators of the 'offer of Catalan' – that is, using the terminology of the policy-to-outcome path, the supply of opportunities to use the language.[7]

In most actual cases, rather less information is available, either under the form of these indicators themselves, or under the form of more or less convenient replacements ('proxies') for those indicators. Therefore, a full-fledged evaluation exercise will usually require fresh information to be generated, either through *ad hoc* surveys or by piggybacking on other, larger surveys – or even national censuses, which in theory yield information with the highest degree of reliability. Table 6.2 contains a list of relevant indicators of the position of a regional or minority language, arranged with respect to 'capacity', 'opportunity' and 'desire'. It is important to note that what matters is not so much the figures themselves, but how the figures *change* over time, in part as a direct or indirect result of policies.

Several comments are in order with respect to Table 6.2, regarding the nature of the indicators as well as the procedure according to which they are produced. Turning first to the former set of questions, we should note the following.

1. First, although it considerably exceeds the amount of information usually available regarding the use of a regional or minority language, the above list is not exhaustive. Other indicators not mentioned here

can be relevant in specific cases; therefore, it is up to the bodies concerned, preferably a specialised language planning agency, to define appropriate indicators and collect the corresponding data.

2. Second, an important feature of these indicators is that they constitute an attempt to go beyond a self-evident, or circular approach to policy effectiveness that would be content with reporting the direct outputs of policy measures. This point has already been made in Chapter 5, using the example of a voluntary programme of language teaching targeting civil servants. It would clearly not be relevant to use, as an indicator of the success of a policy, the number of civil servants who have enrolled for the course, because it would not tell us if, as a result of the course, civil servants are more inclined than before to use the regional or minority language in their dealings with the public. It would also not tell us if the frequency of use of the language in dealings between the civil servants and the public has increased – which is the outcome that we are ultimately interested in. Even an indicator of the evolution of the civil servants' level of skills (which is featured in Table 6.2) should be seen as a very incomplete element of information, for the same reason.

3. Third (and in accordance with the structure of the Charter), these indicators may need to be differentiated regionally. For example, the fact that a state undertakes to make official forms available in a regional or minority language does not imply that this must be the case throughout the territory under its jurisdiction. Article 3 of the Charter allows states to designate those parts of the national territory where specific protection and promotion measures will apply.

4. Fourth, the list of indicators presented above can lend itself to various forms of 'structuring' – that is, some are more generic than others, and some can be considered as describing a subset of the larger issues described by others. In particular, these indicators can be arranged in terms of supply-side and demand-side policies and help to understand the inner workings of policy intervention.

5. The indicators listed in Table 6.2 can be located more or less far along the policy-to-outcome-path. For example, indicator 103 (the percentage of official forms available in a regional or minority language) is probably a direct output of a programme of bilingualisation of official forms, whereas indicator 101 (the number and percentage of oral interactions between civil servants and the public taking place in a regional or minority language) is a perfectly valid final policy outcome.

6. As regards the production of indicators for the selection, design, implementation and monitoring of language policies, the principles

that generally apply in such endeavours will also be relevant here. First of all, indicators ought to be systemic, in the sense that they must proceed from an analytical framework in which key variables are identified, and the essential relationships between them are formulated. In this book, the policy-to-outcome path fills this role, along with the underlying model of language behaviour. The function of a particular variable in this analytical framework is what establishes the relevance of the corresponding indicator. Indicators must therefore be seen as part of a *system* of indicators, and as part of the design of such a system, it is useful to locate each of them explicitly along the policy-to-outcome path.

7. Further desirable qualities for individual indicators include: (i) *the ease of collection* – that is, it should be possible to gather the information without excessive effort or monetary expense; and (ii) where data gathering occurs at regular (e.g. yearly) intervals, the sensitivity of indicators to social change or to policy intervention.

Even if some indicators are closer to direct policy outputs, while others provide information about the final outcomes of a policy, it should be clear that the former are only a stepping-stone to the latter. This insistence on the importance of the concept of final outcome is that it paves the way for a broader comparison between very different policies, because they all share the same goal, namely, to contribute to the maintenance of a certain regional or minority languages. It is therefore time to move on to the problem of generalised effectiveness comparison.

Generalised effectiveness comparison

The procedure for comparing policy alternatives depends on the range of alternatives considered. If we are within a given domain such as the media, two policies (say, *A* and *B*) will logically be characterised by the same set of indicators. For example, policy *A* could support the setting up of a separate television channel operating in a regional or minority language, while policy *B* could support broadcasts in the language as part of the programming of an otherwise majority language station (an approach often referred to as 'mainstreaming'). In both cases, it is possible to collect figures on the audiences of minority language programmes, to compare those figures, and to conclude that (at least on the basis of this particular indicator) one policy is more 'effective' than the other – recall, however, that the question of cost has been put aside for the moment.

The procedure no longer works, however, when we have to compare rather different policies, for example one supporting the audiovisual media and the other the written media. They both share the same philosophy ('diversity is good and regional or minority languages should be protected and promoted'), the same general goal (presumably, 'restoring and maintaining a self-priming mechanism of language reproduction'), and even the same type of target (primarily the condition of 'opportunity'). Yet a fairly natural indicator of the effects of a policy of support to the audiovisual media is audience figures, while a fairly natural indicator of the effects of a policy of support to book publishing is book sales. Audience figures and book sales are completely different matters – how then is comparison possible?

One possible approach (and to our knowledge, the only one that has been tried to date in language policy) is to convert all the indicators included in the comparison into one particularly interesting unit of measurement: time. The underlying rationale is simply that time is necessary for all activities in human life. Furthermore, each activity can conceivably be carried out in the majority or in the minority language; this is particularly true in the case of members of minority language communities, who are typically bilingual. Watching television takes time, and so does reading a book. Hence, television audience figures can be converted into time figures, and so can book sales.[8] Moving from the basic indicators to the corresponding time figures would, in theory, require fairly specific data that are typically not available. Hence, they have to be replaced by plausible estimates; we have seen, in Chapter 2, that this can be an acceptable procedure, particularly in the absence of any alternative. A variant of this method, however, can be recommended: instead of taking *one* estimate, *two* estimates can be used (an upper and a lower one), yielding a *range* within which the actual value is more likely to fall.

Let us consider, for the example, the case of television programmes. Suppose that policy support for minority language programming results in the introduction of one programme, lasting one hour, aired every weekday (but not on Saturdays and Sundays). Further assume that audience surveys indicate that this programme is watched by 25 per cent of minority language users, in a community of, say, 100,000 people. The total *time of minority language use per year* generated by the policy is given by: 1 [hour per day] × 5 [days per week] × 52 [weeks per year] × 25,000 [viewers on average], that is, 6,500,000 person-hours per year of television watching in the language concerned.

Let us now consider a policy of subsidising the publication of books in the same regional or minority language. Suppose that thanks to this policy, 50 titles are published every year, on any subject. Suppose now that each book sells 2,000 copies; that each book *is* read and takes, on average, 25 hours to read; and that because people share and lend books to each other, each book is read, on average, by 1.4 people. The total time of minority language use per year is given by: 50 [books per year] × 2,000 [copies sold per book] × 25 [reading hours per book] × 1.4 [readers per book], that is, 3,500,000 person-hours of reading per year in the language concerned.

On the strength of those numbers, one would conclude that subsidising a television programme is more *effective* than subsidising book publishing, because it results in a higher number of hours during which the regional or minority language used – but this still tells us nothing about the respective cost-effectiveness of both schemes, since cost figures have not, at this stage, been taken into account.

Remember, however, that this type of estimations is *not* supposed to constitute a perfect measurement, and even less to dictate the choice to engage into a policy instead than another. At best, such calculations generate knowledge about policy choices, and they can be used in the debate about how best to allocate limited resources to language protection and promotion. When comparing the effects of policies, it is important to keep in mind the following points.

1. First, we have so far only considered the outcomes of the policies; their cost has not been taken into account (although it will in the following section); it may be, therefore, that subsidising the publication of 50 books per year is so much cheaper than subsidising the production of one hour of television per day that the *per hour cost* of minority language use generated by supporting book publishing instead of television programming is considerably lower. Hence, taking cost into account, the better policy might be to subsidise publishing.

2. Second, estimations of language use in time units are dependent on the reliability of the information (or on the validity of the assumptions) used to move from the basic indicators to the time figures. It may be, however, that television watching or book reading generate conversations between friends on the following day, that these conversations take place in the regional or minority language, and that they would not have taken place if the programme had not been aired, or the book not published and read. Hence, there are potentially important *indirect* time effects, which are presumably positive. Such indirect effects, incidentally, are not necessarily positive; it may be that television viewing and book reading keep people away from

other activities that *would have taken place in the minority language*, like meeting with friends and spending the evening with them in conversation. It is difficult enough, however, to assess direct effects, and virtually impossible to take indirect effects into account. Given that some are potentially positive and others potentially negative, it is acceptable to assume that they cancel each other out to a significant extent, and to compare policies on the basis of direct effects alone.

3. Third, a policy is likely to affect the effectiveness of *other* policies, which takes us back, although from another, 'reciprocal' perspective, to the question of 'cross effects' discussed above. For example, television programming (say, a current affairs programme) is a very effective way of disseminating certain words typical of formal domains, for example those related to government and administration. Hence, this facilitates the use of the language by the public in their dealings with civil servants, and enhances the effectiveness of policies that aim at providing bilingual public services. This argument can be generalised: by demonstrating that a regional or minority language is perfectly worthy of being used on television, support to television programming in that language does not only provide an opportunity to use it: it also improves the image of the language, and hence people's willingness to use it on a variety of situations. Again, these cross-effects are virtually impossible to assess, and it is difficult to justify the choice of one policy over another *because* of these effects, but it should be clear that they also exist.

4. Fourth, the time indicator is an essentially quantitative one, which says little about quality. Quality issues occur in two different ways, namely, *internally* and *externally*. First, at the internal level (that is, within a set of similar measures), quality may differ. For example, a difference can be made between two types of television programmes, say a football match, where commentary will typically mobilise a relatively limited range of concepts and vocabulary, and a current international affairs programme. However, it is far from clear *how* such a difference affects patterns of language use – or even *if* this difference should be taken into account at all in the evaluation. Second, quality differences may arise *between* different policies with a similar aim, such as improved language competence. One might argue that, all other things being equal, the types of language skills developed through television watching and book reading are not the same; advocates of reading may claim that the second type of activity imparts better productive skills (that is, 'speaking' and 'writing') than the first. This, again, is an empirical question.

5. Fifth, and more generally, the effectiveness of any policy is largely dependent on context, and policy selection must pay due attention to historical, cultural, economic and political factors. For example, it may be the case that the audiovisual media have, for a long time, been closely controlled by the state, or even been perceived as an instrument of oppression of the minority. If programming in a regional or minority language is to have a significant effect on language use, it is important for public confidence in this media, first of all, to be restored. This observation harks back to the issue of 'success conditions'. The notion of success conditions can prove useful where lack of comparable data precludes the formal analysis of the workings of a policy. Instead of fully-fledged indicators, analysts can fall back on the 'softer' strategy of inferring, from the observation of cases, factors that have arguably exerted a major influence on the more or less successful outcome of a policy. For example, it may be that success owes much to the presence of a committed avant-garde which, through political activism or intellectual involvement, have pushed minority language issues higher on a parliamentary agenda.[9]

Generalised effectiveness comparison is therefore an exercise requiring, in addition to fairly extensive data, the adoption of a number of assumptions that may not seem quite satisfactory, or at any rate unrealistic. It is useful, however, to put this methodology in context. Let us remember that pronouncements about the relative effectiveness of different policies are often issued by the specialist and the layman alike, on the basis of limited or impressionistic information. Firm conviction often seems to take the place of clear-headed analysis, and Kaplan and Baldauf open their treatise on language policy by noting that 'language issues have many of the characteristics of sex – everyone does it, and consequently everyone is an expert'. The methodology of generalised effectiveness comparison sketched out above is not an answer to all the difficulties of the enterprise, but a way of arriving at more transparent evaluations.

Assessment of policy-specific effects

Last but not least, the evaluation of policy effectiveness requires us to deal with a particularly difficult question, namely, that of the effects that can *specifically* be assigned to a policy.

It may be, for example, that a programme encouraging civil servants to learn a regional or minority language does result in higher average language competence among them, and that interaction between civil servants and the public takes place, more than before, in the language. However, it is conceivable that this evolution would have taken place anyway, even without the policy.

Consider once again the policy offering incentives to civil servants to learn the regional or minority language, or to brush up on their skills. Suppose that this policy proves successful, in that the frequency of interactions taking place through the medium of the language does increase. Suppose now that a significant proportion of civil servants come from families where the language was used on a daily basis two or three generations before, and that a renewed sense of pride moves them to reclaim the language and use it whenever possible in their professional duties. An increase in minority language use in the civil service would have occurred anyway. To use another example, suppose that a new language teaching method is introduced in primary schools. A proper indicator of its success is *not* the level of competence achieved by learners taught through this method, but the *difference* between their competence and what this competence *would have been* in the absence of the new method.

The problem there is the identification of a starting point, or reference point against which we assess the effect of a policy. This reference may be called a 'counterfactual'. This notion of counterfactual must not be understood as implying anything contrary to reality; rather, it pertains to what has not happened or is not the case – but *could have been the case* under other conditions, such as the *non*-implementation of a particular policy.

There are no ready-made guidelines to solve the problem of picking a suitable counterfactual. In fact, a full 'solution' would require not only identifying and measuring all the effects, positive and negative, of a particular policy, but also doing the same for the counterfactual. In practice, the choice of a counterfactual may be more or less difficult depending on the type of policy considered. In many cases, there will be no choice but to rely on common sense and make educated guesses about what would have occurred in the absence of a policy. In some cases, however, the comparison can be controlled, provided extensive data are available. In order to clarify this point, let us return to the example of the choice between different language teaching programmes.

Before any such programme is introduced in the entire school system, the programme must be run through a pilot phase. Specifically, a small number of selected classrooms will be taught under the pilot programme *A*. The achievements of learners in those classrooms at the end of a school year (or whatever duration is relevant for the programme in question) can be compared with those of other students who have followed the 'normal' or traditional programme. Using standard methods of multivariate analysis, it is possible to standardise the observations in terms of other variables such as family background, prior language competence, classroom composition, and so on; this methodology allows the analyst to single out, to a significant extent, the effect that a particular programme has had. This procedure can be carried out, in parallel, with a different pilot programme *B*. Programmes *A* and *B* can then be compared with each other, as well as with the traditional programme. If the data are of adequate reliability and in sufficient number, multivariate analysis can isolate differences in achievement that are directly associated with the respective programmes and therefore assess which of the two is more effective.

Despite the methodological effort and significant data needs involved in this type of estimation, it is always useful to at least *formulate* the problem in explicit terms, so as to minimise not only the risk of crediting a policy with a success it is not really responsible for, but also that of discarding a policy as intrinsically ineffective, even though its failure may be due less to faulty design that to unfavourable conditions.[10]

Effectiveness evaluation probably represents the most demanding step in a policy evaluation exercise. However, policy choice requires some further steps to be taken. In particular, we need to take account of the cost of the alternatives considered in order to compute their respective cost-effectiveness. This question is examined in the next chapter.

Notes

1. The Welsh bilingualism campaign, with name tags and signs on civil servants' desks indicating to the public that either English or Welsh can be used may be interpreted as a measure whose function is to encourage positive attitudes, at least as much as to provide opportunity to use Welsh.
2. On transfrontier cooperation in minority language policy, see Héraud (1997). Cost-effectiveness assessments of this type of interventions are proposed in Grin, Moring *et al.* (2002).
3. For example, Churchill (1986); Hornberger (1994); May (1994); Hamers and Blanc (1999); Skutnabb-Kangas (2000); Baker (2001).
4. Fortunately, the rising interest in language policy, as well as the growing awareness of the fact that it does not boil down to language teaching, is reflected in the development of specialist language policy journals such as *Language Problems and Language Planning, Current Issues in Language Planning,* or *Language Policy.* Many of the most targeted information sources about language policy are in languages other than English; mention should be made in particular of the Catalan review *Llengua i ús* (Language and use) published by Catalonia's *Direcció general de política lingüística* (Directorate General of Language Policy; see http://cultura.gencat.es/llengcat/publicacions/sumliu23.htm), or of the *Indicateurs linguistiques* (Linguistic indicators) published by Québec's *Office*

de la langue française (French Language Office; see http://www.olf.gouv.qc.ca/ ressources/sociolinguistique/index.html#indicsolf). Generally, the publications of language boards are the main sources of information about experience in non-education related language policies. A list of further internet resources is provided in the Appendix.

5. See e.g. Taylor Fitz-Gibbon and Tymms, 2002.
6. See http://www.olf.gouv.qc.ca/index.html. 'Certification' refers to a legal provision whereby companies above a certain size (minus those exempted from the law) have to demonstrate ability to operate in French, including for internal communication. A similar provision applies to the administration.
7. See Faba *et al.* (2000); for a succinct presentation of Catalan language planning, see Solé (1997). The Consortium can be accessed through http://www.cpnl.org/presentacio/welcome.htm.
8. The importance of time as an indicator of behaviour has been extensively modelled in economic analysis following the work of Becker (see e.g. Becker, 1976). Applications to language use are developed in Grin (1990, 1992, 1993) and Grin and Vaillancourt (1998).
9. An example of policy intervention in the perspective of 'success conditions' can be found in Grin and Vaillancourt (1999), who identify seven conditions, namely 'avant-garde', 'redistribution', 'normalcy', 'technical effectiveness', 'implicit price', 'individual language maintenance' and 'strict preference'. This set of seven conditions has been used again by Grin, Moring *et al.* (2002) in a review of the measures adopted by the European Commission in support of regional or minority languages.
10. Cooper (1989: 96) addresses this problem with an interesting twist: policy makers may shun policy evaluations precisely because 'they suspect that their policies have failed (or at least not succeeded very well) and thus they may avoid confirming their suspicions'.

7
Costs and Cost-Effectiveness

Understanding and measuring costs

Measuring policy costs is no easy task, and the broader the scope of a policy, the more difficult it is to assess its cost. At first glance, costs could be regarded as 'the monetary value of the resources' devoted to a policy (Stokey and Zeckhauser, 1978: 151), but evaluating them usually entails a much more intricate exercise. In what follows, I shall not attempt to develop a full account of the concept of cost, which can be found in most introductory textbooks in microeconomics, public finance or policy analysis. However, a selection of some key dimensions of the concept of cost needs to be presented.

Cost v. expenditure

Expenditure is directly related to the purchase of a good, service or production factor, and it is therefore associated with the various *inputs* into a process. For example, we could talk about 'expenditure on minority language textbooks'. Cost, by contrast, attaches to the direct *outputs* or to the final *outcomes* of the process. For example, we would talk about the cost of increasing the percentage of a certain age group who is fluent in the minority language. Typically, generating a certain output (for example: setting up a bilingual education stream at primary school level) requires the combination of several inputs. The fact that all of them need to be taken into account does not, as such, raise conceptual problems. Difficulties arise because it is not always sufficient to simply add up the expenditure on several inputs. The reason is that some inputs are used jointly for several outputs, and it is not always clear how these inputs (and a corresponding proportion of the expenditure on those inputs) must be allocated to different outputs. This difficulty is, of course, more acute if we try to evaluate a final outcome rather than a direct output, because the cost has to be tracked down through the successive links that relate the various inputs all the way down to the final outcome.

Suppose for example that we wish to estimate the cost of providing not just unilingual, but bilingual education. Civil servants working at the national ministry of education (in countries sufficiently centralised for such a ministry to exist) spend *part* of their time dealing with questions originating in the bilingual programmes of the education system, while the rest of their time is devoted to the management of other sides of the education system. What share of their salary should then be considered as an element of the total cost of the bilingual stream? Even if each civil servant in the ministry performs only one task, office space is allocated among them, and this carries a certain cost, which is part of a per-person overhead. How then is the cost of office space, office supplies, etc., to be allocated to different activities of the ministry?

Again, clear-cut calculations are rarely possible. Even approximations require a well-developed collection and processing of statistical data. At the time of writing, only a small clutch of countries would be able to deliver reliable estimates of how the time of their civil servants is allocated to the management of different streams in the education system. A considerable amount of experience in the measurement of education costs has been accumulated in the field education economics.[1] However, expenditure figures are not calculated in relation to the language dimensions that concern us here. Such figures are usually apportioned to various tiers in the system (e.g. pre-school, primary, secondary, and tertiary), to various 'streams' or 'pathways' (e.g. pre-university v. vocational education), to different types of tasks carried out within the system (e.g. teaching, research and administration), to different categories of expenditure (e.g. wages v. capital investment) or to different sources of financing (e.g. national, regional and local authorities).[2]

Some pilot studies in education economics include a methodology for the evaluation of total public spending *by subject*, including foreign languages;[3] this yields an estimate of the cost of a policy of teaching a given set of foreign languages. As regards other forms of language policies, estimates of the costs of specific policy programmes are occasionally calculated.[4] Barring such exceptions, however, few are the cases where language-related expenditure has been processed in order to provide estimates of the costs of policies addressing language issues. In practice, rough calculations, possibly using an upper-bound and a lower-bound estimate, will often have to be accepted as a fallback solution, always trying to relate information on what is being spent (expenditure) to what is being produced, at a certain cost, combining various items of expenditure.

Opportunity cost

Even if the above questions have been answered to satisfaction, it is important to reconsider critically whatever evaluation has been arrived at. The problem hinges on the meaning of cost figures obtained. The relevant measure is the cost of using a resource in a certain way *instead of using it in another way*. This is known as the *opportunity cost*. It is a fundamental concept in economics and in project evaluation, and it must be understood as a decision-making rather than an accounting concept. Let us clarify this with an example.

Suppose that a certain stretch of land could be used to build a new school to serve the minority-language population of a city of 50,000. Suppose that the land was purchased 20 years before by the city authorities at the cost of €50,000. The opportunity cost of using this land for the school is not €50,000, but the value of the *best alternative use* to which this land could be put – a park, a retirement home, or simply the option to keep the land unused and available for some future, yet undefined use; the land might also be sold to private developers. If the value of the best alternative is €200,000, the opportunity cost of building the minority-language school is €200,000. If the city has no potential use for the land, the opportunity cost of the stretch of land is its original purchase price, that is, €50,000.

Opportunity cost is a potentially important dimension of language policies. Consider for example the decision to introduce the regional or minority language as a subject in the school syllabus. The total cost of the project includes not only the salary of the teachers who would be hired to teach it, but also (if the total endowment of school hours per week is fixed at, say, 30 hours per week) the value of the knowledge that would have been acquired in whichever course will have to be phased out of the syllabus in order to make room for the teaching of the regional or minority language.

Clearly, the issue of opportunity cost raises the problem of the identification of the 'counterfactual' once again (see Chapter 6). On the one hand, one can say that introducing the regional or minority language as a subject does carry an opportunity cost as just described. On the other hand, one could equally well say that *not* offering the language as a subject would entail a no less relevant cost, namely, the disenfranchisement or alienation experienced by members of the regional or minority language community who are prevented from acquiring competence in their own language. The choice of a counterfactual is therefore not a self-evident one. The implication is that the estimation of the opportunity cost must be made with respect to an explicit counterfactual, whose choice needs to be strongly and transparently argued.[5]

Macro-economic effects

A general problem of policy cost evaluation is that large-scale policies have an impact on the economy, in particular on the prices of the goods and services used (supplies, etc.) and on the production factors (particularly the workforce) it requires. This question is generally not a major one in language policy, because the relative and absolute magnitude of the costs of language policies tend to be modest and so is, accordingly, their impact on the economy as a whole, even if some sector-specific effects can arise. Of course, some elements of some language policies entail presumably far-reaching consequences. However, available estimates from the few cases that have been documented are modest. For example, the total cost of Quebec's far-reaching language policy, put in place under the *Charter of the French Language* adopted in 1977, has been estimated at less than half a percentage point of the provincial domestic product.[6] By implication, the macroeconomic costs of less extensive language policies is lower, and in general, the analyst can safely decide to ignore this form of cost.

However, it is useful to observe that such effects may, in specific cases, drive a wedge between *ex ante* and *ex post* policy costs. For example, promotional policies that require minority language-speaking TV producers, translators, and so on, are likely to bid up the price of their services. The resulting labour market prices are appropriate elements of cost, if evaluated *ex post*. In *ex ante* evaluations, however, allowance for price increases may be built into the projection, by multiplying the unit price of the factors concerned by a coefficient larger than one – for example, 1.2 if a 20 per cent increase in the wages of a particular type of personnel is anticipated.

The issue of macroeconomic costs remains, however, very little-known, and a number of theoretical issues deserve further examination until rough estimates are ventured. For example, the more or less deliberate choice, by most European countries, to teach English as the first foreign language in their national school systems is echoed by the relative neglect for foreign language teaching in many English-speaking countries, which simply rely on the fact that others will just learn their language. This translates into a lower investment in second languages as school subjects, correspondingly freeing time and money, in the English-speaking countries concerned, for investing in the development of other skills. To the extent that the latter promote economic growth, the readiness of other countries to give English this leading position amounts to a financing of part of the economic growth of English-speaking countries by all the others.[7]

Negative benefits

Many of the relevant costs take the form of unfavourable impacts, which can be seen as negative benefits; these affect people who are not participating in the market transaction. Suppose that a new cultural centre is opened, in which minority-language theatre plays are given. Assume that this results in the manifestation of a strong pent-up demand among the population hitherto deprived of this form of entertainment. Several 'negative benefits' may arise. For example, people attending theatre plays will no longer consume other forms of entertainment, such as videos or films dubbed or subtitled in the minority language – assuming such videos can readily be purchased or rented. If this results in a noticeable drop in the demand for dubbed or subtitled films, distributors may decide to reduce the output of such goods, thereby giving rise to a negative effect on the opportunities to use the regional or minority language. Some forms of negative impacts are unrelated to minority language use. For example, the opening of the cultural centre may lure people away from other forms of entertainment whose suppliers may find themselves facing a sharp drop in their business. This carries a social cost, linked perhaps to resulting unemployment in the corresponding sectors, and is likely to cause a drop in fiscal revenue.

There is no fixed rule regarding which indirect costs ought to be included in the calculation, and if so, whether this inclusion should be full or partial. In practice, a decision in this respect may be influenced by whether the losers will require (and receive) compensation; this is largely a question of political influence and image of the sectors concerned.[8]

Some unfavourable impacts can be linked quite directly to the practical implementation of a policy. Suppose for example that the cultural facility induces such a rise in demand that the facility turns out to have insufficient capacity. It will be impossible to satisfy demand, generating frustration. Even though such frustration may be less acute than that experienced previously in the *absence* of minority language entertainment, it is a form of cost, which could arguably come in deduction of the value of the project.

Non-market costs

Most public policies entail non-market costs; incidentally, many of the 'negative benefits' just described are of a non-market nature. Non-market effects (whether benefits or costs) arise *outside* of a market, in the sense that these effects are not reflected in the defining variables of a market, that is, prices and quantities bought and sold. An example from the realm of the natural environment will clarify this. Consider the project to build of a power plant, which would generate much-needed electricity, but would also have negative environmental impacts, whether in terms of noise, air pollution, or damage to the scenic beauty of a region. These costs are largely of the non-market kind, because they will not be reflected in market variables – or only in part through lower property prices. These costs are not given direct market expression because the quality of life in a region is not, *as such*, 'bought' or 'sold'; they arise from the reduced enjoyment of that region's physical amenities.

Non-market costs, however, are no less real, and have major importance in language policy, largely because it affects our *linguistic environment*, and because language itself, although it might be called a 'commodity', is intangible. It is often the case that the cost is *symbolic*, and this term will also be used in this book. The symbolic nature of those costs is often evidenced by the political dimensions involved. For example, measures in favour of regional or minority languages are liable to meet with resistance in disgruntled segments of majority opinion, because it reduces the relative dominance (or hegemony) of the majority culture and language. In particular regions where members of the majority community constitute a majority, there is a risk that feelings of disenfranchisement would arise. This issue, for example, has often been raised in the case of some segments of the English-speaking community of Quebec, which makes up about 8 per cent of the population in a province where a far-reaching language policy has been put in place through a succession of Acts, particularly since the 1970s.[9] Similar concerns have sometimes been voiced in the case of speakers of Castillian in Catalonia – not to mention members of the Russian-speaking community in states that were formerly part of the Soviet Union, notably Estonia and Latvia.

These costs are not to be taken lightly. However, even if, in theory, they ought to be computed and included on the cost side of the ledger, their evaluation is often tricky. The general approach to their measurement rests on the notion of 'willingness-to-pay': the true costs of the unfavourable impacts of a policy are the total amount that people would be willing to pay to *avoid* the policy being implemented. This approach, known as the *contingent valuation* method,[10] typically requires surveys in which people are asked how much they would be willing to pay to avoid the implementation of a policy they dislike, or how much they would require in compensation to agree to it. While this method is acceptable in the case of environmental policy, it would be difficult to countenance in the case of language policy, because it also lends itself to another interpretation, namely asking people to state how far they are willing to *resist* the granting of language rights to the minority.

Such costs can be minimised by not casting minority language policies in a light such that it might be perceived as gratuitous challenges to the majority. The text of the Charter reveals a clear awareness if this requirement, by insisting, in its Article 5, that nothing in it 'may be interpreted as implying any right to engage in any activity or perform any action in contravention of the purposes of the Charter of the United Nations or other obligations under international law, including the principle of the sovereignty and territorial integrity of States.' In practice, measures in favour of a regional or minority language (for example, subsidies to cultural products in the language) can be complemented by accompanying measures benefiting cultural production at large, irrespective of the language in which they are produced. This type of accompanying measure can help to make clear that the allocation of resources to a regional or minority language does not come at the expense of such allocation to a majority language. The costs of such accompanying measures should of course be budgeted. It does not follow, however, that they should be considered part of the cost of the policy in favour of the *regional or minority language*, because what makes them necessary is the unwillingness of some segments of majority opinion to countenance a loss of dominance, rather than an intrinsically necessary component of the policy.

Total, average and marginal cost

Let us now put aside the issue of non-market costs, or assume that the policy measure considered is sufficiently simple and self-contained for complicated cost implications not to arise. Still, two types of situation may appear. In the first (and simpler) situation, a choice must be made between two policies, both of which have a 'yes-or-no' character: either policy *A* or policy *B* will be adopted. In the second situation, each policy can be carried more or less far, and costing the policy requires some understanding of how cost will vary according to 'how much of it' is engaged in. Let us consider both situations in turn.

In the simple 'yes-or-no' case, the cost estimates for each policy can be compared with each other and a policy decision proposed on this basis. Suppose that the authorities are considering two ways of offering one hour a day of local television programming in the regional or minority language. This could be done either by airing the programme on a separate channel (policy A), or by including one daily hour of programming on a local majority-language television channel (policy B). Suppose that the first option carries a direct monetary cost of €180,000 per year, and the second a direct monetary cost of €100,000 only. Further assume that in either case, this hour of programming would be aired in prime time, which implies that under policy B, majority viewers would be deprived of the possibility of one hour of prime time viewing on their local channel; this carries a non-market cost which can be taken into account – for example by estimating how much majority viewers would, in total, be prepared to contribute in order not to be deprived of this hour of television in their language.

Assuming an average 'willingness-to-pay' of €0.5 per person and a potential majority audience of 200,000, an additional *non-market* cost of, say, €100,000 would have to be taken into account in the cost of policy B. Other elements of costs might be added (for example, a drop in the sales of video shops selling films dubbed in the minority language), but we shall ignore them for simplicity.

Taking the direct market cost and the non-market cost into account, the total cost of policy A is still €180,000 per year, and the total cost of policy B is €200,000 per year. Since both policies generate an identical amount of programming and, by implication, make a similar contribution to the vitality of the regional or minority language concerned, policy A can be chosen over policy B simply because it costs €20,000 less per year. Assume (in line with the example provided in the section of Chapter 6 on 'generalised effectiveness comparison') that this hour of programming in the regional or minority language is watched by 25,000 viewers on average. This yields a per-viewer cost, with policy A, of €7.2 per year (180,000 ÷ 25,000).

Consider now another situation. A minority television channel already exists, and airs one hour of regional or minority language programming every day. Suppose that this is considered inadequate, and that a proposal is tabled to increase the offer of programmes. As the number of hours of programmes in the regional or minority language increases, costs will increase as well. However, costs will not always increase at the same rate. How they do exactly is, again, an empirical question. In some industries, the rate at which costs rise as output increases is fairly constant; in others, cost increases may be rapid at first, then slow over a certain range, then very pronounced beyond a certain point. What matters is that the *average* cost of an hour of television (the average cost being equal to total cost *divided* by the number of hours produced and aired) is likely to be variable, and dependent on the number of hours produced. It is important to note that the average cost of programming may be lower if 20 hours of programming are offered every week than if only two hours are offered – for example, because some administrative overhead can be spread over a higher number of hours of programming.

This is shown in the two panels of Figure 7.1, where the number of hours h^* corresponds to a minimum average cost.[11] This is not to imply that the authorities should aim at offering precisely h^*; for any number of reasons, levels below or above h^* may be preferable. However, when calibrating a policy, it is important to gain knowledge of the evolution of costs, also for levels of provision of the policy *other* than those considered at first, because this may help identify potentially attractive volumes of output where a large effect can be obtained at a unit cost lower than might have been assumed otherwise.

Even more important is the concept of *marginal* cost. Marginal cost denotes the cost of one *additional* unit of the good or service produced – or, putting it slightly differently, the increase in total cost brought about by the production of one more unit. In our example, this may be defined as the cost of one additional hour of programming in a regional or minority language. The level of marginal cost depends, of course, on the evolution of the total cost function – or, equivalently, on the shape of the total cost curve as shown in the left-hand side panel of Figure 7.1 Marginal cost corresponds to the slope of the tangent to the total cost

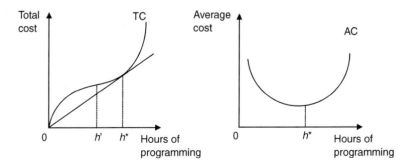

Figure 7.1 Total and average cost curves

curve, and programming hour h' (at which slope of the total cost curve is less than at any other point) is therefore the cheapest hour to produce. Assuming the quite standard evolution of total cost described there, marginal cost will first decrease, then increase. This means that over a certain range, each additional hour of minority language programming will cost *less* than the preceding hour, but that beyond a certain point (indicated by h' in the left-hand side panel of Figure 7.1), each additional hour will cost *more* than the preceding one. This does not mean that the appropriate number of hours to supply is h'. However, the notion of marginal cost is useful for two reasons.

First, it is generally an important feature of the evolution of costs, and one which it is advisable to know in order to fully understand the cost structure of a proposed policy.[12] Second, it helps to identify *relevant* elements when estimating the cost of a policy, because it draws attention to the notion of *incremental* units of a good or service produced, and to the corresponding *incremental* cost. Let us clarify this point with an example.

Suppose that the state, in accordance with Article 10, paragraph 1.b of the Charter, decides to make available all administrative forms in a given regional or minority language. This includes tax return forms, and the state engages in a 'Tax Form Bilingualisation Programme', whose costs we shall now try to evaluate.

Let us first assume a total resident population of 6 million people made up of 4 million households (that is, an average household size of 1.5 persons). Households matter because they represent the relevant tax-paying unit and, for some public services, the relevant consumer unit. In order to serve this population, some 4,100,000 tax return forms are printed every year in the majority language (4 million corresponding to the number of resident households, plus a 2.5 per cent security margin), at the cost of €0.5 per form, that is, €2,050,000. Assume now that under the new policy, taxpayers can request tax return forms either in the majority language or in the regional or minority language. Further assume that users of the regional or minority language make up 20 per cent of the national population, and that 80 per cent of taxpaying households in this community avail themselves of this choice and do request forms in their language. This means that 640,000 forms (16 per cent) will no longer be needed in the majority language, but in the regional or minority language. With a similar security margin of 2.5 per cent, this means that on average, 656,000 forms will have to be printed in the regional or minority language ($4,000,000 \times 0.2 \times 0.8 \times 1.025$).

Material production costs are identical at €0.5, which implies spending €328,000 on tax forms in the regional or minority language, *plus* the cost of producing, revising and finalising a quality translation. Assume that the cost of these translation tasks amounts to €150.000, payable once (that is, in the current year only, because once the translation is ready, it can be re-used in subsequent years).[13] Ignoring for now the problem of time (which will be discussed in a moment), what is the cost of offering tax forms in the minority language as well – instead of making them available only in the majority language – for the year considered? One might be tempted to evaluate this cost at €328,000 + €150,000 = €478,000. This, however, would be a gross overestimation of cost, because tax forms would have to be printed anyway for the *total* number of households, irrespective of the language in which these forms are filled. In other words, the cost of the 'Tax Form Bilingualisation Programme', during the year considered, is only the *incremental* expenditure necessary, that is, €150,000. Given that, in our example, users of the regional or minority language make up 20 per cent of the total population (that is, 1.2 million people), the cost of the programme is, *during the year considered*, €0.125 per head (12.5 cents).

The notion of incremental cost can therefore be a very helpful one when identifying policy costs; we shall return to it in Chapter 9, which is devoted to an extensive policy evaluation exercise. At this time, however, it is important to move on to another question, which has just been mentioned in passing, namely, the problem of time.

Time and discounting

In the preceding paragraphs, I have pointed out that calculations were being made for the current year only. Let us recall that some elements of expenditure on a policy generate results over many years. This point has already been mentioned in Chapter 5, in our preview of the principles of effectiveness, cost-effectiveness and democracy, and it is time to examine it more closely.

Let us once again take the example of the 'Tax Form Bilingualisation Programme'. Assume now that the tax system is fairly stable, and that a general overhaul of the tax forms is necessary only at 10-year intervals. However, minor adaptations are made every year. The cost of these adaptations is made up of a certain proportion of the working time of civil servants at the Ministry of Finance, say, 20 per cent of the time, throughout the year, of a 20-person team; this amounts to four full-time jobs – but since such adaptations are taking place anyway, their cost is not part of the cost of the 'Tax Form Bilingualisation Programme'. Let us now assume that under the programme, these minor adaptations also have to be worked into the minority language version of the tax return form. This task is entrusted to a freelance translator, whose work is then checked at the Ministry, at a total cost of, say, €45,000 per year. Clearly, the 'updating cost' part of the 'Tax Form Bilingualisation Programme' includes *only* those translation costs, because the updating cost would have to be incurred anyway.

We are now in a position to move on to a more precise calculation of this cost. First, the €150,000 spent on translating the tax form is an expenditure whose value must be spread over a 10-year period, implying a per-year cost of €15,000. Adding this to the yearly updating cost of €45,000, we get a total cost for the 'Tax Form Bilingualisation Programme' of €60,000 – that is, 5 cents per year and per user of the regional or minority language, infants and elderly people included.[14]

This estimation procedure is appropriate in the case of expenditure that has to be renewed on a regular basis. This is the case for the greater part of the cost of the hypothetical project presented here (€45,000 out of a total of €60,000 per year). However, some projects are of a different nature, and imply a major expenditure at time *t*, whereas the effects of the project will make themselves felt over a longer period. The evaluation of expenditure accruing in the more distant future requires specific treatment. This problem is known in project evaluation as 'discounting', and because it is presented in any economics or project evaluation textbook (not to mention those in the field of finance), I shall confine myself to a very succinct explanation, again using a simple example.

Let us consider a possible measure under Article 12 of the Charter ('Cultural activities and facilities'), whose Paragraph 1.a requires the authorities to 'encourage types of expression and initiative specific to regional or minority languages and foster the different means of access to works produced in these languages.' To this end, the Ministry of Culture is promised a grant of €10 million. This sum is the only budget allocation of this kind that will be made by Parliament for a period of 10 years with respect to Article 12 of the Charter. Suppose that the Ministry wants to support cultural activities in a provincial town of the region where the target language is used; let us further assume that the region has a population of one million, of which half are users of the regional or minority language. Hence, financial support to cultural activities in this region will, in principle, benefit a pool of 500,000 potential users.

Suppose that two projects are proposed. One is to build a cultural centre for live arts performances; the other is to build a public library, which will serve not only the general public but will also be used by local schools operating through the regional or minority language. Either would operate on a non-profit basis, although they may be allowed to charge for the services provided (for example, entry tickets to shows may be sold, and use of the library facilities may carry a modest membership fee; we shall, however, ignore this possible revenue for the time being).

Let us assume that both projects imply a total expenditure roughly estimated *ex ante* at €10 million. However, their respective cost structure is likely to be different. The reason is that expenditure takes place at different moments in time, as shown by Table 7.1. In this table, I assume that either facility will take one year to build, that the buildings will be amortised in linear fashion (straight-line depreciation), and that they will operate at constant cost over the same nine-year period. What happens beyond this initial 10-year period is ignored for simplicity. Inflation is also assumed away, as is the residual value of assets (for example, buildings, equipment, etc.) in either project at the end of the period considered.

The cost difference between both projects is related to the fact that the further away in time a cost (or a benefit) is, the less it should weigh in the balance. The rationale goes as follows (in the case of costs): expenditure that takes place in the more distant future is uncertain; furthermore, the money *not* spent now, but which will have to be spent later, can in the meantime be invested and yield interest (one further reason for discounting future money flows is inflation; recall, however, that inflation is kept out of the example for the sake of simplicity).

Table 7.1 Cost structure over 10-year period

Project	Cultural centre	Library
Nature of up-front cost in year 1	Building of the new theatre/arena, fittings, etc.	Building of the library, acquisition of computer system, etc.
Up-front cost* in year 1	3,700,000	2,800,000
Nature of operating costs	Paying for productions (administration, artists' fees, props, decors, costumes, printing of programmes), etc.	Administration, book purchases and renewals, periodicals subscriptions, administration, etc.
Operating costs* per year from year 2 through year 10	700,000	800,000
Total current cost	10,000,000	10,000,000

* *Costs expressed in current €; costs are assumed to be incurred on 1 January of each year concerned.*

Suppose that money not spent now can be saved, yielding 5 per cent interest per year. This means that the *present* value (on 31 December in year 0) of €700,000 to be spent on 1 January in year 2 is equal to the amount that should be saved *now* in order to get exactly €700,000 at the beginning of year 2, that is, $700,000/(1 + 0.05) = 666,667$. The figure can also be calculated the other way around: the sum available in year 2 would amount to 666,667 *plus* the interest earned during the 365 days of year 1 $(666,667 \times 0.05 = 33,333)$, exactly totalling €700,000. In the case of an amount of €700,000 that will be spent only in year 3 (again, on 1 January), interest can be earned two years in row (during year 1 *and* during year 3) on a sum set aside on 31 December of year 0. This implies that for savings to add up to 700,000 by the beginning of year 3, a total amount of $700,000/(1 + 0.05) = 666,667$ should be invested over year 2, or $666,667/(1 + 0.05) = 634,921$ over year 1 already. This latter amount is the present cost of 700,000 to be spent on 1 January of year 3, and can also be calculated directly as $700,000/(1 + 0.05)^2$.

Note that the difference between the final amount of €700,000 and its present value $(700,000 - 634,921 = 65,079)$ corresponds to the total interest gained. Because the €634,921 × 0.05 = €31,746 earned over the first year can be reinvested for the second year at the same interest rate, an additional €33,333 (that is, 31,746 × 1.05) can be earned, yielding a total interest gain of 65,079. Hence, the present value of a constant expenditure of €700,000 declines year after year. Generally, the present value PV_K, on 31 December of year 0, of an expenditure K to take place on 1 January of year t, given a constant interest rate r, is given by:

$$PV_K = K/(1 + r)^{t - 1}$$

This general formula can be applied to estimate costs over the entire duration of both projects, as shown in Table 7.2.

Taking account of time reveals a difference in cost linked to the possibility of investing money not spent right away. The savings over the 10-year period are in the order of €1.3 million if the cultural centre is built, and over €1.5 million if the library is preferred. The net difference of €189,219 can be invested in other support policies.

Of course, if there is a flow of revenue generated by either project, the net cost of the projects will be less. Presumably, building a cultural centre is more promising, because proceeds from ticket sales are likely to be higher than a membership fee to access the services of a library. It goes without saying that the revenue generated in either case must be discounted in the same way. Because revenue further away in the future is worth less than immediate intakes, any amount earned L has to be

Table 7.2 Present cost* of projects

Project →	Cultural centre		Library	
Year ↓	Current cost	Present cost	Current cost	Present cost
1	3,700,000	3,700,000	2,800,000	2,800,000
2	700,000	666,667	800,000	761,905
3	700,000	634,921	800,000	725,624
4	700,000	604,686	800,000	691,070
5	700,000	575,892	800,000	658,162
6	700,000	548,468	800,000	626,821
7	700,000	522,351	800,000	596,972
8	700,000	497,477	800,000	568,545
9	700,000	473,788	800,000	541,471
10	700,000	451,226	800,000	515,687
Total	10,000,000	8,675,476	10,000,000	8,486,257
Savings		1,324,524		1,513,743

* *Present cost values rounded to nearest €.*

expressed in terms of its present value PV_L. If calculations are made on 31 December of year 0, and earnings in year t will be in the till and available at the end of the that year, the formula to apply to calculate the *present* value of revenue L to be obtained in year t, assuming a constant interest rate r, is:

$$PV_L = L/(1 + r)^t$$

If revenue is secured at the beginning of each period (that is, on 1 January instead of 31 December), then the periodicity of expenditure and income coincide; the formula for discounting revenue would then be:

$$PV_L = L/(1 + r)^{t - 1}$$

Given that the focus of this chapter is on costs rather than benefits (although benefits *can* be interpreted as negative costs), I shall dispense with an example on the discounting of future revenue.

The issue of discounting, which is of foremost importance in the evaluation of large-scale projects, will be of consequence only for the costing of certain types of language policy measures. First, many language policy measures do not imply a major capital expenditure at the outset; they often do not have the structure of a project with a fixed financial endowment, and for which cost projections need to be made over a finite period. For example, paying teachers who speak a regional or minority language and are hired to teach it in schools implies a steady flow of expenditure, just as in the 'majority' school system. In other words, a large range of language policies increase mainly current expenditure on an annual basis, making the application of discounting procedures unnecessary. It is important, however, to be aware of the role that the time-expenditure profiles may have on the actual cost of some policy measures.

Cost-effectiveness evaluation

Once the costs of a policy have been properly estimated, it becomes possible to combine this information with indicators of the effectiveness of a policy, as discussed in the preceding chapter. By dividing an appropriate measurement of the cost of a policy by an appropriate (that is, corresponding) measurement of its effectiveness, we obtain a ratio which is simply the unit cost of the policy. The lower the unit cost, the more cost-effective the policy is. This intuitive explanation, however, deserves closer examination.

The analytical definition of cost-effectiveness

A production process or a policy can be considered cost-effective if, given a certain amount of resources invested in it, the outcome is as high as possible, or if, given a certain result, it is achieved at the lowest possible cost. In this section, to avoid repetition, I shall relax somewhat the distinction between the words 'output' and 'outcome'; furthermore, the word 'result' will also be used as a synonym for either.

This is easily seen graphically (Figure 7.2). Let us put ourselves in the position of a language policy office and start from point A, where expenditure is x_2 (say, €20 m per year for a language revitalisation programme) and results are at level y_1, denoting, say, a certain *frequency* of language use among the population. How can policy become more cost-effective? A concern for economising resources while still ensuring the same result would lead us to try to move to point B (where a lower amount x_1 of resources, say €5 million per year instead of 20, is spent, while still securing an unchanged frequency of language use y_1). Alternatively, reaching the best possible result (that is, 'as much minority language use as possible') with an unchanged amount of resources induces a move to point C (where the unchanged expenditure of €20 m per year now yields a higher result y_2, meaning for example that more members of the community use their minority language, and/or do so much more frequently – according to Figure 7.2, almost twice as much as before). This figure must be compared with Figure 7.1. Figure 7.2 actually represents the inverse of the

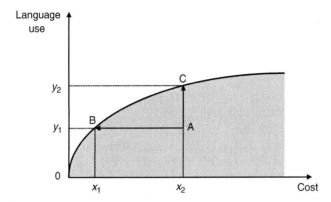

Figure 7.2   A graphical representation of cost-effectiveness

total cost curve in Figure 7.1, except that only the latter part of that curve is now taken into consideration. The range kept here corresponds to decreasing marginal productivity of resources, and therefore focuses on what is, in most cases, the more relevant part of a production process.

Feasible outcomes are located in the shaded area in Figure 7.2. This 'feasible area' is located below the curved line called the *effectiveness boundary*. It is a boundary in the sense that is not possible for any policy to be *more* cost-effective. When a policy is characterised by an output level and a cost such that it is 'on the boundary', it is not possible to achieve a better result with the same amount of resources. Alternatively, it is not possible to reach the same result while also spending less.

This figure explains why cost-effectiveness implies that the best possible result is reached at a given cost *or* that in order to achieve a given goal, no resources are wasted. Although this point may seem rather obvious, it is often overlooked in language policy, largely for lack of information about the costs and the effects of policies.

Cost-effectiveness has very practical relevance for two reasons. The first is a simple one of public finance: sound principles of management suggest that the best possible use should be made of scarce resources. The second is that the acceptability of policy measures in favour of regional or minority languages, particularly in the eyes of majority opinion (which will generally make up the majority of taxpayers) is likely to be higher if the authorities can demonstrate that such measures are cost-effective.

Cost-effectiveness is a convenient criterion in policy evaluation, not least because it can be seen as a simplified (or truncated) form of *cost–benefit analysis*. The cost–benefit analysis of a policy plan requires all the effects of a policy, whether negative or positive (that is, whether they represent costs or benefits) to be identified, measured, *and* expressed in a common unit of measurement, usually monetary units such as euros, dollars, and so on. Translating not only costs, but also benefits into monetary units is not an easy task, because it adds a difficulty to those identified earlier. We have already seen that identifying and measuring cost is an exercise that goes well beyond the mere tallying up of expenditure figures. Identifying and measuring benefits may be even more complex, particularly in the case of language policy, whose ultimate function is to affect the linguistic environment in a welfare-enhancing direction. A cost–benefit evaluation would then require us to put a monetary value of those benefits – but what is the monetary value of the visibility of a regional or minority language? How many euros is the very survival of a language worth? Even though there are some methods (generally derived from environmental economics) which can help us address these questions, they remain extremely arduous ones.

In this book, we can eschew the difficulties of cost–benefit analysis, because the type of problems likely to arise in the implementation of the Charter require a relatively narrower comparison of policy options. Under the Charter, the general purpose of state intervention is clear (implementing the Charter); the goals are also fairly well-defined (taking measures that will contribute to making a language viable in the long run). The problem then is not to choose between completely different measures (for example, in the field of education *or* culture), but to select policy measures *within* a certain category of measures (for example: 'education', 'media', 'culture', etc.). It follows that we can compare policy alternatives in terms of their outcome (or 'effectiveness') and, between two policies with equivalent outcome, select the one with the lower cost.

Of course, comparison requires the outcomes of policy *A* and policy *B* to be expressed in the same units (such as the number of hours of television programming in the minority language; the number of clients served in the minority language; the percentage of ads in a magazine that use the minority language, etc.). Only then does it become possible to compare their effectiveness. In the same way, the costs of policy *A* and policy *B* need to be expressed in the same units – usually, monetary units, which is generally regarded as a natural way of expressing costs; the respective costs of both policies can then be compared.

Cost-effectiveness indicators

Cost-effectiveness is, all other things being equal, a desirable characteristic of policy measures. Given the definition above, it can be expressed in different ways, which will be illustrated with the example of the 'Tax Form Bilingualisation Programme'. We have seen that the cost of the policy is €60,000 per year. Its counterfactual is the *absence* of a policy, and the continuation of the earlier practice of providing tax forms in the majority language only. This amount of €60,000 is made up of two parts: a per-year share of the cost of producing, every 10 years, the translation of a completely overhauled tax form; and the cost of producing, every year, limited updates to the regional or minority language version of the tax form. We have also seen that these translation costs should be taken into account, but *not* the cost of designing the tax form in the first place, or the cost of printing and distributing it, because those costs would have to be incurred *anyway*, even if tax forms were available in the majority language only.

The question now is to select an appropriate effectiveness indicator with which this cost figure can be associated. Of course, we have seen that these €60,000 correspond to an output of 656,000 forms in the regional or minority language – but the issue there is not how many forms are *produced*, but how many are *used*. In our example, 80 per cent of households using the regional or minority language request a form in their own language;[15] and users of the regional or minority language make up 20 per cent of the total number of households (assuming that average household size is identical across all language groups in the country). Given a total population size of 6 million and an average of 1.5 persons per household, we get a total of 4 million households, of which 800,000 (20 per cent) are users of the regional or minority language. This yields a figure of 640,000 users of these forms (where $640,000 = 4,000,000 \times 0.2 \times 0.8$). Cost-effectiveness can be expressed as 640,000/60,000, that is, just over 10 users (10.67) per euro spent in this programme.

Such a figure can be directly compared with a similar evaluation of an alternative policy (say, offering citizens forms in a regional or minority language for applications for passports, travel documents, etc.). Let us call this the 'Travel Document Application Bilingualisation Programme'. Assume that the per-year cost of offering those forms in the regional or minority language as well (instead of offering them in the majority language alone) is €20,000. The nature of cost components can be the same as for the tax forms, but I am assuming this new programme to cost less because initial translation costs are lower (it being a shorter, simpler form), and updates less frequent or extensive. On the other hand, the number of people who apply for travel documents (or renewal of the validity of those documents) is likely to be relatively low (not everybody engages in international travel). If travel documents have a validity of five years, renewals are necessary at intervals of five years or more, because an expiring passport need not be renewed immediately if no foreign travel is planned. Let us assume that in any given year, 10 per cent of the population (minors included) requires a new passport or validity extension, and that this percentage applies irrespective of language. Further assume that 80 per cent of users of the regional or minority language concerned by the programme will choose to fill applications in their language. The number of users of application forms in this language will therefore be 96,000 per year (6 m × 0.1 × 0.2 × 0.8). This amounts to 4.8 users per euro spent.

In other words, in terms of number of users, the cost-effectiveness of the 'Tax Form Bilingualisation Programme' is higher than the cost-effectiveness of the 'Travel Document Application Bilingualisation Programme'. Actually, the former is at least twice as cost-effective as the latter. If the problem is to choose between one or the other, and if resources are available for the more expensive of the two (but not for both), the first programme should be chosen, even if its per-year cost is three times as high (€60,000 as compared to €20,000).

However, our estimate of the relative cost-effectiveness of these two programmes crucially depends on the choice of the effectiveness indicator. Instead of just counting users, we might for example have evaluated the *time* that they spend using their language when filling out different types of forms. Suppose that filling out the travel document application form takes about 30 minutes, while filling out the tax form takes four hours. The number of hours of regional or minority language use generated by the bilingualisation of tax forms would be 2,560,000 hours (assuming only one person in each household fills out the form); the number of hours of regional or minority language use generated by the bilingualisation of travel document application forms would be 48,000. Hence, the number of hours of language use generated per Euro spent is 42.7 for tax forms, against a mere 2.4 for travel document application forms. The cost-effectiveness ratio between both programmes is no longer 2 to 1, it is now almost 20 to 1.

This underscores the importance of a very clear and well-argued choice of an effectiveness indicator, not only for its own sake, but also because it will affect the cost-effectiveness evaluation. If cost-effectiveness is a consideration taken into account when making policy recommendations (or when actually deciding to implement one or another policy), the computation of cost-effectiveness certainly matters. First, it may influence the rank-ordering of policy options; second, it may influence the decision to adopt a policy or not, depending on the constraint on resources (this latter point will be addressed shortly).

We should also recall a point made in Chapter 6, namely, that the selection of an appropriate effectiveness indicator affects the mutual comparability of policies. Suppose that we are comparing two measures with different types of outcomes, such as financing a minority language cultural centre or a minority language library. The effects of such measures *could* be estimated, in the first case, as the total audience size per year, and in the second case, as the total number of books lent per year. These, however, are likely to be very unsatisfactory indicators for a comparison, because the respective effect of 'one more person in the audience at a traditional dancing event' and of 'one more book in the regional or minority language borrowed' are quite far apart, particularly if we are interested in an effect in terms of its contribution to the revitalisation of a language, or in terms of actual language use. The language contents of the cultural event can be high or low; the book may be read or not read; it may be read by more than one person (the borrower); it may take more or less time to read; it may more or less effectively stimulate the reader's linguistic competence; both the cultural event and the reading of the book may prompt conversations between friends later, and these conversations may take place in the minority language; and so on.

Whenever possible, it is therefore advisable to transform basic effectiveness indicators into a less direct, but probably more relevant indicator. A very general one is the amount of language use generated by a policy, where language use would be estimated in time units. This allows a link-up with existing theoretical models of language use and has been used in previous effectiveness comparisons between alternative language policies.[16] Generally, transforming direct effectiveness indicators into more fundamental ones, such as time use, will also allow for more interesting cost-effectiveness evaluations and more useful comparison of the respective cost-effectiveness of different policies.

Cost-effectiveness, available resources and decision-making

The use of cost-effectiveness information in policy choice raises two types of questions – some political, some technical; let us begin with the latter.

When implementing the Charter or considering measures for its cost-effective implementation, the technical questions that can arise will typically be of two forms: one is to adopt or to reject a policy proposal; the other is to select one policy proposal among many. These questions must be handled in conjunction with the issue of resource availability. I shall not investigate this latter question in detail, because it opens up a whole new range of issues which would exceed the scope of this book, and we shall content ourselves with an overview of some key points.

The first question (adopting or not adopting a policy, when only one is considered, for example in application of a given paragraph of the Charter) requires:

1. demonstrating that the measure is likely, to the best of the analysts' knowledge under the information available, to 'make a difference' – that is, given the definition of the word adopted here, to be 'effective';
2. making sure that the resources available make it possible to put the policy in place.

Suppose that under Article 10, the 'Tax Form Bilingualisation Programme' is the only measure proposed at a given time; remember that according to Article 2, parties to the Charter need not select more than one paragraph of Article 10 ('Administrative authorities and public services'), although of course they are encouraged to do more. Under the assumptions of our example, tax forms in the regional or minority language are likely to be used by 640,000 households and to generate 2.5 m hours of language use; hence the programme is 'effective' in terms of the definitions used in this book. It requires a budget allocation of €60,000. If this amount *is* available for the policy, then the programme can be recommended as a valid proposal.

Let us now turn to the second question. Suppose that several distinct policies are considered in the field of 'Administrative authorities and public services' and that more than one can be adopted, subject to a certain budget constraint for measures falling under this heading. Let us compare the effectiveness and cost-effectiveness of measures in Table 7.3, in which we are considering one more programme, namely the 'Social Security Questionnaire Bilingualisation Programme'. By assumption, this other programme concerns the adult population of working age (say 60 per cent of the population), in gainful employment (say, 75 per cent of people in the relevant age bracket); persons meeting both conditions are required to fill a questionnaire every year on their professional activity and earnings; this information will serve to calculate the benefits they will be entitled to after retirement under a national social security scheme. Because this information needs to be processed, and some of the processing will need to take place through the regional or minority language and hence require *additional*, language-specific resources (for example for the translation of answers to open questions), cost per year is estimated at €100,000.

Table 7.3 A comparison of effectiveness, cost and cost-effectiveness, of bilingualisation programmes in official forms

Programme	TF	TDA	SSQ
Potential users group	20% of RML-using households	10% of RML users	75% of 60% [= 45%] of RML users
Number of potential users	800,000	120,000	540,000
Actual users (80%)	640,000	96,000	432,000
Time cost per form	4	0.5	1
Time use effect (hours)	2,560,000	48,000	432,000
Yearly monetary cost (€)	60,000	20,000	100,000
Potential users per euro spent	13.3	6	5.4
Actual users per euro spent	10.7	4.8	4.32
Hours of language use per euro spent	42.7	2.4	4.32

RML: Regional or minority language
Users of the regional or minority language make up 20% of a total population of 6 m, that is, 1.2 m
TF: Tax Form Bilingualisation Programme
TDA: Travel Document Application Bilingualisation Programme
SSQ: Social Security Questionnaires Bilingualisation Programme

Assume now that the funding available for the implementation of measures corresponding to Article 10 is equal to or greater than €180,000 per year. All three programmes could be adopted. However, problems of choice will arise if the budget allocation is lower. In this case, we would rank-order the projects in terms of their cost-effectiveness and keep selecting projects as long as financial resources allow it.

A special difficulty arises because in practice, analysts will be confronted with 'lump projects', that is, projects that cannot be fragmented or implemented only in part – each project can simply be adopted or not. In such cases, if the budget cannot be stretched and if resources cannot be transferred to the following year, a relatively more cost-effective project may have to be skipped in favour of the next one in the ranking, so that the largest total effect is achieved with the resources available. This is summarised in Table 7.4.

Table 7.4 brings to light several interesting facts regarding the general decision rule and the effect that budget allocations may have on its application. Reciprocally, budget allocation decisions can be informed by the cost-effectiveness indicators. Clearly, more money increases the range of possible options, and hence the results that can be achieved. At the same time, not *all* budget increases will result in such increases.

Table 7.4 Rank-ordering of projects by cost-effectiveness and project choice under various budget constraints

	Potential users per euro spent	Actual users per euro spent	Hours of language use per euro spent
Rank-ordering of projects according to cost-effectiveness			
1	TF	TF	TF
2	TDA	TDA	SSQ
3	SSQ	SSQ	TDA
Project(s) selected according to budget size, in euro x 1,000			
$20 \leq B < 60$	TDA	TDA	TDA
Effect achieved*	120,000	96,000	48,000
$60 \leq B < 80$	TF	TF	TF
Effect achieved*	800,000	640,000	2,560,000
$80 \leq B < 100$	TF + TDA	TF + TDA	TF + TDA
Effect achieved*	920,000	736,000	2,608,000
$100 \leq B < 120$	TF + TDA	TF + TDA	TF + TDA
Effect achieved*	920,000	736,000	2,608,000
$120 \leq B < 160$	TF + TDA	TF + TDA	TF + TDA
Effect achieved*	920,000	736,000	2,608,000
$160 \leq B < 180$	TF + SSQ	TF + SSQ	TF + SSQ
Effect achieved*	1,340,000	1,072,000	2,992,000
$B \geq 180$	all three	all three	all three
Effect achieved*	1,460,000	1,168,000	3,040,00

*: *Effect measured in terms of effectiveness indicator relevant to each column; figures from Table 7.3*
Users of the regional or minority language make up 20% of a total population of 6 m (1.2 m)
TF: Tax Form Bilingualisation Programme
TDA: Travel Document Application Bilingualisation Programme
SSQ: Social Security Questionnaires Bilingualisation Programme

1. We can first observe that because of the 'lump' nature of the programmes, we may be led to advocate a relatively *less* cost-effective programme, in order to achieve the highest result with the funds available. This is why a budget allocation in the €160,000 to €179,999 range requires the adoption of programmes TF and SSQ, but not TDA, even though TDA is more cost-effective than SSQ *according to the ranking established in terms of potential or actual users*. If our decision rule is based on hours of language use, no such conflict arises.
2. Suppose now that initially, €80,000 per year are earmarked for measures under Article 10 of the Charter. No matter which cost-effectiveness indicator is used, programmes TF and TDA should be adopted. However, no budget increase will make any difference unless it is sufficient to

cover the third programme (SSQ). Hence, it is not always wise to spend all the budget available. If the budget is in the €100,000 to €159,999 range, it is preferable to implement programmes TF and TDA at a total cost of €80,000, and not to use the remaining sum (€20,000 to €79,999). The reader can easily check that implementing programme SSQ (and exactly exhausting the budget, if it is equal to €100,000) or programmes SSQ and TDA (if the budget is in the €120,000 to €159,999 range) will yield *lower* results, no matter which effectiveness indicator is used.

3. In this example, the choice of programmes to be implemented under various levels of budget allocation is the same irrespective of the cost-effectiveness criterion adopted for the ranking of programmes. However, it is also possible, in a more complex case than the one presented here, that the choice of programmes is dependent on the criterion chosen. Suppose first that the Social Security Questionnaires need to be filled not all at once, but partly in two or three occasions, totalling a per-question-naire time of seven hours instead of one; let us, however, leave all the other assumptions unchanged. This will, of course, affect the correspon-ding time use effect in Table 7.3, which would then jump from 432,000 to 3,024,000 hours. Accordingly, the 'hours of language use per euro spent' would also increase from 4.32 to 30.24. Note that this will *not* affect the rank-ordering of projects in terms of their cost-effectiveness, as indicated in the top panel of Table 7.4. However, under *some* budget configurations, the choice of measures will no longer be the same. For example, with a budget allocation in the €100,000 to €119,999 range, decision-makers would recommend spending all the money on proj-ect SSQ alone, *if the cost-effectiveness indicator is based on the hours of language use*, because it generates over three million hours of language use, instead of the 2.6 million generated by the joint implementation of the other two programmes. This case is presented in Table 7.5, in which I report only the rows corresponding to budget allocations in which a different decision will be made depending on the outcome indicator selected.

4. Let us now return to our interpretation of Table 7.4. The decision rule may also be affected by bringing in other cost-effectiveness indica-tors. Suppose for example that a representative survey of residents' attitudes is taken, indicating that they *expect* to derive the highest satisfaction from the TDA programme, followed by the SSQ pro-gramme and then by the TF programme; it may be because travel documents, which open up onto an international dimension, are per-ceived as symbolically more important, thereby giving a push to the

Table 7.5   Rank-ordering of projects by cost-effectiveness and project choice under various budget constraints, with alternative assumptions on SSQ' programme

	Potential users per euro spent	Actual users per euro spent	Hours of language use per euro spent
Rank-ordering of projects according to cost-effectiveness			
1	TF	TF	TF
2	TDA	TDA	SSQ'
3	SSQ'	SSQ'	TDA
Project(s) selected according to budget size, in euro x 1,000			
100 ≤ B < 120	TF + TDA	TF + TDA	SSQ'
Effect achieved*	920,000	736,000	3,024,000
120 ≤ B < 160	TF + TDA	TF + TDA	SSQ' + TDA
Effect achieved*	920,000	736,000	3,072,000

*: *Effect measured in terms of effectiveness indicator relevant to each column; figures from Table 7.3*
   plus alternative assumptions regarding programme SSQ'
Users of the regional or minority language make up 20% of a total population of 6 m (1.2 m).
TF: Tax Form Bilingualisation Programme
TDA: Travel Document Application Bilingualisation Programme
SSQ': Social Security Questionnaires Bilingualisation Programme with extended time requirement

popularity of the TDA programme. Depending on the *relative degree of importance* that residents give to these various programmes in their evaluations, it may then be that a budget allocation of €120,000, for example, should be allocated to programmes TDA and SSQ, instead of projects TF and TDA. Ranking programmes in terms of *one or another* cost-effectiveness indicator then becomes a political decision, in which a policy analyst or a politician makes a deliberate choice to pay more attention to expected results in terms of numbers of users, or patterns of language use measured in time units, or preferences directly expressed by residents. Such a choice must be convincingly – and transparently – argued.

5. Even in a context, as in Table 7.4, where no such ambiguity arises, it is hardly conceivable politically that a measure, once put in place, could be rescinded because a budget increase would make it possible to replace it by a more cost-effective one. Suppose a TDA programme has been in place for four years, to general satisfaction, with a budget allocation of €25,000 per year (which means that €5,000 per year are unused and returned to Treasury). Assume now that a further €35,000 per year (which means a total allocation of €60,000) are earmarked for Article 10 measures. Although this would apparently require abandoning the policy of offering travel document applications in the regional

or minority language in order to offer this facility for tax forms instead, such a decision could probably not be countenanced for political reasons. In practice, an increase up to €80,000 (that is, €55,000 more) will be required, so that *both* the TDA and the TF programme can operate.

Closing considerations on cost-effectiveness

Apart from the technical questions just discussed, a number of more political issues arise.

It should be clear by now that cost-effectiveness evaluation, apart from being a demanding exercise, does not yield ready-made policy recommendations. Much depends on context and actual conditions, and it would be futile to attempt to provide a general treatment here. Nevertheless, I hope to have alerted the reader to the caution that needs to be exercised when using this type of instrument. The virtues of the approach, however, remain: it forces analysts, elected politicians and decision makers in government to clarify the implications of their choices, and enables them to compare, debate and choose options on the basis of detailed knowledge and careful consideration.

It bears repeating that many critics of the technical approach sketched out in this chapter are liable assert, often using rather tenuous arguments, that a particular option is necessarily the best course to follow. Such pronouncements often turn out to be logically flawed, either as a result of a deliberate exclusion of some aspects of the question, or because commentators are simply not aware of the logical implications of their own recommendations. For the sake of transparency and, consequently, democracy, the choice of cost-effectiveness indicators needs to be clearly argued and justified, and subjected to tests of logical consistency. It is only if this effort is also made that it makes sense to recall that policy choice remains, ultimately, a political choice. Cost-effectiveness analysis, therefore, is merely an instrument to encourage analytical rigour and transparency in this political process.

Contrary to what is often all too rashly assumed, a cost-effectiveness analysis in no way implies that support to regional or minority language should be stingy or grudging. Taking cost dimensions into account, as such, gives no grounds to dismiss policy proposals because they would be 'too expensive'. From an economic standpoint, there is no such thing as 'too expensive' in the absolute. A very costly policy programme may be justified, if the benefits expected from it are higher than the costs. This book does not discuss the issue of benefits, because I have assumed that the political context is one in which a decision of principle has been made to implement the Charter or a set of measures comparable to those proposed in the Charter, even if they are not formally presented as such. Expressed differently, this assumption implies that the expected benefits from minority language protection and promotion are considered sufficient to justify spending a certain amount on them; this amount, however, has to be spent wisely. By clarifying more rigorously the cost implications of proposed measures, cost-effectiveness evaluation reinforces the credibility of these measures and of their proponents. Therefore, it may actually create conditions for *more* resources to be allocated to minority language protection and promotion.

Finally, several issues not addressed in this book also play a part in policy choice. They will not be discussed in detail (although I return to them in the concluding chapter), but deserve mention here. They are linked to the issue of financing and redistribution.

The question necessarily arises of how language policies will be financed. As a general rule, one would assume that policy costs will be covered out of tax revenue, which is levied on the resident population as a whole. It is possible, however, for some services to be financed in part by users. For example, even if the authorities support the creation of a cultural centre where theatre performances in the regional or minority language will take place, part of the costs of the operation may be recouped through ticket sales. This is not to say that the cost should be *wholly* covered by users. If they were in a position to do so, one could expect (as explained in Chapter 2) that such facilities would already exist. The 'market failure' context justifies state support in policy analysis perspective – and not just because of minority rights considerations. It is important to note, however, that the issue of financing opens up a broad range of questions, and that these may be handled in very different ways depending on the nature of the policy concerned.

Financing is, of course, intimately connected with redistributive effects. Just about any public policy has redistributive effects, because there never is perfect correspondence between those who pay for it and those who stand to benefit from it most directly. Run-of-the-mill examples include roads (which are financed out of tax revenue, but benefit owners of cars more than others) or education, which is also financed by all taxpayers, whether or not they have dependent children, but primarily benefits families with school-age children. The same is true of policies in favour of regional or minority languages. One may argue that these primarily benefit minority language users themselves, and if these policies are financed by all residents, there is a transfer in favour of members of the minority.

Plentiful anecdotal evidence suggests that members of the majority are quite sensitive to assumed or real redistribution effects (and are often inclined to overestimate them); complaints about measures in favour of minority languages (deemed expensive of wasteful by their opponents) are often heard.[17] It is therefore important to have adequate understanding of the rationale and cost structure of language policies. This enables social actors to explain or to realise three important points: first, that financial support to language policies is *necessary*, because the preservation of diversity, as explained in Chapter 2, raises problems of 'market failure' and consequently cannot be left over to 'free market' forces; second, that some benefits may accrue to members of the majority themselves, even if such benefits are, on a per-capita basis, probably lower than those accruing to minority language users; third, that language policies are typically quite inexpensive anyway, which means that the actual extent of redistribution between groups of actors is limited.

Notes

1. See e.g. Psacharopoulos (1987) or Lemelin (1998).
2. See e.g. the OECD's 'Education at a glance' series of indicators.
3. Grin and Sfreddo (1997).
4. Vaillancourt (1978, 1996); Grin and Vaillancourt (1999); Grin, Moring *et al.* (2002).
5. This problem is frequently illustrated through the following anecdote: at an international conference in which representatives of the Sámi community were taking part, all the debates were conducted in English. A well-intentioned representative of an international organisation, himself a native speaker of English, approached one Sámi representative, asking him whether he would need simultaneous interpretation. The answer he received was: 'I speak English and *I* don't need interpreting, but *you* might if we spoke my language at this conference!' Clearly, the potential cost of simultaneous interpretation *into Sámi* arose *because* a choice had been made to use English at the conference, and would not have arisen if Sámi had been the working language. This raises the question of why English was *a priori* chosen to fill this role – and, more generally, draws attention to the importance of critically considering the counterfactual used as a basis for the estimation of costs.
6. Vaillancourt (1978).
7. This question is addressed in Durand (2001).
8. It is unlikely that tobacco companies would be able to secure compensation from a drop in sales caused by a successful campaign targeting teenagers and promoting sporting activities.
9. In particular Bill 22 (1974), Bill 101 (1977), Bill 57 (1983), Bill 178 (1988), Bill 86 (1993), Bill 40 (1997) and Bill 171 (2000). See http://www.olf.gouv.qc.ca/charte/reperes/reperes.html.

10. See e.g. Mitchell and Carson, (1989) or Cornes and Sandler (1996, Ch. 18); for an application to language policy, Grin (1994). Contingent valuation methods are of course relevant for the evaluation of the *benefits* of policy measures, and therefore a useful tool in cost-benefit analysis. In this book, however, I shall only use cost-effectiveness evaluation (which may be interpreted as a truncated form of cost–benefit analysis; see below) The methodology of benefits evaluation is therefore outside the scope of this book.

11. Average cost at any given point on a total cost curve corresponds to the value of the slope of a straight line from the origin (0) to the point considered.

12. Depending on the mode of delivery of a good or service, for example if it is sold to the public at a price, marginal cost yields useful information about the amount of the good or service that ought to be produced, if resources are to be used judiciously. This rule, however, which is fundamental for private sector producers operating on a competitive market, is not systematically relevant for public (e.g. state) decision-makers.

13. For the sake of the example, I ignore possible further costs, such as a certain share of the working time of civil servants at the Ministry of Finance whose task is to supervise the production of a translation and the general administration of the bilingualisation scheme.

14. To use another indicator, we might want to compute the cost per minority language household which actually uses minority language tax forms. Under our assumptions, there are 640,000 such households (6 million inhabitants × 20 per cent belonging to the minority community × 80 per cent of them who choose to use minority language forms). The cost per form used is €0.09375 (a little over 9 cents). Collecting costs would then hardly justify billing the service to users.

15. For simplicity, we assume that households use either one or another language.

16. Grin (1992); Grin and Vaillancourt (1998, 1999).

17. On the alleged wastefulness of policies in favour of Scottish Gaelic, see for example McLeod (2001).

8
Democracy

Democracy and policy choice

Democracy is an issue addressed in most policy analysis textbooks. However, it is often treated as an afterthought, or simply assumed away, as if the practice of policy analysis (because it largely revolves around the comparative evaluation of the benefits and costs of policy alternatives), should be divorced from the examination of the more or less democratic character of these alternatives.

The fact that a full chapter is devoted to it here reflects this book's concern for the conditions of application of basic policy analysis instruments to minority language policies. Putting it differently, the technical dimensions of policy analysis should not lead us to overlook aspects that can significantly affect the success of policy decisions.

My starting point is the fact that the application of policy principles such as effectiveness and cost-effectiveness does, in itself, raise questions which should be addressed in conjunction with a certain interpretation of what democracy is. This question alone could set off a fully-fledged discussion of the basics of democracy as a political system, but this would far exceed the scope of this book, and readers who wish to study fundamental issues of democracy in policy development will find useful materials in the references quoted in the footnotes. I shall not, however, address these broad issues and confine my discussion to narrower aspects that are necessary to clarify the requirements of 'good policy' in a policy analysis perspective. This need for clarification must be understood in relation to a point made in Chapter 5, where I have criticised the notions of 'good policy' and 'best practice' as ambiguous, and sometimes meaningless. I have already proposed to define them in terms of effectiveness and cost-effectiveness but in this chapter, I shall go one step further, and submit that if our quest for 'good policies' is to be fruitful, their more or less democratic character also needs to be considered.

Let us start out with general notions, before moving on to the more specific issues.

Democracy is nowadays professed as a universal value and it is accepted, if not as a realised feature, then at least as a priority goal, in the official discourse of state governments and international organisations. There are some exceptions, namely a small number of countries where western-type democracy is explicitly rejected by authorities as alien or contrary to local ethics or cultural traditions – which are, in turn (though not systematically) liable to be legitimised by religion. In addition to its intrinsic value, democracy is increasingly presented as a condition for stability and peace in international relations, as well as for economic prosperity. Democracy is usually embodied in a representative system. A minimum criterion for a regime to be considered democratic is that power not only requires consent by the people, but that the people be the recognised source of power through a system of representation (Lauvaux, 1990). Direct democracy constitutes a theoretical alternative to representation, but one that has little practical relevance in a world where the modern nation-state remains the bedrock of international order.

Whatever the practice, the formal endorsement of democracy is overwhelming, even if actual practice often belies discourse. Our concern here, therefore, is not so much with the existence of formal democratic institutions, or respect for the rule of law – even though the latter does not automatically proceed from the former. For our purposes, the existence of democratic institutions can be postulated (at least in principle) as the context within which the Charter is being implemented or its signature and ratification considered. Sovereignty of the people, free and fair elections, appropriate representation, equality before the law, general application of the rule of law, may of course be interpreted in different ways and justify extensive discussion. For example, who is recognised as belonging to 'the people'? What does 'appropriate' representation exactly mean? However, these questions are outside the scope of this book, and our focus here is on another question: *assume* that we find ourselves in a political setting presenting all the normal institutional characteristics of representative democracy, and that, in particular, language policy choices *are* made according to democratic procedures. Further assume that these policy choices are demonstrably effective and cost-effective in the sense in which these concepts have been defined in the preceding chapters, and that, as a consequence, they can confidently be expected to meet the objectives of the Charter in what appears to be the best possible way. Is this enough to conclude that we are in presence of 'good policies' – whatever such an expression is taken to mean?

While all this would constitute an extremely promising start, it is still not clear that the standards of democracy applied in the above example would meet more than formalistic criteria. This limitation has been mentioned at the end of Chapter 5 and alluded to again in Chapters 6 and 7, and it harks back to the issue of 'technocracy'. Consider a case where policy development is entirely handed over to well-trained analysts. These analysts are assumed to have been appointed by a democratically-elected executive, and to carry out their tasks with a genuine concern for the accomplishment of the welfare-increasing objectives set by the legislator (that is, in representative democracies, by Parliament). The resulting policy development process, however, may turn out to be democratic only in a limited, and potentially unsatisfactory sense. The source of this limitation is that many (if not most) citizens may be shut out from the discussion over the specific contents of the policy options that will, ultimately, affect them.[1]

This concern might point in the direction of a classical discussion on the limitations of standard forms of democracy, namely, the representation and 'effective participation' of minorities. This category of issues, however, is not my concern in this chapter. Although it refers to serious matters, it has already been the object of a considerable amount of literature, whether in the legal perspective of minority rights and the political analysis of institutional arrangements to accommodate those rights,[2] given a context of nationalisms with conflicting claims,[3] or in the political-philosophical perspective on democracy and difference in plural societies,[4] which has been discussed in Chapter 5. I shall not return to those questions here. Rather, the next few pages will be devoted to the relevance of participatory democracy. In particular, I shall examine whether, in the context of language policies, participatory democracy could serve as an ingredient in the definition of 'good policies'.

Participatory democracy and the evolutionary character of democracy

Democracy as a form of political organisation has taken a long time to emerge: textbook presentations of democracy usually trace its roots back to the oligarchic democracy of cities in ancient Greece, and routinely mention the American revolution (particularly 1776 to 1778) and French revolution (particularly 1789 to 1792) as watershed points in its evolution. It was not until the twentieth century, however, that democracy was generally professed as the model of government to which all nations could normally (and legitimately) aspire. The fact that though not universally practised, it is now at least seen as a legitimate claim of all peoples, should not obscure another fact, namely, that democracy remains an evolutionary reality. Putting it differently, the fact that democracy has crystallised in a set of generally identifiable, formal institutions and procedures does not imply that democracy cannot be improved – or 'deepened'. This brief section is concerned precisely with this issue of the 'deepening' of democracy in the context of language policy.

The term 'democracy' is often heard in legal and institutional discourse, for example in documents published by international or non-governmental organisations addressing issues of human rights or minority rights. In such documents, it usually refers to the existence of a certain number of features of social and political organisation pertaining to the acquisition and exercise of power, the relationships between governments and citizens, and the relationships between citizens.[5] The dimensions of democracy at issue here are different, and pertain to the *actual* (and often informal) participation of citizens in policy processes. These processes include selection, design, implementation and evaluation. This is not to say, however, that there is a sharp or essential analytical break between the institutional traits of democratic systems and the less formal modes of operation of democracy on the ground – often referred to as democracy 'from below'.[6] Rather, practical democratic processes on the ground may be viewed as a natural counterpart of formal democratic institutions, depending on one's criteria for regarding a system as genuinely democratic. The term 'natural' should not be understood as expressing a value judgement, but rather the notion that depending on the definition of democracy adopted, the development of structures for the participation of grassroots movements in political processes can be perceived as a likely or normal evolution. In other words, there is, arguably, a *continuum* between formal democratic institutions and the possibility for citizens to be directly involved in policy development. This notion of continuum can be approached in two complementary perspectives.

First, a broad definition of democracy might include not just its institutions, but the processes through which it operates for political decision-making, down to the practical procedures applied for policy implementation. This raises the question of the relationship between the formal institutions of democracy and the arrangements made to facilitate the active participation of citizens in policy processes. In practice, such arrangements may need to operate at the periphery of formal institutions.

Furthermore, they may not be fully captured by established systems of 'direct democracy', as embodied for example in the 'initiative' and 'referendum' systems which exist in some countries. If the full exercise of formally recognised civil and political rights is interpreted as implying the opportunity to be directly involved in the debate over policy choices, additional arrangements may be necessary. Some possibilities in this direction are opened by the notion of *participatory democracy*.

'Participatory democracy' may be understood in very different ways. For some, it involves little more than more extensive information provided by the authorities to the residents living under their jurisdiction. A stronger requirement would be that of regular communication channels between the authorities and the public for information to circulate both ways. The next level of participatory democracy supposes various, but fairly stabilised, procedures of consultation and consultation between the authorities and the public. A yet further-reaching interpretation of participatory democracy implies a direct influence of citizens, whether speaking in their personal name or through independent organisations, on policy processes. In this chapter, I adopt a definition of participatory democracy implying relatively demanding standards, as exemplified by the case of the city of Porto Alegre in the Brazilian state of Rio Grande do Sul (see below).

Although 'participatory democracy' has no fixed meaning, it requires at the least, for most commentators, that people get a hearing in expressing and supporting their claims to political attention. The practical modalities of this hearing, furthermore, give citizens an opportunity to learn from one another, in addition to enabling the authorities to be informed of their constituents' concerns, and to act on this basis. The formulation of these concerns, which if acute enough can be seen as 'needs', is certainly facilitated by public discussion and exchange of information, conflicting views, and analyses. All this gives democratic processes their 'constructive importance';[7] it also indicates that practical arrangements for communication and exchange may be seen as part and parcel of a democratic system and can operate, in particular, through civic forums for public discussion and debate. Furthermore, these forums can be granted advisory competence and have an input in decision-making.[8] For lack of a formal definition, I shall henceforth take it to mean a structure with a certain degree of permanence over time, whose chief aims are (i) to offer residents the opportunity to express their concerns over policy issues; and (ii) to relay these concerns to the authorities with a view to encouraging the authorities to take these concerns on board. In this definition, a civic forum must be independent from the state, even if it may be instituted with support from the state; it follows that access to public speech is not regulated other than by normal rules of procedure. Furthermore, in order to qualify as a structure that enhances participatory democracy, a civic forum should be plural- ist, in the sense that it must be independent of organised political forces (even if the latter are many, but operate in formal or informal coalition). This applies whether the political forces in question are political parties or other forms of organisations, associations, and so on.

At the same time, the evolutionary nature of democracy can be approached from another angle, with reference to some developments in the theory of social movements. Democracy as a set of institutional or infor- mal arrangements may need to be seen in conjunction with *democratisation*, which would then be defined as a process whereby democracy is continu- ously expanded and deepened.[9] If so, it follows that macro-level social evo- lution embodies a long-term trend towards 'deeper' (and, relatedly, 'more genuine') democracy, also in the form of participatory democracy.

This trend is, in turn, reflected in more articulate expectations by citi- zens to be able to voice their opinion about the policies that affect them, including language policies. The logical implication for policy develop- ment in general, including in the case of language policies, is that one should not expect successful policies to result solely from the selection, design, implementation and evaluation of policies in ministerial offices or specialised agencies – but to emerge *also* from ideas debated and from con- sensus-building in civic forums, regularly held estates general, and so on.

The relevance of democratisation may be illustrated by the growing popularity of the concept of 'governance'. It is described as a recent trend,[10] which 'give[s] rise to a new demarcation of power within con- temporary societies, between governments and citizens'; it is reflected in the fact that 'national, linguistic and cultural minorities are increasingly being included in government administration, leading to a rethinking of the old vertical forms of authority and accountability'.[11] Governance is demarcated from traditional statist and centralizing approaches; power is no longer 'the monopoly of the all-powerful State', and relies more on coordination and networks linked by negotiation and 'expresses interdependence between the powers of the institutions involved in collective action'.[12] In order to link together the various concepts discussed here, we may say that participatory democracy pro- poses modalities through which civil society can be integrated in gover- nance as defined above.

It is risky to venture generalisations about the conditions that enhance the feasibility of participatory democracy. It appears likely, all other things being equal, to be easier to implement in institutionally decentralised settings, where even in their absence, the law provides for some decisions to be made regionally or locally. This multiplies the levels at which practical arrangements can be designed for individual citizens and grassroots movements to make their concerns heard. This also applies to matters of language policy. Examples of decentralisation in language policy are many and range from small European countries like Switzerland, where language competence is vested with the cantons (and, in some cantons, delegated to municipalities),[13] to very large ones like India, whose daunting linguistic diversity is managed with 16 constitutional languages, but where municipalities can intervene in the linguistic domain and declare a co-official language in a given district, normally when a minority ethnic group is present in sufficient numbers.[14] Another related generalisation is that the effects of decentralisation on the fortunes of regional or minority languages are not systematically favourable, since decentralisation may prevent the central government from adopting the large-scale policies often required for the effective protection or promotion of some languages.

Nevertheless, there is a growing number of instances of authorities setting up structures which allow for a more direct participation of minorities in public policy. An integrative overview of this experience in very different settings remains to be written. In the concluding section of this chapter, I shall mention selected examples in which an effort is explicitly made at experimenting with designs that, without voiding standard representative democracy, attempt to complement it.

Participatory democracy and language policy

The question remains of how participation can be implemented in practice, and which areas of policy it may affect; let us therefore take a closer look at these practical modalities.

The by now well-known case of the 'participatory budget' in the city of Porto Alegre in southern Brazil is a model of urban governance based on a partnership between the local government and civil society. In this model, residents of different city neighbourhoods can determine the criteria for the allocation of budget resources to various municipal investment projects. The choices of citizens' assemblies are forwarded to the city council, who then turns them into a budget law with formal legal validity. Some decisions, however, are not subjected to this procedure and are made according to standard legislative procedures; this is for example the case for the hiring and firing of civil servants, operating expenditure, and so on. In practice, the system requires three types of assemblies: regional assemblies meeting twice a year, neighbourhood meetings and regional topic-related forums.[15]

The political principles underpinning this system can be transposed to the selection, design, implementation and evaluation of language policies. Clearly, the practicality of participatory democracy in the form just described is likely to be more restricted in the case of policies that are meant to apply to a large region or a country as a whole, as often occurs in language policy. However, various features of participatory democracy can be built into most contexts of language policy development. In the case of large-scale policies affecting an entire state, structures such as regularly held 'Estates general of language policy', or rounds of open consultations in which citizens and groups send written submissions on matters of language policy, can provide regular opportunities for them to express their concerns and priorities. The authorities, whether the various ministries in charge of policy development or a specialised language office, can present their policy proposals to citizens, obtain reactions to these proposals from individuals and organisations, solicit counter-proposals, and generally ensure that citizens have the possibility to be directly involved in this process. Estates general may be geographically decentralised for easier access, and benefit from the experience generated in other countries in similar endeavours.[16]

Many useful aspects of the Canadian experience in the governance of (official) linguistic minorities are embodied in the so-called 'Canada-Community agreements'. These are defined as framework agreements between the Department of Canadian Heritage and the official minority language communities themselves and set out a 'framework for cooperation to advance the vitality and development of the communities'.[17] The minority communities that are party to these agreements are represented by various sectoral, regional and provincial associations. Representatives of these associations take part in a *provincial or territorial roundtable*, whose role is to establish priorities for community development and to promote coordination between the various agencies involved in it. These priorities are integrated in a development plan, which is then forwarded to an *Agreement Management Committee*. This is a joint committee that includes an equal number of representatives of the Department of Canadian Heritage and of the roundtable. In addition to receiving the priorities formulated by the roundtable, it supervises the implementation of the development plan, and advises the Department on how programme and project funding should be allocated. The Canada-Community agreements can therefore be seen as an alternative to the top-down, hierarchical form of support by the federal government to minority groups.

The first of these agreements was signed in 1988 with the Francophone community of the province of Saskatchewan; agreements with other communities were signed over the 1994–96 period, and a second round of agreements negotiated in 1999–2000, to last until 2004–05; the average funding for the 1999–2004 period is estimated at some CAD 27 m per year (the exchange rate between the Canadian dollar and the Euros is roughly 1 : 1). These agreements cannot, however, be considered an unqualified success. Not only have they taken place in a context of budget cutbacks, in which responsibility for the apportioning of cuts was shifted from the federal government to the minority communities themselves; institutional problems (particularly in relation with the issue of accountability in this more diluted power structure) also are not fully solved. Nevertheless, the operation of the Canada-community agreements has generated a wealth of hands-on experience in new forms of governance. Citizen participation may be less direct, in the context of these agreements, than in the context of Porto Alegre's participatory budget; however, it can provide pointers for the development of complex and innovative formulas in which civil society organisations have the possibility to influence policy choices.

Not all cases lend themselves to the development of relatively complex systems like the Canada-community agreements. In countries where explicit policies for the protection and promotion of regional or minority languages are only just beginning (as is the case for some 'transition countries' in Eastern and Central Europe or in the CIS), as well in countries where a longstanding language policy tradition exists, but the need is felt to undertake a major overhaul and start again with a clean slate, simpler approaches to civil society participation may be advocated.

A recent example on the national-level orientations of language policy can be found in the work of an eight-member *Coimisiún na Gaeltachta* (Commission for the Irish-speaking regions of Ireland, jointly designated as 'the Gaeltacht') which was established in April 2000 by the government of the Republic of Ireland to review the needs of the Irish language and the effectiveness of the policies and bodies serving the Gaeltacht. The Commission held 28 public meetings throughout Ireland between November 2000 and February 2001 (including two in Northern Ireland), in which more than 1,500 people took part. Notices and announcements were also placed in the media seeking written submissions from the public. Submissions were entered by 76 organisations and 70 individuals. In addition, the opinions of young people in secondary schools were sought, and a website was opened for information and debate. Of particular interest, of course, is the range of issues raised at the public meetings. Participants observed in particular that there were glaring inconsistencies regarding the language in which public services were delivered in Gaeltacht areas; that the setting up of special educational structures was a necessity across the system,[18] from the *naíonraí* (Irish-medium pre-school) to the tertiary level; that various structural conditions (pertaining for example to land planning or regional industrial development) amounted to hurdles preventing local youth from staying in Gaeltacht areas and in fact quickened the demise of the language; and that Irish-language radio and television should be improved, particularly in terms of addressing some audience segments and as regards the quality of the language used on the air. These queries are reflected in the recommendations made to the government by the Commission.[19]

In the case of small-scale policies with regional or local effects, or for the practical implementation, at regional or local level, of nation-wide policies, more direct modes of participatory democracy can be designed. The 'participatory budget' system, for example, can be applied in the case of cultural promotion. Consider for example the decision, examined in Chapter 7, to build a cultural centre for live arts performances in a regional or minority language, or to build a public library acquiring and lending books in the regional or minority language. The principles of participatory democracy require the citizens of the region concerned to be associated closely with the choice to adopt one promotional project or the other.

A wealth of relevant experience at the local level has been accumulated by the Welsh *Mentrau Iaith*, or language initiatives, which are dedicated to the promotion of Welsh in economic and social life. The first *menter* (the singular form of the plural '*mentrau*') was established in 1991 with funding from the Welsh Office, that is, the Westminster government. There are now 13 *mentrau* operating under the aegis of the Welsh Language Board. The *mentrau* are grass-roots organisations that have grown out of the aspirations of people in various localities to safeguard the future of the Welsh language in their areas. The internal organisational structure of the *mentrau* may differ, but they all rely on volunteer work, and they focus in particular on:

- helping to ensure adequate opportunities for children, young people and adults to use Welsh in their leisure time;
- providing information about Welsh medium playgroups and schools;
- advising new parents on raising their children bilingually;

- helping public, private and voluntary organisations to use Welsh;
- undertaking translation work, or putting you in touch with translators;
- providing information about Welsh for Adults courses and helping to ensure that learners can practice their Welsh outside the classroom;
- increasing the use of Welsh in the Welsh tourism industry;
- offering practical advice and help, often free of charge.

The *mentrau* are therefore strongly embedded in local communities and, through their links to the Welsh Language Board and to the local administrative authorities, they function as community agencies relaying the concerns of communities to the political structures.[20]

It seems evident that participatory democracy is likely to function better, all other things being equal, if information circulates freely and if, in particular, the authorities provide citizens with descriptions of their policy proposals – along with their reasons for putting forward any particular proposal – with adequate detail, yet in accessible language. This may be viewed as part of a general effort towards transparency. In the case of regional and minority languages policies, this means not only that the information provided ought to be jargon-free (while the more technical documents unavoidably associated with any detailed policy development can be made available separately); it also means that the information must be provided in a language that those concerned will understand; in some cases, this implies providing the relevant documents in the regional or minority language(s) concerned.

If citizens receive appropriate information and if appropriate civic forums are created for language policy options to be debated, the question then arises of how the preferences expressed by citizens can make their way into the legally enforceable Acts of democratically elected authorities. The most direct path is probably the one just described in the case of participatory democracy in the Brazilian city of Porto Alegre – the recommendations of citizens' assemblies are forwarded to the authorities, who then give them their official stamp. In strictly legal terms, however, they have no obligation to do so, since the assemblies from which these recommendations proceed are not elected.

Other, less direct avenues are also possible. The fact that the policy measures to be adopted in application of the Charter concern, most directly, the situation of people belonging to *minority* groups indicates that particular caution must be exercised: a classical limitation of democracy is that in its elementary form of majority rule, it is insufficient to safeguard the rights of minorities. In such situations, state authorities are likely to find themselves in the position of protector of relatively powerless groups in society, including users of regional or minority languages. This general limitation also applies to participatory democracy, and this could precisely be seen as an argument to *insulate* from participatory democracy all decisions affecting the status of regional or minority languages!

Such a restriction may be required in cases where the majority shows particular resistance to the granting of the conditions for the full exercise of individual rights by fellow citizens who happen to have another mother tongue (in other words, they are unwilling to allow them access to the 'context of choice' from which *they* benefit as majority language users; *cf.* Ch. 5). The fact that legal instruments for the protection of minorities are needed at all is evidence enough that there is no guarantee that majorities will cheerfully endorse measures in favour of regional or minority languages. However, in the absence of such animosity, there is no *a priori* reason for not including *some* language policy choices (such as the choice of building a cultural centre or a library) in the set of those processed through participatory democracy – including with respect to its particular dimension discussed here, namely, the inclusion of citizens' recommendations in formal administrative decisions. One safeguard which can be applied (and which is already embodied in the Charter itself) is to stipulate that no recommendation made by a civic forum or citizens' assembly may be accorded political legitimacy (let alone binding legal force) if it contravenes to the Charter – particularly Article 4, paragraph 2, which states that its provisions 'shall not affect any more favourable provisions concerning the status of regional or minority languages.'

Circumstances may justify restricting consultation on particular policy projects, as well as the right to formulate recommendations about them, to those people who are actual or potential users of a regional or minority language. This, for example, can be the case for the practical implementation of measures in the field of minority-language education. An example can be found in Canada, where Article 23 of the Canadian Charters of Rights and Freedoms gives Canadian citizens of official mother tongue residing in a minority community the right to administer minority-language educational institutions. Parents meeting the criteria for being recognised as eligible to this right (as part of a broader set of minority education rights) may take advantage of the services offered, and be involved, as members of a *community*, in the administration of schools. This amounts to a system that provides the possibility for individuals to affect language policy more directly, *qua* members of a group sharing certain language-related characteristics, and therefore represents a departure from the usual workings of formal democratic institutions.[21]

It would be naïve to assume that participatory democracy is any more exempt from conflict than the usual political game in formal democratic institutions. Conflicts of interest and values between citizens or groups of citizens will undoubtedly arise in civic forums, whether the issue under discussion is land reclamation, the expansion of city parks or the promotion of a regional or minority language. In the preceding paragraphs, we have seen that participatory democracy (which, taken to its logical conclusion, would amount to nothing less than the full self-management of communities) is no excuse for depriving the relatively weak of the protection of the state against the relatively strong. However, diverging interests will manifest themselves even when some issues, possibly for human rights or minority rights reasons, are kept out of the reach of civic forums. What arguments can then be brought to bear to arbitrate between such diverging interests?

This question raises fundamental problems in political and economic theory, and in the absence of definitive solutions, some guiding principles should be invoked. To the extent that issues in the debate surrounding them have been mentioned in Chapter 5, they will not be repeated here. Such principles may include 'consistency', in which conflicting claims are evaluated using similar criteria – that is, the 'rules of the game' are identical for all; it is important to recall, as we have seen before, that this principle is perfectly compatible with a differential treatment of people in different situations. This latter observation is also relevant to assess the role of other principles for processing conflicting claims. For example, one may attempt to derive trade-off rules between conflicting claims according to principles explicitly embodying some *moral* preference[22] – for example, 'equity' or 'justice'. These notions, however, are not sufficient for a final arbitration between conflicting interests expressed by different groups of citizens in a public forum. It is widely accepted that equity requires treating equally people who are in the same situation, and treating differently people who are in a different situation. This will, of course, raise the problem of identifying and measuring *relevant* similarities and differences, as well as the extent of compensatory measures to be adopted to make up for those differences.[23] Hence, giving participatory democracy an important role in governance does not, far from it, imply the demise of the state. In fact, 'the removal of government from the process ... appears to remove any real possibility for real accountability'.[24]

Whereas in the case of the principles of effectiveness and cost-effectiveness, I have aimed to present more rigorous, at times somewhat technical instruments for policy development, it may not be possible to replicate this approach when participatory democracy is at issue. This, of course, reflects the simple fact that there are no generally applicable rules for *grading* practices in this area. However, and perhaps more importantly, the question is that by definition, 'democracy' as discussed in this chapter may not fit neatly into fixed categories. Taking full measure of its evolutionary character requires that citizens themselves discuss and develop various modes of social participation. Hence, though no rules can be put forward at the close of this chapter, it is useful to formulate four questions, which can serve as a check-list for policy analysts who are concerned with developing arrangements for direct participation by the public in the selection, design, implementation and evaluation of policies.

1. How relevant and extensive is the information regarding minority language policies made available to citizens?
2. How, and through what mechanisms and institutions, are minority language policies discussed in the public arena?
3. How are citizens' concerns regarding minority language policies 'taken on board' and integrated into policy decisions?
4. How does the system arbitrate between the conflicting interests voiced by different citizens and groups of citizens regarding minority language policies?

The scope of participatory democracy must be limited, if only to allow the state to fulfil its function of protecting the relatively weak, an issue that undoubtedly presents particular cogency in the case of regional or minority languages. Hence, one absolute precondition for developing institutions of participatory democracy as a tool for democratic policy development is to ensure that the political context ensures that these institutions cannot be instrumentalised by members of the majority in order to curtail the rights of users of regional or minority languages. If such a condition can be met, scrutinising the policy measures considered not just in terms of effectiveness and cost-effectiveness, but also in the light of the four questions just formulated, will generally help to move towards more successful language policies.

Finally, in the form of a coda, it is useful to recall that 'civil society', as well as the individuals and groups who may, through forms of participatory democracy, influence language policy processes, need not be restricted to members of the minority language community affected, or to residents (no matter their language repertoire) of an area that would be affected by a language policy. Other associations (such as language teacher associations) may have valid and legitimate proposals to make, and may have a role to play themselves, particularly in raising people's awareness to the importance of linguistic diversity.[25]

Notes

1. This concern is particularly manifest in the context of the building of the European Union; see various contributions in Smith and Wright (1999).
2. See e.g. Hannum (1990, 1993); Tomuschat (1993); Lapidoth (1996); de Villiers (1994); Brunner and Meissner (1999); de Varennes (1999); etc.
3. See e.g. McGarry and O'Leary (1993); Hutchinson and Smith (1994); Gellner (1997); Schöpflin (2000); O'Reilly (2001), etc.
4. See e.g. Taylor (1992); Kymlicka (1995a,b); Benhabib (1996); Shapiro and Kymlicka (1997); etc.; well-known work on consociational democracy by Lijphardt (1977) may be said to fall between these contributions and those mentioned in the preceding footnote.
5. No distinction will be made in the present discussion between 'citizens' and the broader group of 'residents'.
6. See contributions in Kaldor (ed., 1991) on the role of civil society organisations in the 'democratic revolutions' of 1989 in Eastern and Central Europe; see also Wydra (1999).
7. Sen (1999).
8. On forums and participatory democracy, see e.g. texts published by the Centre for Consensual Democracy on http://www.consensualdemocracy.org. There is no fixed definition of 'civic forum'.
9. On this question, see Rossiaud (1996, 1997). Democratisation occurs as part of a natural, broader process of societal evolution, and is related to the rise of subjectivity, both individual and collective, as one of the socially valid and politically legitimised levels at which values and choices are formulated and acted upon by social actors. Rossiaud further considers that we are witnessing a 'universalisation' of democratic aspirations and models, and that this aspect is an essential dimension of the process of globalisation.
10. Cardinal and Hudon (2001).
11. Ibid., p. 9.
12. Stoker, 1998: 20.
13. See e.g. Voyame (1996); Schoch (1999); Grin (2000a).
14. On India, see e.g. Pattanayak (1990). For an extensive catalogue of language legislations around the world, see the web site of the International Research Centre on Language Planning (CIRAL) in Québec/Canada under http://www.ciral.ulaval.ca/alx/amlxmonde/accmonde.htm.
15. On the Porto Alegre experience, see Genro and de Souza (1998).
16. For example the 'consensus conference' model pioneered by Denmark since 1993; similar models are applied in other countries, in various forms. Generally, the method of such 'conferences' is to involve ordinary citizens in a panel together with experts and to provide conditions for common work between them (see http://www.loka.org). One well-known example is the

'National Issues Forum' in the United States, which describes itself as a 'nationwide network of educational and community organizations that deliberate about nation-wide issues ...; NIF is non-partisan and does not advocate a specific solution or point of view. Rather, deliberative forums provide a way for citizens to exchange ideas and experiences with one another, and make more thoughtful and informed decisions' (see http://www.nifi.org).

17. Cardinal and Hudon (2001: 22).
18. For example, some communities complained about the Irish language proficiency of some primary school teachers who had graduated from training colleges.
19. See *Coimisiún na Gaeltachta* (2002). The report is also available on-line on http://www.coimnagael.ie.
20. Information about the *Mentrau iaith* is available on-line on: http:// www.mentrau-iaith.com/prif/index.html.
21. On the organisation of official minority language education in Canada, see Martel (1991, 2002).
22. For a discussion, see Saward (1994).
23. This question can be analysed in terms of the combination of 'efficiency' and 'fairness' in language policy. For a formalised application to the choice of official languages in multilingual states, see Pool (1991) or Van Parijs (2001).
24. Peters (2001: 48), quoted by Cardinal and Hudon (2001), who point out that 'the State, without taking over the network [of civil society organisations] must work to orient its action so as not to lose sight of the broader public interest' (2001: 10).
25. This point is made, among others, by the President of the FIPLV (Fédération internationale des professeurs de langues vivantes); see Cunningham (2002).

9
A Walk-Through Example: Language Education Policy

Methodology

Part III of this book emphasises the presentation of analytical instruments with the help of examples, largely avoiding theoretical considerations. The moment has now come to propose a general recapitulation of these instruments with one integrative example. In this chapter, we shall follow a language policy analysis process all the way along the 'policy-to-outcome path' presented in Chapter 2, using the principles presented in Chapter 5 and the evaluation instruments presented in Chapters 6 and 7. Key elements of the policy context will be derived from the Charter, presented in Chapters 3 and 4. Several methodological choices need to be made first.

1. Because my focus is on language *policy*, not language *politics*, considerations about the political dimensions involved will largely be side-stepped. However, literature about them is abundant[1] and one sub-section in this chapter is devoted to 'language *politics* assessments', less to analyse and describe them than to characterise their practical role and usefulness in an overall policy evaluation procedure; following this, I move on directly to the policy analysis issues.
2. The question arises of whether this integrative example should be taken directly from reality, or suggest a fully hypothetical one. I have opted for the latter solution for the following reasons. First, there are few evaluation exercises of actual policies,[2] and not much would have been gained by simply presenting once again one or another of such cases. Second, picking another real-world case would necessarily have carried with it the problem discussed in the introductory chapter: each case is a special case, and what can be learned

about one may not always have direct relevance to other cases, and the realities of a particular real-world situation would have distracted our attention from the exercise proposed here. Third and relatedly, because the purpose of this chapter is, in a sense, pedagogical, certain priorities follow – more precisely, the application of a set of tools can be explained most clearly with a tailor-made example, in which reference is made only to the analytically essential features.[3] Fourth, doing justice to a real-world case would call for a fully-fledged study in its own right, raising problems of data availability, while also requiring me to leave out certain aspects which some readers would have considered essential.

3. This does not mean, however, that the example should be completely pure, in the sense that it would be stripped of all the contextual features that necessarily define real-world policy problems. Hence, the example presented below is embedded in a (hypothetical) demographic, cultural and political context, which also serves to exclude *a priori* some policy questions which would, in a general theoretical approach, have to be discussed as well.

4. Finally, it would not have been possible – lest this book become considerably longer – to analyse the application of the three principles of effectiveness, cost-effectiveness and democracy to many, let alone *all* of the measures proposed in paragraphs of the Charter, and a choice had to be made. I have decided to focus on measures in the field of education, and to investigate 'language education planning' (LEP). This choice is explained by three main reasons. First, education is arguably the single most important area of intervention in language policies, as shown in the analytical framework in Chapter 2. Second, it is one in which states *must* step in, in compliance with the undertakings to which they subscribe as parties to the Charter. Third, it has been relatively little used in the preceding chapters of the book.

Linguistic environment

The demolinguistic context

Let us consider a country of six million people, of which 20 per cent, that is, 1.2 million, are actual or potential users of a regional or minority language X. The majority language Y is known by the entire population, although it may be known at a low degree of competence by elderly members of the X-speaking group.

The regional or minority language X is spoken by *most* of the 1.2 million people who make up the 'pool' of actual or potential users, though with varying degrees of proficiency ranging from 'low' to 'fluent'. Characterising levels of fluency raises theoretical and empirical difficulties which will, however, not be discussed here.[4] Out of this pool of 1.2 million people, we shall assume that 80 per cent (960,000) claim to speak the language, but that only 196,000 of them are fully fluent in it and feel at least as confident (or even *more* confident) using X than Y. Out of the same group of 1.2 million people, 300,000 speak X well, but feel more confident using Y, particularly in writing. The remaining 500,000 only have basic knowledge of X. For example, they may only know simple expressions learned with grandparents or in other family contexts. The demolinguistic breakdown of the country is summarised in Table 9.1.

The 'pool' of actual or potential users of X (that is, 1.2 m people) coincides with the people who associate with a regional or minority language community, usually (though not necessarily) because of their own family background, ancestry, or marriage with a member of this community. Let us remember, however, that in the spirit of the Charter, what matters is not ethnic identity, but actual or potential language use.

Let us assume that actual or potential users of language X live in one particular part of the country, in which they constitute a local majority (the 'RML region'), as well as in the country's capital city, in which they constitute a minority. For simplicity, the example further assumes that there are no additional autochthonous languages, no non-territorial languages, and no immigrant languages – or at least, not in numbers of any consequence.

Language X is engaged in a spiral of decline ('language shift') in which X-speaking parents often decide not to teach their children language X, nor to encourage them to learn it. While such a pattern is not assumed

Table 9.1 Population distribution by language skills

Total population	6,000,000
'Majority' population (speakers of Y who do not know X and claim no intergenerational ties with the X-speaking group)	4,800,000
Actual or potential users of Y	1,200,000
broken down by competence levels in X as follows:	
Fluent	196,000
Good	300,000
Basic	500,000
None	204,000

to be systematic, it may result, in some families, in children having limited or no competence in *X*, while their grandparents have limited or no competence in *Y*. At the same time, a large number of people have basic competence in *X*, which is why the corresponding group is assumed to be larger than that of people who have no knowledge of it. Generally, the percentage of fluent or good speakers is higher in the older age brackets, and the percentage of poor speakers or non-speakers is higher in the younger age brackets.

Finally, I shall assume that language *X* has a longstanding (if quantitatively limited) literary tradition and has a clearly identified and unified written form, even if oral usage may vary between parts of the RML region; this means that language 'corpus' questions (choice of a writing system; lexical development) do not arise, or at least not to a greater extent for *X* than for *Y*.

Language *X* across domains

Suppose that the use of language *X* has long been tolerated by government in the public space, but not encouraged. As a result, there are no provisions for the use of *X* in courts, in the administration or in the publicly-held media. However, there exists one *X*-language local radio station in the RML region, as well as one weekly magazine in language *X*. The same company which produces this magazine also publishes, without state support, a small number of books in language *X* every year, mostly children's stories, some literary works by *X*-speaking authors, and textbooks for *X*-language learning (mostly destined for primary schools and pre-school education – see below). Cultural activities in language *X* (theatre plays, music festivals, other cultural events) may be organised, but typically do not (or only marginally) benefit from state support. Language *X* may be used (but this only rarely occurs) in written form in business and commerce. For example, some shops may label their products in language *X*, although the law requires labels and all signs in shops to be in language *Y* (though not exclusively in *Y*). Language *X* is typically not used on commercial forms, operating instructions for goods, lists of ingredients on packaging, safety instructions, and so on.

Suppose that until the Charter comes into force in the country considered, language *X* is only offered as an optional subject (but not as a medium of instruction), and this only in a limited number of schools in the RML region. Education is decentralised through primary and secondary school, and regional authorities are entitled to decide whether they will or will not provide such classes, and in which establishments. There are no provisions for the training of teachers of language *X*, who typically are language teachers (normally teaching *Y* or some foreign language) who also happen to be good or fluent speakers of *X*; they teach *X* in addition to their normal teaching load – but are paid for this work.

Clearly, the setting just described is a hypothetical and relatively simple one, yet it is not at variance with what may be observed in several European cases; it largely corresponds to the upper reaches of stage 5 or the lower reaches stage 4 in Fishman's *Graded Intergenerational Disruption Scale*. Readers who want to examine at closer range the implications of a different context will, however, find ample materials in the sociolinguistic literature where real-world cases are described.[5]

What works?

Policy options and the language politics assessment

In our hypothetical example, national authorities intend to sign and ratify the Charter, and are contemplating policies in the area of education. A range of options is provided in the first part (1) of Article 8, covering pre-schools (letter a), primary education (b), secondary education (c), technical and vocational education (d), university and other higher education (e), and adult and continuing education (f). Within each tier of the education system, a choice is proposed between offering education through the medium of the regional or minority language (in our example, language *X*); offering part of the curriculum (that is, a selection of subjects) in *X*; teaching *X* as a subject as part of the curriculum; or to apply one of the above measures 'at least to those pupils whose families so request and whose number is considered sufficient'. At least three paragraphs must be selected from Article 8 (which also includes additional provisions on: the teaching of the history and culture reflected in language *X*; teacher training; supervision of educational provisions; and the teaching of *X* in regions other than those where it is traditionally used).

Let us assume that two general policy orientations are considered, namely: (i) policy *A*, in which *X*-language classes are made available, on an optional basis, to all in the RML region (and not just in the accidental school); and (ii) policy *B*, in which *X*-medium primary education for all subjects is offered, as an optional stream, to all in the RML region. We shall suppose that these two policies are considered for compulsory education, which by assumption concerns primary education and secondary education up to the age of 15. This would, typically, not include technical and vocational education, which some young people enter after completing their compulsory education. Suppose therefore that compulsory education covers nine years of schooling, normally from age six to age 15.[6]

Even before engaging in the full identification of the resources that a policy will require, and of the results it is expected to deliver (my primary concern in this book), a *preliminary* review of the relevance of the policy should be carried out, in the form of a general language *politics* assessment (as distinct from language *policy* analysis). This language politics assessment (LPA) is that part of an overall evaluation which is, in most cases, most commonly carried out. The main reason for this is probably the following: in that it directly connects political issues with sociolinguistic ones, it can draw on long-established fields of specialisation.

There is, however, no standardised way to carry out an LPA. Its methodology will tend to be hermeneutic, inductive and qualitative, rather than formalised, deductive and quantitative; its thrust is to develop a *convincing interpretation* of selected social phenomena, rather than to propose a formal proof that these can be explained through a given set of causal relationships. Some useful elements for an LPA can be found in the so-called 'seven success conditions' mentioned in Chapter 6, as part of our discussion on policy effectiveness.

The emphasis of an LPA would normally be on the relationship between language, power, and ideology. It should seek to identify and explain the positions and actions of different groups of actors – who typically have unequal access to political, economic and symbolic resources – *vis-à-vis* language matters: what are the confronting views in society about the respective status of different languages? Who (that is, which groups defined in terms of language, social class, profession, educational level, region of residence, etc.) holds what views, and for what reasons? Should the divergence of views be interpreted in terms of conflict, domination or oppression? What are its historical and political roots? Can certain views hostile to policies in favour of language *X* change of their own accord, following their own dynamics? Should they be expected to change only in response to deliberate action undertaken by the state (for example, by directly advocating, or even 'marketing' a 'bilingual society')? Answers to the above questions must then be processed in order to assess how the proposed language policy measures can earn acceptance among various groups in society – both in terms of the use of material and symbolic resources they entail and in terms of the results they are intended to reach. This may, in turn, significantly influence analysts' preference for policy *A* or *B*. The 'language politics assessment' is therefore not divorced from language policy analysis; they may be seen as two sides of a coin, just like some political scientists contrast 'results-oriented' with 'interaction-oriented' policy research.[7]

Because the range of issues that can prove relevant in an LPA is practically limitless, let me attempt to clinch this point with a simple illustration. In our example, although policy *B* goes further than policy *A*, either of them would constitute a notable change for the demolinguistic perspectives of language *X*. Both may therefore be considered desirable from the perspective of diversity promotion, as well as from the perspective of the group interests of actual or potential users of *X*. However, the choice of policy *A* or policy *B* may generate heated public debate, not only among actual or potential users of *X*, but also in the population as a whole, even though members of the majority (unilingual *Y*-speaking) population would for all practical purposes remain unaffected by these policy developments. Policy *B* may (much more than policy *A*) be perceived as a watershed, raising fears in some segments of majority opinion that it may signal a radicalisation of inter-community differences, with attendant threats to the integrity of the state. Reciprocally, depending on the prevailing political context, it may be that policy *B* is necessary to preserve the integrity of the state, since it would formally recognise the legitimacy of language *X* as a fully-fledged component of the country's identity. Investigating these points would, in such a context, be among the main functions that an LPA would serve.[8]

Suppose now that following an LPA, policies *A* and *B* still stand as valid options. We can now turn to the application of policy analysis instruments to the comparison between them.

Examination of goals

By adopting the Charter, state authorities undertake to engage in a policy compatible with the spirit of the Charter. This already clarifies the goals pursued to a significant extent. For reasons discussed previously, language policy should aim at restoring a self-priming mechanism of language reproduction, which constitutes the overarching goal of the policy.

In our example, the initial situation of language *X* is one where the language receives virtually no support from the state, and where the observable patterns of language shift pose clear threats to its future; furthermore, toleration of language *X* falls far short of the conditions necessary to guarantee its long-term vitality. Education plays a crucial role in the restoration process, since it makes up one of its three necessary conditions, namely, the capacity to use the language, the other two being 'opportunity' and 'desire'. Let us call policy interventions in the sphere of education 'language education planning' (LEP). LEP may operate in two different ways, which in practice occur jointly, but may be distinguished analytically: 'acquisition planning' and 'skills development'; I use both expressions in a specific sense that needs to be explained.

'Acquisition planning' aims to increase the number of users, whether in relative or in absolute terms (this distinction is discussed below). Successful acquisition planning results in an increase in the number or proportion of persons who can use the target language *at a given level of competence*, without culling these people from lower competence groups. I shall assume this level of competence to amount to fluency, which I define here as levels C1 ('effective proficiency') and C2 ('mastery') on the six-point scale used by the Council of Europe in its language education projects.[9] Deliberately simplifying this assessment scale, we can say that this refers to the ability to communicate effectively and precisely in most circumstances, making the language mastered to that degree an adequate tool for cognitive processes and communication.

'Skills development', by contrast, focuses on increasing the skills level of users, without necessarily increasing the absolute number or percentage of the latter. Skills development means, for the persons concerned, moving up from a lower to a higher level of competence on an evaluation scale, such as the Council of Europe scale just mentioned. Both acquisition planning and skills development may target adults as well as young learners, although the emphasis of this example – in keeping with the Charter – is on people of school-going age.

Of course, increasing the number (or the percentage) of speakers logically implies that the level of language skills of the persons concerned will increase – hence, both forms of LEP cannot always be distinguished in practice – but skills development can focus on a fixed number of persons, that is, it does not imply an increase in that number. In the formal modelling of minority language use, these two types of intervention have analytically different effects, even if the expected final outcome in terms of language vitality is the same. In policy evaluation, it therefore makes sense to distinguish them and to clarify whether the goal pursued is primarily an increase in the number of speakers of X, or an increase in the competence in X of a given number of speakers.

Let us now assume that given the observed pattern of decline of language X, people are most concerned with its transmission to the younger generations, particularly in view of the fact that large-scale language teaching, all other things being equal, is more effective if begun at a younger age. This validates, in our example, the *a priori* consideration of policies *A* and *B*, both of which are directed towards language acquisition by young people. Clearly, both policies would result in a net increase in the number of competent users; they would also result in an increase of the percentage of competent users in the target population, unless the growth rate of the population exceeds that of the number of users. The difference between the evolution of the demolinguistic weight of users in absolute or relative terms is analytically relevant, because one may argue that in order for a language to survive, even a high absolute number of users will not constitute a sufficient safeguard, if those users, many as they are, are diluted in a much larger population of unilingual *Y*-users.[10] However, barring particularly high fertility rates in the unilingual *Y*-speaking portion of the *X*-identified population, it is only deliberately ineffective modes of implementation of these two policies that would result in higher absolute numbers but a lower percentage of *X*-language users. We can therefore assume that either indicator can be used as a measuring rod of a policy's success.

The question now arises of which of the two policies considered is likely to meet this goal more effectively. To ascertain this point, we need to look more closely at the way in which they operate.

Identifying relevant cause-and-effect relationships

I have just defined 'acquisition planning' as the policy of increasing the demographic weight of competent users of the language in a given target population, through a concerted language-teaching effort operating via the education system. In the terms of the policy-to-outcome path, the direct goal of acquisition planning is 'capacity development', which can be considered as a direct proof of success. However, this reference to the direct character of the proof must remind us of the necessity, discussed in Chapter 6, of considering its induced effects in order to assess the ultimate outcomes of a policy. Let us therefore briefly characterise each, before investigating them at closer range.

The first-level criterion of success is self-evident, both under policy *A* and policy *B*: the policy should result in an increase in the number of speakers at a given level of competence (in this example: 'effective proficiency' and 'mastery' in the Council of Europe's terminology). The success of the policy implies that this increase obtains as a result of it, that is, that the persons concerned would not have become competent users in the absence of the policy. Ascertaining this causal link and evaluating its magnitude requires an internal effectiveness evaluation, where the word 'internal' refers to the fact that the critical link is one that operates within the education system.

Before discussing procedures for international effectiveness evaluation, it is worth noting that such first-level success can obtain only if a preliminary condition is met – quite simply, if the policy is sufficiently attractive. Investigation of this point is not normally within the scope of standard internal effectiveness analyses, and may be included in the language politics assessment described earlier. Recall that both policy A and policy B offer optional education streams; analysts should in particular consider which of the two policies is likely to result in the highest level of enrolment. On the one hand, parents may consider policy A as attractive, because it would equip youngsters with competence in X without introducing too sweeping a change from the pre-existing situation. In particular, if all subjects save X are still taught through Y, they can expect their children to be proficient in X without running the risk of being excluded from the dominant-language labour market for inadequate competence in Y. If this perception is widespread, we would expect policy A to have more appeal than policy B, and until this perception does change, policy A would be considered superior to B in terms of its capacity to increase the number of competent speakers of X, owing if nothing else to attitudinal reasons.

However, let us remember that the ultimate goal pursued is to restore and safeguard what has been called a self-priming mechanism of language reproduction. Therefore, even if the number of people who are able to use X increases markedly, the mechanism can hardly be considered self-priming if people do not actually use it! Hence, what matters is whether the potential users 'produced' by the education system under policy A or B do use the language in their everyday life – and also if they pass it on, as parents, elders, teachers and the like, to the next generation. Assessing this particular point raises the question of external effectiveness evaluation – where the adjective 'external' indicates that the crucial effects now operate outside of the education system.

Let us now examine in turn internal and external effectiveness evaluation.

Internal effectiveness evaluation

Internal effectiveness evaluation examines processes taking place primarily within the education system, where some resources are transformed into certain results. The resources in question are immensely varied. Consider the case of policy A. This includes a certain endowment of hours during which language X is taught in the weekly programme; the production and provision of books and other teaching materials; the use of school premises, including a certain proportion of the cost of running and maintaining them; a certain proportion of the managerial and organisational resources devoted to the education system; and a certain number of teachers, who have to be paid a certain salary, and have, at an earlier stage, cost a certain amount of resources to train. These resources are transformed into outputs by the teaching and learning process, whose outputs are the skills acquired by learners. The notion of resources can be extended to incorporate the conditions under which they are invested. For example, equally well-trained teachers may not be able to foster the same progress among their pupils depending on whether classrooms are homogeneous or heterogeneous in terms of the general scholastic abilities of the pupils.

In the case of policy B, the range of resources tallied up must be appropriately expanded to include for example the availability and quality of textbooks for various school subjects in language X.

The assessment of the effectiveness with which inputs are transformed into outputs is a classical field of investigation in education economics, on which a considerable literature exists,[11] even if a tiny fraction of it focuses on the analysis of language-learning processes. This means that there are comparatively few established statistical results on the way in which the range and amount of resources invested in a language teaching and learning process affects results (which are defined, for reasons discussed above, as an increase in the number of competent users, whether potential or actual).

A fully-fledged presentation of internal effectiveness evaluation would deserve a detailed treatment, whether in general or in the case of language skills. Let us therefore content ourselves with sketching out the exercise: usually, the examination of the underlying pedagogical or psycholinguistic processes is side-stepped, and statistical procedures (in particular multivariate analysis) are used in order to isolate the relative contribution of various inputs to the desired output, by comparing the results achieved by learners schooled under the policy being evaluated with those of learners from a control group. For example, does a group who has been taught language X using a new textbook perform better, on average and all other things being equal, than a control group who has been using a standard textbook? Do classrooms that have been split in sub-groups according to ability or inclination achieve higher competence, on average and all other things being equal than heterogeneous classrooms?

What can internal effectiveness evaluation mean in the context of our example, namely, the comparison between policies *A* and *B*?

One first needs to consider the issue of data availability. Authorities confronted with the problem of choosing a policy in order to fulfil their obligations under Article 8 of the Charter would not be in a position to test the relative success of models which do not, in their country, exist yet – in our example, there is at the outset virtually no teaching of, let alone *in* language *X*. Depending on time and political context it is, however, possible for a state to subscribe to lower-level objectives in Article 8 and simply to offer only the teaching of language *X* as a subject (policy *A*), while pursuing higher-level objectives on a trial basis in some pilot schools. The latter could for example operate wholly through the medium of *X* (policy *B*). This opens the door to comparative testing and the later decision to stick to policy *A* or shift to policy *B* and, in this latter case, to upgrade the degree of protection and promotion afforded language *X* in the initial ratification instrument.

However, because these policies are significantly different, it may not be most relevant to organise the comparison of their effectiveness (in terms of the resulting language competence of learners) with respect to specific input combinations. Rather, one would move on directly to a cost-effectiveness evaluation, in which the increase of the number of speakers generated under policy *A* and policy *B* respectively (comparing, of course, an identical number of pupils) would be divided by the expenditure entailed by each. This, however, raises questions of cost identification, cost measurement and cost-effectiveness, which are addressed later.

In contexts where it is not possible to create the conditions for a systematic comparison of the internal effectiveness of *A* and *B*, the decision to adopt one or the other may be guided by the experience acquired elsewhere, particularly in those cases where a choice between streams exists, and where each stream is characterised by a greater or lesser extent of minority language use, for example the 'A', 'B' and 'D' models in the Basque Country.[12]

External effectiveness evaluation

External effectiveness evaluation starts out from the outputs of internal effectiveness evaluation and treats them as inputs. In our example, the increase in the number of competent speakers of *X* made possible by the policy (whether *A* or *B*) would be assumed to be one of the causes giving rise to certain effects (which are then treated as outputs). The effects we are interested in, then, are precisely the ultimate goals of the policy, or some indicator that is as close as possible to these ultimate goals.

As noted before, the ultimate goal is the restoration of a 'self-priming mechanism of language reproduction'. Though this points to a fairly clear (if complex) reality, it remains too broad to pin down *as such*; hence, it is rational to evaluate external effectiveness with indicators approximating this reality. Candidates for this role have been proposed in the presentation of 'generalised effectiveness comparison' in Chapter 6: they include for example the change in frequency with which language X is used. Hence, external effectiveness evaluation can take the form of an assessment, through representative surveys, of whether persons who have learned language X as a subject (policy A) use language X in their everyday life more or less readily than persons who have been schooled through the medium of language X (policy B). Other indicators could include the range of domains in which people consider (as may be revealed by an opinion survey) that it is 'normal' to use language X.

If policy B generates, all other things being equal, a stronger increase in the frequency with which X is used, B will be considered more effective. This, however, does not tell us if it is more cost-effective, or if B should be adopted. As shown in Chapters 6 and 7, further steps need to be completed in the analysis before such a conclusion (or the opposite one) can be accepted and acted upon.

Again, data are likely to be lacking, particularly when considering policies that have not been implemented. However, it is possible to poll people on what they think they *would* do – that is, which language they would use, for what activities, and at which frequency – if they spoke language X better than they do, or if more people around them did. This provides contingent evaluations of the external effectiveness of policies that aim to increase the number of competent users. If the practical situation precludes the taking of surveys of any kind, and therefore no statistical analysis is possible, relevant information on patterns of use of regional or minority languages that have benefited from a longstanding investment in teaching will provide useful pointers. Well-known examples in Western Europe include Catalan, Basque and Welsh.[13]

One of the main virtues of quantitative analyses is that they may be used to shed light on the critical role of certain intervening variables in a causal relationship. Strictly speaking, statistical analysis does not reveal, let alone prove *causality*: what it does is to reveal (with a higher or lesser degree of likelihood), the presence and strength of *associations* between variables; theoretical analysis is then used to propose plausible explanations for observed associations. In the same way, statistical analysis can help check whether particular variables have a determining influence on whether or not a causal relationship seen as likely *a priori* actually occurs.[14] Such information is particularly useful given that in much of the literature where this type of question is identified, propositions remain very general, noting for example that language use will 'also depend on' one or another factor, without attempting to ascertain the strength of this conditionality.

These remarks about the underlying links between variables, however, apply at all stages of the evaluation. This point has already been made in a slightly different way when discussing the policy-to-outcome path of Chapter 2: increased capacity to use the language will result in an increased use of the language only if 'opportunity' and 'desire' are also present. These very general variables find expression in much narrower ones that lend themselves to easier testing. For example, an increase in the number of children who are taught language X may result, in some establishments, in an equivalent increase of linguistically competent speakers at age 15, and in other establishments, in a negligible increase. The statistical evaluation of effectiveness may indicate that the two types of establishments in which the evaluation is carried out are identical in most respects (socio-economic profile of pupils and teachers, expenditure per head, etc.), except that the pedagogical materials used are different. This would create as a strong presumption that the materials used in the better-performing establishment explain, at least in part, different results.

The causal relationships discussed so far can be summarised in a two-way table (Table 9.2). In column 1 of each row, I indicate the direct policy input. There exists a relationship (characterised in column 2) which links, on the one hand, the direct policy-determined input with other inputs (the 'intervening variables' in column 3) and, on the other hand, the result or output of the policy (column 4). A policy will be considered successful (column 5) if this result reaches a certain level. The reader will note that the success criterion relevant to external effectiveness amounts to a broader policy *outcome*, namely, reaching the ultimate goal of the language policy as a whole.

One objection frequently made to effectiveness evaluation exercises is that they tend to neglect contextual elements. However, there is nothing to prevent us from introducing them at one or another stage in the overall procedure. For example, information gathered during the LPA about parental attitudes can be used to contextualise the role of specific variables intervening downstream in the policy process.

Table 9.2 Cause-and-effect relationships in language education planning

Direct policy input	Relationship	Examples of critical variables in the causal relationship between input and output	Policy result ('output')	Success criterion
(a) General policy appeal Offering X as a school subject or as a medium of instruction in primary and secondary schools.	Evaluation by parents and youngsters of the attractiveness of the educational option offered.	Expected skills in X and Y resulting from education; Language-based differences in labour market access; Parents' political opinions; Orientation of media coverage; Attitude of political parties.	(Expected) enrolment figures in educational option made possible by the policy.	As many families as possible should choose to send their children to schools in which X can be learned.
(b) Internal effectiveness Percentage of children starting primary school with fluency in X.	Internal effectiveness of education process in terms of X language acquisition.	Number of hours per week when X is taught (A) or taught and used (B); Teacher-pupil ratio; Teacher training and teacher experience; Educational methods and pedagogical materials; Classroom composition; Per-capita spending; Support for out-of-school language use.	Percentage of young people completing secondary school with fluency in X.	The highest possible number of pupils should acquire (through the educational option considered) fluency in X – which they would not have otherwise achieved.
(c) External effectiveness Percentage of young people completing secondary education with fluency in X.	Use of X-language skills in every day adult life.	Opportunities to use language X in public and private life ('supply-side factors'); Desire to use language X in public and private life ('demand-side factors').	Frequency of use of language X in public or private life (see indicators in Table 6.2).	Language X is used in a large number of domains, by a large number of people, with high frequency; the use of language X in all domains is considered 'normal'.

Let us note that the effectiveness of policies is likely to depend on accompanying measures; these are mentioned in Table 9.2. Suppose for example that holiday camps are set up, where young people can spend part of their holidays in X-speaking surroundings, or that an awareness campaign stressing the importance of intergenerational language transmission is set up. Both types of measures will generally enhance the effectiveness of the process as well as the contribution of other explanatory variables to the resulting number of users or to their average skills level. The comparison between policies A and B makes sense if such accompanying measures are taken into account, as characteristics of one or another policy plan. By the same token, they need not be considered if they are present in both or neither of the two policies and if so, are also likely to have comparable effects on each.

Summing up, the type of investigation described here cannot be expected to generate an exhaustive evaluation of effectiveness. This reservation does not detract from the fact that the information so obtained is significantly better than no information at all, or information whose patchy and partial nature is concealed by sweeping general pronouncements. Although Table 9.2 contains no more than examples of the critical variables and relationships between them, it can already generate a broad range of questions which deserve examination in order to evaluate whether a particular language education policy plan is likely to be more or less effective.

Costs

The analysis of educational costs constitutes a major chapter of education economics;[15] unfortunately, there are relatively few applications to the cost of teaching a particular language as a subject, or of using a particular language as a medium of instruction. Hence, there is relatively little experience to go by, and in order to propose procedures to estimate the educational costs generated by the implementation of given language policies, we have to enter largely uncharted territory. This enterprise deserves sustained attention, and probably requires the development of potentially sophisticated techniques, as in the case of the (more circumscribed) question of the estimation of expenditure for foreign languages.[16] However, my objective here is not to engage in a detailed investigation of the technical problems posed, but to rough out a simple approach suitable for a first approximation.

In this cost assessment, the identification of the 'counterfactual' (see Chapter 7) plays a particularly crucial role. More precisely, we need to identify the situation that would prevail if a particular policy were *not* adopted. Consider first the case of policy A, in which language X is offered as a school subject. If the alternative is *not* to offer it at all, the cost to be considered is that of adding one subject to the curriculum. The following elements would then need to be taken into account to estimate the expected *per-year* cost for one particular cohort, assuming a 40-week school year throughout primary and secondary I school:

1. *per-hour* salary W of an X-language teacher (including employer's contribution to pension schemes, social security, health insurance, etc.), which one can assume (unless information is available about it to the contrary) to be similar to an average salary figure derived from existing public accounts;
2. average weekly number of hours H during which the X will be taught throughout the nine years of schooling affected by policy A;
3. enrolment E by each cohort in the optional X-language courses;
4. average teacher–pupil ratio R in the school system;
5. average teaching load L per language teacher and per week;
6. average career duration D per teacher;
7. average per-language teacher training cost T, which can be assumed to be similar to the cost of training teachers of other subjects;
8. average per-hour share S (assumed to be similar across all school subjects) of total infrastructural and managerial costs of the education system;[17]
9. average per-subject and per-syllabus year cost M for the development and printing of teaching materials (which can, again, be assumed to be similar to the cost of materials development for another *language* taught as a subject).

The product $E \times R$ therefore represents the number of X-language classes in the system. If this expression is multiplied by H, the weekly endowment for this subject, we get the number of periods per week during which, in the entire system, language X is taught as a subject. In order to get a yearly figure, this needs to be multiplied by the number of weeks in the school year (in our example, 40). Hence, the number of lessons per year in the system is $40 \times H \times E \times R$. The 'lesson' often is a relatively convenient unit for education accounting purposes, because it is a very common (if not universal) concept, corresponding to a situation in which a teacher is in charge of a group of pupils. The number of lessons per year must now be multiplied by its unit cost. Two elements of this unit cost are easily identified – at least conceptually. The first is the average per-hour salary of teachers (*W*). The second is a share (*S*) of the infrastructural costs of the system. Yet another element of cost can be associated with each lesson, namely, a fraction of the total teacher training cost. We denote by *T* this total training cost. If, in this first stage of our calculations, we focus on the cost of the system for the *first* year of its introduction, this cost will have to amortised entirely over the first year (this assumption, however, will be relaxed later). Hence, *T* must be divided by the number of lessons that an average teacher will teach during the year, namely, 40 multiplied by the average weekly teaching load. Consequently, the three elements of hourly cost read as: $W + S + T/(40 \times L)$. Now that we have an estimation of the total number of hours concerned and of the per-hour cost, we only need to multiply them, and add to the product other (fixed) costs. Thus, in the *first* year of the introduction of policy, the total cost of policy *A*, TCA_1, can be estimated at:

$$TCA_1 = \left\{ [40 \times H \times E \times R] \times \left[W + S + \frac{T}{40 \times L} \right] \right\} + M \qquad \text{(Eq. 1)}$$

We can now turn to the estimation of the long-run per year cost. For this purpose, let us assume for simplicity a similar total cost structure (that is, unchanged values for each of the variables entered in the cost equation) in each successive school year, from year 1 through year 9, in which language *X* is introduced as a subject. The nine-year span is adopted because it is a fairly standard value for the duration of compulsory education, corresponding to the primary and secondary I levels of many education systems; however, there is nothing to prevent us from replacing '9' with any value 'J' applying to a particular education system. The same is true, of course, of the number of weeks in the standard school year.

This mode of calculation means in particular that the size of each entering cohort remains constant and that drop-out and repetition rates are zero. Total cost therefore increases from $1TCA_1$ in the first year of implementation to $9TCA_1$ in the ninth year: because additional teachers have to be trained to teach younger cohorts entering the system, the corresponding teacher training cost has to be borne in full for each year. The same applies to the development of educational materials, to the extent that these materials are specific to successive curriculum years.

As of year 10, the complete system is in place, and the per-year cost then remains equal to $9TCA_1$ *minus* the cost of materials development and teacher training that will no longer be as high: pedagogical materials have a life-cycle of several years. In the same way, once a sufficient number of teachers has been trained to serve the entire school population, no *additional* teachers need to be trained – other than for the replacement of teachers retiring or resigning. Let us therefore assume that pedagogical materials are completely overhauled every 10 years, which means that on average, one tenth of the cost of developing them can be assigned to each year (the material, however, is course-specific through the 9-year syllabus, which means that the amortised cost of materials development must be multiplied by 9). Given that all schoolteachers are assumed to work for D years, a proportion $1/D$ of the cost of the per-hour cost of training the total X-language teaching workforce can be assigned to each year. The long-run total cost of policy A, TCA_{LR}, 10 years and beyond from the introduction of the policy, is then equal to:

$$TCA_{LR} = 9 \times \left\{ [40 \times H \times E \times R] \times \left[W + S + \frac{T}{(40 \times L \times D)} \right] \right\}$$

$$+ 9 \times \frac{M}{10} \qquad \text{(Eq. 2)}$$

For an estimate of the average yearly cost, we can simply divide this equation by 9 and obtain:

$$\overline{TCA_{LR}} = \frac{1}{9} TCA_{LR} \qquad \text{(Eq. 3)}$$

Equations (2) and (3) certainly represent a simplification, which can only yield an approximation of what it would cost to engage in policy A instead of no policy at all. For a more precise estimation, each of the variables featured in the equation ought to be parsed in order to:

1. allow for numerous manifestations of variability (for example, between primary-school and secondary-school teaching loads);
2. establish the reliability of average estimates (for example, the spreading of infrastructural and administrative costs on school hours);
3. take account of the dynamic nature of school systems, in which some learners repeat classes or drop out of the system altogether;
4. allow for change over time, which range from parental attitudes and demographic figures (both of which would influence E) to the average price level (which will influence W).

As explained above, the formula used here is, apart from the cost of pedagogical materials development, essentially a product of two terms: a number of hours that must be taught (by a teacher) in the system per year, namely, $[40 \times H \times E \times R]$, and a per-hour cost, namely, $[W + S + T/(40 \times L \times D)]$. This implies that the analytical unit used for the costing exercise is the lesson, or hour, or period of teaching of language X.

However, another unit might have been chosen to construct cost, such as the individual student, who in the course of his or her nine years of compulsory schooling will 'consume' $H \times 40 \times 9$ hours of X-language instruction carrying a certain hourly cost, plus a share of the cost of materials development, given by $[M/(10 \times E \times 9)] \times 9 = M/10E$.

Experience suggests, however, that the knowledge gains derived from ever more precise calculations tend to decrease rapidly with increasing complexity. Hence, unless most of the parameters in the equation are seriously wrong *at the same time*, a simple formula such as that proposed for TCA_{LR} will yield a useful figure for a rough cost assessment. As pointed out in Chapter 7, it is possible to replace single-value parameters by lower-bound and upper-bound values; this will generate a *range* within which the *actual* cost is more likely to fall.

The question remains of the interpretation of a cost figure such as TCA_{LR} as a guide for decision-making in language policy, for example in the context of the implementation of the Charter. As shown before, a cost figure means little on its own, and requires interpretation. As a first step in this direction, let us divide this figure by another, such as the number of young people in the target population, or the number of young people actually enrolled in X-language classes. This, however, would nudge us in the direction of cost-effectiveness evaluation, which is addressed below. At this point, it is particularly relevant to divide TCA_{LR} by total education spending *without* policy A. This will show, in percentage terms, by how much total education spending is affected by adopting the policy, and therefore yield the *marginal cost* of introducing language X as a subject in the education system.

Estimates are difficult to come by. In the case of Switzerland, with four distinct language regions (and no less than 26 education departments, given the high degree of decentralisation of the country), about 5.4 per cent of total education spending for primary, secondary I and secondary II education (ISCED levels 1, 2 and 3) is devoted to the teaching of L2, that is, the *first* language other than the dominant language of the region of residence.[18] Total spending for the teaching of second or foreign languages (including national languages other than the locally dominant language, as well as English) stands at about 10.5 per cent of total education spending. Estimates of the cost of introducing a particular regional or minority language, as would be the case under policy A, are unlikely to be markedly different. As a rule of thumb, a 4 per cent to 8 per cent range can be assumed.

However, let us remember that in our example, policies A and B would apply to a fraction of the total population. The above percentages are reasonably indicative if we wish to estimate the extra cost over and above what would be spent on the *same number* of pupils in the absence of any policy, because they have been calculated on the basis of spending figures for the entire school-going population (in that case, in Switzerland). However, let us recall that in our example, we are assuming that only a part of the school-going population would actually enrol in X-language classes. Hence, the cost increase over total education spending in the country as a whole would be lower than the 4 per cent to 8 per cent range indicated above. For example, if only one quarter of all young people in the relevant age bracket enrol in X-language courses, the cost increase, in relation to total (national) education spending would be more likely to fall in the 1 per cent to 2 per cent range.

Consider now the case of policy B, under which a choice is offered between Y-medium and X-medium education for primary and secondary I education. Although this is a much more sweeping reform, the estimation of its cost is, paradoxically, not more complicated. The reason for this can be traced back to the identification of the counterfactual and in particular the relevance of the concept of marginal cost, as shown in Chapters 6 and 7.

Let us remember that if schools do not offer an X-medium stream, young people will still have to be educated, though in a Y-medium stream. Hence, the cost of policy B must be understood only as the cost of *bilingualising* the education system. This requires identifying (and taking account of) only those components of total education spending which are made necessary by bilingualism. If teacher–pupil ratios are identical in the various models, if teachers working through the regional or minority language command the same wage rate as those who teach through the medium of the majority language, and if other characteristics (teachers' career duration and teaching load; per-hour share of infrastructural cost; etc.) are the same, expenditure per student is not part of the cost of policy B. Typically, relevant cost items need only include the following:

T: per-person cost of teacher training for language teachers;
f: number of X-language teachers; f is a function of enrolment E in the X-medium stream;
M: average per-syllabus year cost of development and printing of language teaching materials;
V: per-person cost of language-specific pedagogical training for teachers of other subjects (in order to enable them to teach through the medium of X);

g: number of non-language teachers teaching through the medium of *X; g*, just like *f*, is a function of enrolment *E*;

Z: average per-syllabus year cost of development of *X*-medium teaching materials for each non-language subject (for simplicity, I assume that the same number of subjects is taught in each of the nine school years, although they need not be the same subjects);

s: number of subjects taught apart from language *X*, totalling a weekly endowment of *Q* hours;

P: additional organisational cost per year entailed by running a bilingual system or indeed bilingual school establishments.

Some of these terms can of course be re-expressed in terms of their underlying components. In particular, we can define *f* and *g* as follows:

$$f = 9 \times (H \times E \times R)\frac{1}{L} \qquad\qquad \text{(Eq. 4)}$$

$$g = 9 \times (Q \times E \times R)\frac{1}{L} \qquad\qquad \text{(Eq. 5)}$$

The term *f* can therefore be computed as the ratio between the total number periods per week during which, in the entire system, language *X* is taught as a subject (i.e., the expression $9 \times H \times E \times R$) and the average weekly teaching load per teacher *L*. As for the term *g*, it is similarly constructed, except that the relevant number of hours is *Q* instead of *H*. This of course assumes that teacher–pupil ratios are identical across all subjects, and that the weekly endowment for language *X* remains unchanged during the entire curriculum.

Again, allowance must be made for the period during which human and non-human resources are used in the system. Let us assume that teaching materials are overhauled every *n* years, and that a fraction $1/k$ of the total teaching force needs to be trained each year in order to enter their teaching career and exactly meet the hiring needs of the education system. Then the long-run *per-year* cost of policy *B*, $\overline{TCB_{LR}}$, is given by:

$$\overline{TCB_{LR}} = \frac{(fT + gV)}{k} + \frac{9(M + sZ)}{n} + P \qquad\qquad \text{(Eq. 6)}$$

Introducing equations (4) and (5) into equation (6) and rearranging, we get:

$$\overline{TCB_{LR}} = 9 \times \left\{ \frac{(HERT + QERV)}{kL} + \frac{(M + sZ)}{n} \right\} + P$$

which simplifies to:

$$\overline{TCB_{LR}} = 9 \times \left\{ \frac{ER \times (HT + QV)}{kL} + \frac{M + sZ}{n} \right\} + P \qquad \text{(Eq. 7)}$$

Although it may look somewhat complicated, this expression offers the advantage that it allows us to estimate the cost of the policy on the basis of more simple components, many of which can be obtained from standard school statistics – or roughly estimated on the basis of such statistics without major difficulty.

The value so obtained can be used in different ways. In particular, we may divide it by the number of young people in the target population or by the number of pupils in the X-medium stream. However, it is particularly important, as pointed out above, to compare this figure with total education spending.

Calculations have been made in the case of the teaching through Basque[19] and through indigenous languages in Guatemala;[20] both arrive at a cost estimate in the 4 per cent to 5 per cent range.[21] Such figures probably represent upper-bound estimates, because item V in the equation is likely to taper off after a few years. The reason is that once it becomes normal for teachers to be trained to teach either in X (for some) or in Y (for others), there is no reason why it should be more expensive to train them to teach in X rather than Y. Hence, no additional cost related to the use of language X as a medium of education need arise because of specific teacher training needs. Furthermore, in the case of our example, the X-medium stream is optional, and expected to attract a certain proportion of school-goers, but only from potentially or actually X-speaking households. The figures just reported pertain to a much higher percentage of the target age group (in the case of the Basque country, for example, half of the people in the entire school system are schooled partly or wholly through the medium of Basque). If a smaller share of a target group is enrolled in X-medium streams, the number of teachers needed will be less: since both are an increasing function of E, parameters f and g in the calculation of TCB_{LR} will be lower. As a percentage of total educational cost, the extra cost entailed by adopting policy B is more likely to be closer to 3 per cent.

Here again, it is unlikely that numbers would differ markedly, in other contexts, from those mentioned above. Particularly striking, however, are the following twin facts: the cost of engaging in policy A or policy B (instead of engaging in *neither*) is modest; in percentage terms, the cost of both policies is fairly similar.

Cost-effectiveness

Once effectiveness indicators have been selected and calculated, and cost estimates made for both policies, cost-effectiveness comparison is a fairly straightforward business in an *ex post* evaluation. In an *ex ante* situation, available effectiveness indicators are fewer, and the projections with which they can be replaced less reliable. The principle, however, remains the same: one would simply divide the value of a particular indicator of the success of a policy by its cost, and compare the result for both policies.

Suppose for example that out of a population of some 1.2 million actual or potential speakers of X, the school-going population between the ages 6 and 15 (targeted by either policy) living in the RML area (in which these policies would be implemented) represents 150,000 persons (12.5 per cent). Of these, 10 years after the introduction of the policy, two-thirds (100,000) are expected to be receiving some form of X-language instruction. They may be enrolled in X-language courses (policy *A*) or in the X-medium stream (policy *B*). Further assume that one fourth of these 100,000 learners (that is, 25,000 young people) would have completed their ninth school year as bilinguals anyway, thanks to their own family environment. This figure is compatible with those provided in Table 9.1, where a little over 16 per cent of the minority population is made up of fluent language X users; one can assume that children from fluent X-speaking households will be over-represented among those enrolled in the X-language courses or streams. This means that at most 75,000 people may *become* competent bilinguals *because* of the language education policy.

Assume now that policy *B* is expected to be more effective, because it amounts to a full language immersion programme;[22] such programmes have a record of success that is generally superior to the teaching of a language as a subject, all other things being equal. To take account of these aspects, let us therefore conservatively assume that out of the total number of people enrolled in the first nine years of the school system at any one time, 50,000 can be expected to *become* competent bilinguals if policy *A* is adopted, and 70,000 can be expected to *become* competent bilinguals in the case of policy *B*.

On the cost side, let us assume that average per pupil spending in compulsory education stands at about €6,000 per year (a not at all unreasonable figure).[23] Suppose that the total number of young people aged six to 15, out of a population of 6 million, is 750,000 (where this proportion of 12.5 per cent applies to the minority and to the resident population as a whole). Therefore, €4,500 million is spent on their education every year. Assume now that the extra cost entailed by policies *A* and *B* is estimated, under the set of assumptions above, at 2 per cent and 3 per cent of *total* (national) education spending respectively. We arrive at a total cost of €90 million for policy *A*, and €135 million for policy *B*. The total cost of obtaining one more bilingual is therefore equal to €1,800 (€90 million divided by 50,000) for policy *A* and €1,929 (€135 million divided by 70,000) for policy *B*. Now, further recall that this cost is spread over nine years of schooling, assuming away repetition and dropout. The cost per school year and per bilingual created is therefore €200 in the case of policy *A*, and €214 in the case of policy *B*.

Reassessing cost–benefit evaluations

The relevance of this type of figures emerges on two different planes – apart from the banal fact that policy costing is a requirement of sound state budgeting.

First, it is useful for national authorities taking steps to implement the Charter to compute estimates of the likely effect of alternative policy plans, and to associate cost figures with these effects. Even if, for lack of data, the estimations can only be rough ones, this type of exercise can greatly help to clarify the options available and to map out policy development in an orderly way.

Second, such figures can help to steer the language policy debate away from the surprising, sometimes downright absurd pronouncements that often characterise it, in political speeches as well as in op-ed columns. Language policy is an area in which, as Pool observes, people can hold 'extraordinarily stubborn beliefs',[24] and figures, particularly in relation to costs, can exert a much-needed sobering influence.

Before closing this chapter, it is important to recall three more points. Even if they have been made in preceding chapters, experience suggests that they bear repeating, in order to pre-empt one form of criticism which, though perfectly valid in principle, often reflects inadequate understanding of the type of instruments presented in this book, and of the motivations for using them.

First, the evaluation procedures presented in this chapter (and, for that matter, throughout Part III) are a simplified procedures; reality is more complicated. Hence, these procedures should not be seen as ready-made solutions. The role of this walk-through example is to familiarise the reader with the logic and methodology that can be applied in the evaluation of the effectiveness, cost and cost-effectiveness of alternative language policies – and specifically, in the case of Chapter 9, language education policies. Direct application of the steps described above will yield rough estimates, which can only serve as a first approach. However, more precise estimations will generally take the form of refinements on the above, rather than a fundamentally different procedure.

Second, my insistence on the importance of cost, and hence of a cost-effectiveness evaluation of the measures considered, cannot be interpreted as advocating niggardly policies, or as an excuse for *not* engaging in the protection and promotion of regional or minority language. The often-made criticism that because of the ineffable nature of the dimensions of human experience they target, policies affecting language (or culture) should eschew any financial considerations is as logically flawed as it is strategically ill-advised. It bears repeating that even relatively *expensive* policies can be perfectly worthwhile. The point is to understand (and explain to others!) *why* they are worthwhile. The aim of the exercise goes well beyond intellectual satisfaction, because it can claim direct strategic relevance. Ultimately, constraints on available resources bear upon all policy decisions. If a language policy office requests a certain budget allocation from ministerial authorities in order to develop and implement particular policy measures, it needs to be able to justify the amounts requested. In turn, budget allocations have to be defended, ultimately before Parliament, if not voters. This implies, for example, that the authorities must be able to explain why a certain sum is devoted to language promotion, whereas the same amount could easily have been spent on road improvement, training schemes for the unemployed, or health care for the elderly. There is no way to make such a point convincingly without providing evidence that one has taken cost implications into consideration, and that the choice to divert resources away from other legitimate social goals has been carefully pondered.

Finally, I wish to repeat that the numbers generated by the estimation of costs and the quantitative approach to effects are in no way meant to dictate any policy decision. They are, quite simply, politically crucial (and also, one might add, analytically interesting) informational elements. Their role is to provide useful, though often overlooked elements of knowledge which are eminently relevant to a better-informed, and hence more democratic political debate.

Notes

1. As distinct from legal analyses, discussions of the political, social and cultural arena in which language policies developed can be found in Calvet (1987, 1996); Guillorel and Koubi (1999); Kontra *et al.* (1999); Labrie (1993);

Maurais (1987a); May (2001); Ricento (2000a); Schiffman (1996); Schmid (2001); Skutnabb-Kangas and Phillipson (1994); Skutnabb-Kangas (2000); Tollefson (1991); etc. These questions are also discussed in books that focus more specifically on the operation of language policy and planning, e.g. Cooper (1989), Fishman (1991), Kaplan and Baldauf (1997), etc.

2. Grin and Vaillancourt (1999); Grin, Moring *et al.* (2002).
3. On the pedagogical value of abstraction in the study of language issues, see Pool (1991b).
4. On the measurement of bilingualism and language skills, see e.g. Baker (2001, Ch. 2), Schneider and North (1997) or Council of Europe (1998b), where a major effort has been made to clarify and standardise representations of levels of language skills in language-learning processes. For a simpler, four-level characterisation of fluency appropriate for large-scale data collection and processing, see Grin (1999a).
5. For a review of cases in the European Union, see e.g. Nelde, Strubell and Williams (1996). For a broad overview of the linkages between many educational and political issues that arise in minority education and pointers to a considerable body of literature, see Skutnabb-Kangas (2000). According to Grin, Moring *et al.* (2002), stages 4 and 5 in the *GIDS* coincide with the situation of the following languages in the *Euromosaic* report (mentioning here 'unique' languages only): Irish in Northern Ireland, Franco-provençal in Italy, Mirandese, Breton, Catalan in Aragon, Friulian, Sorbian, Basque in France, Ladin, Asturian, Catalan in France.
6. This corresponds to ISCED (International Standard Classification of Education) stages 1 and 2 in the OECD classification.
7. See e.g. Scharpf (1997).
8. Useful pointers regarding the topics that an LPA should contain can be found in Cooper (1989: 93–6).
9. See e.g. North (1994, 1999); Schneider and North (1997); for a precise characterisation of skills levels at various stages, see Council of Europe (1998b: 169). For a very extensive evaluation of the experience accumulated to date with the use of the 'European language portfolio', see contributions edited by Schärer (2000).
10. The notion that language decline is not only mirrored, but *determined* by the decline in the *percentage* of speakers has long been a common one in the sociolinguistics literature; see e.g. Ambrose and Williams (1981), criticised in Grin (1993).
11. On internal effectiveness measurement, see the specialised treatment in Hanushek (1986, 1987), or the relevant chapters in textbooks by Johnes (1993) or Lemelin (1998).
12. For information sources on specific European cases, see the list of Internet resources provided in the Appendix. In Euskadi (Basque Country), the 'A' model offers teaching through Castilian, and Euskera is taught as a subject; the 'D' model represents the symmetrical arrangement; the 'B' model offers teaching in both languages, with the share of each language varying between schools.
13. See for example the highly detailed sociolinguistic surveys of the Basque country carried out at regular intervals by the language policy bodies and related publications (Euskal Kultur Erakundea, 1996).

14. For example, a statistically significant pattern of association between X-medium instruction (the 'independent variable') and more frequent use of language X in adult life (the 'dependent variable') may be observed on a given sample. Suppose that the sample includes respondents living in the 'RML area' as well as in the predominantly Y-speaking capital city of the country. A sample split between these two groups of respondents, followed by a reestimation of the effect of the independent variable on the dependent variable in each subsample, may reveal that the relationship holds in one, but not in the other, revealing the conditionality of the effectiveness of X-medium instruction.
15. See e.g. Woodhall (1987); Verry (1987) or Lemelin (1998, Ch. 11).
16. On the costs of teaching of a particular language as a school subject, see Grin and Sfreddo (1997); on the costs of using a particular language as a medium of instruction, see Patrinos and Velez (1996) or Vaillancourt and Grin (2000).
17. A per-pupil estimate may also be used.
18. Grin and Sfreddo (1997: 123 ff.); this figure therefore does not include the teaching of English, since children's first L2, in Switzerland, is supposed to be one of the country's national languages. This general rule did apply at the time of data collection, and even though some cantons have recently reversed the order of introduction of second languages (that is, they moved English before a national language of Switzerland), the general priority still applies.
19. Grin and Vaillancourt (1999, Ch. 5).
20. Patrinos and Velez (1996).
21. Note also that in the case of Basque, figures reflect the bilingualisation of the entire system outside university (instead of compulsory education only, as in our example).
22. The terminology is not stabilised. According to Baker (2001, Ch. 9), if the typical participant in the programme is a member of the minority language community, this might rather be called a 'maintenance' or 'heritage programme', particularly if some of the teaching is provided through the medium of the majority language.
23. The average figure for OECD member countries is USD 3,915 at primary level and USD 5,625 at secondary level. These average figures, however, hide a considerable spread between countries, even after correcting for inter-country differences in price levels. See OECD (2001).
24. Pool (1991b: 7).

Part IV
Conclusions

Summary of Part IV

Part IV contains only one chapter. It is set apart for logical consistency, in order to distinguish the tools and their applications on the one hand from a general assessment and look into future perspectives on the other hand. In this concluding chapter, I sum up the seven core ideas of this book, before commenting on some developments resulting from the coming into force of the Charter in some countries and discussing the role of specialised language planning bodies as they exist for some regional or minority languages in Europe. In a brief concluding section, I return to the role of diversity as a challenge for modern societies at the dawn of the twenty-first century.

10
Assessment and Perspectives

Summary

Let us begin this concluding assessment with a check-list of the main ideas presented in the foregoing chapters. Some of them can be seen as standard propositions derived from a deductive analysis, which lend themselves to empirical testing as well as, of course, further theoretical discussion. Others, by contrast, are merely interpretive, in the sense that they propose to 'understand' a given facet of reality in a certain way. Since both types of statement are present, I stop short of calling them 'propositions' in the formal scholarly sense. I simply wish to submit them as the *seven core ideas* that I hope the reader will, in addition to a few technical tools, retain from this book.

1. The protection and promotion of regional or minority languages requires the use of concepts and methods from different disciplines.

This requirement demands more than simply picking, here and there, tools that look relevant. What is needed is a framework for the targeted combination of these tools, variously developed by international lawyers, sociolinguists, political scientists, occasionally economists, and practitioners of other disciplines. This, in turn, calls for bridge-building between the associated frames of references, or professional cultures in which these tools are embedded. There are, of course, many ways to build bridges, but one approach emerges as particularly relevant. Let us recall that the protection and promotion of regional or minority languages requires *making decisions* (defining goals, setting priorities, adopting specific measures, designing ways of implementing them, allocating resources to these tasks, etc.). Hence, it is quite natural to call upon a theory of choice for this bridge-building exercise. This is why I have adopted a policy analysis angle, which can help to fill a gap between the main strands of literature on language policy. Should the reader retain only one idea from this book, it should be the following: the selection, design, implementation and evaluation of language policies is not only a sociolinguistic question, and even less a legal or institutional question, but largely a public policy question, and as such, one that needs to be addressed with the tools of policy analysis.

2. The policy-to-outcome path, as its name suggests, proposes a set of cause-and-effects relationships between policy measures at one end, and policy outcomes at the other end

It has already proved useful in practical exercises of policy evaluation. Without going into the particulars of the underlying formalised model, we have seen why this analytical frame brings to light one fundamental fact of language policy, namely, that the long-term vitality of a language requires three conditions to be present: people's *capacity* to use that language; *opportunities* to use it; and the *desire* to do so. Capacity, opportunity and desire are then used as a 'read thread' to guide us in the analysis of language policy.

3. The European Charter for Regional or Minority Languages is an instrument which, going well beyond the enunciation of lofty standards, proposes specific measures for the protection and promotion of regional or minority languages

Its focus, therefore, is on achieving results, which puts the Charter directly in tune with the rationale of policy analysis. However, the originality of the Charter is not limited to this emphasis on results. It is also about languages as essential elements of Europe's heritage, in particular its linguistic and cultural diversity. Since the Charter does not advocate the maintenance of linguistic diversity in terms of rights, and hence does not primarily rest on the normative discourse in which legal and institutional approaches are typically rooted, its philosophy must be sought elsewhere. The Charter can be interpreted as a text motivated by a welfare-based ideology, according to which diversity is worth preserving and developing because it constitutes a contribution to the general quality of life. This, again, is directly in tune with the concerns of a policy analysis perspective.

4. **Frequent invocations, usually in political discourse, of notions 'good policy' and 'best practice' typically omit any definition of those terms. A possible way to give them more precise substance is to call upon two key concepts of policy analysis, namely, effectiveness and cost-effectiveness**

The former is defined here as the fact of making an actual, observable difference, while the latter is defined here as reaching a certain result with the least input of resources, or, alternatively, achieving the best possible results with a given amount of resources. Effectiveness and cost-effectiveness can therefore be viewed as principles of good policy. Resources are not confined to material, financial, or 'market' resources. However, a third principle should be added to these mainstays of policy analysis, namely, that of 'democracy', in order to safeguard against the risk of a technocratic policy development from which citizens would be largely excluded.

5. **Effective policies require goals to be clearly set, cause-and-effect relationships identified, outcomes appropriately measured and expressed in units allowing for comparison between policy options, and the specific contribution of a given policy to be distinguished from the effect of other contextual factors**

Spelling out precisely the implications of policy choices is a matter of transparency. It does not only enhance the logical consistency and democratic credentials of the process; it also helps to strive for meaningful changes in the direction desired.

6. **Cost is a crucially important notion, which must be distinguished from expenditure**

Its appropriate measurement requires the application of particular concepts – in particular, that of marginal cost, which helps us to clarify the notion that the cost of a policy must be evaluated by comparison with the cost that would have been incurred in the absence of a policy. Indicators of policy outcomes and indicators of policy costs can then be combined into an assessment of the relative cost-effectiveness of the policy options considered. These concepts have been presented at a fairly high level of generality, eschewing technical developments and illustrating them with examples. The application of these concepts to the realm of language policies calls for additional research work.

7. **Effectiveness and cost-effectiveness are desirable, but not sufficient conditions for good policies; an assessment of the practical modalities of people's involvement in the selection, design and implementation of language policy is crucial**

Even if the formal institutions of democracy provide the political and legal framework within which regional or minority language policies are developed, effectiveness and cost-effectiveness, though valid criteria for policy evaluation, do not suffice to guarantee democracy with adequate depth. Forms of participatory democracy, despite their limits (and potential dangers, particularly when minority issues are at stake) can significantly contribute, by associating civil society more directly to the policy process, to the success of minority language policies.

Implementation of the Charter in practice

At the time of writing (August 2002), the Charter has been signed by 29 countries,[1] and ratified by 17 of them,[2] Cyprus being the latest addition (26 August 2002). In line with their obligations under the Charter, some parties to this treaty have already submitted the first of their *periodical reports* (see Chapter 4). An evaluation of these documents could easily justify a full-length book, and this exercise will not be attempted here. Rather, I shall address one frequent feature of these reports, which reflects the more general experience of countries that have begun implementing the Charter.

This common feature is one that illustrates the observation made in Chapter 1: *language policies* are becoming a significant field of government intervention. Yet authorities (whether national, regional or local) are usually ill-equipped to deal with the questions that arise in the course of such management. These difficulties have to do not only with constraints on financial resources or lack of organisational structures, but also with the rationale with which the implementation of the Charter is approached.

Typically, the reports supplied by parties to the Charter open on a general overview of the legal provisions and of the historical, linguistic and political background that characterise the regional and minority languages used on their territory. This is followed by an overview of the actions undertaken by state authorities, their surrogates, or other organisations whose operations are supported or authorised by the state. These actions are usually presented in correspondence with articles and paragraphs of the Charter.[3] In some countries, the ratification of the Charter has resulted in the adoption of new provisions; in other countries, existing provisions are presented as serving the purpose of complying with the state's obligations under the Charter.

This approach to reporting, although it represents an indispensable starting point, overemphasises formal provisions at the expense of actual outcomes. Putting it differently, it focuses on supply, but tends not to pay sufficient attention in terms of language vitality. As we have seen before, particularly in Chapters 2, 5 and 6, the mere existence of a policy may be a necessary condition, but it is not a sufficient one to ensure that it *will* generate a positive change – in particular, that it will effectively contribute to the maintenance (or, where needed, the restoration) of a self-priming mechanism of language reproduction.

One might counter that, precisely because the Charter is a recent instrument, it is too early to expect results, and therefore justified not to take issue with the country reports for their emphasis on the measures taken rather than on the results achieved. Such an objection, however, would be unconvincing.

In some countries, the measures listed in the initial periodical report have been in place for a long time; one often mentioned example is the Netherlands; this is also the case for Switzerland, where owing to the country's federal structure, competence in language matters largely rests with its constituent cantons rather than with the federal authorities, the trilingual canton of Graubünden/Grischun/Grigioni (whose official languages are German, Romansch and Italian) and the Italian-speaking canton of Ticino have direct responsibility in ensuring that Switzerland's obligations under the Charter are met. For example, the provisions currently enforced which amount to an implementation of Article 8 of the Charter are listed in the report, which points out that in the Canton of Graubünden, it is the communes (municipalities) that have legal competence for the choice of the language of instruction used in primary schools. This arrangement has been in place for decades, which begs for the question of whether it is effective or not. Unfortunately, this question is not brought up in Switzerland's report – perhaps because there is ample evidence to the effect that it is not. On the basis of census returns as well as abundant micro-level information, one would be tempted to conclude that existing measures are simply failing, since Romansch has been undergoing steady erosion ever since federal censuses have been taken.[4] Reservations regarding the effect of language policies in Switzerland can also be made with respect to more recent measures. According to the same report, secondary schools will, following the revision in 1998 of the education Act of the Canton of Graubünden, offer a 'bilingual stream' in which two 'fundamental disciplines' will be taught through the medium of Romansch. One may legitimately ask how many students are expected to choose this possibility, how this will impact on patterns of language maintenance, whether the percentage of fluent speakers will be significantly *higher* than it would have been in the absence of such a measure, and whether stronger accompanying measures might not be necessary to make sure that this particular measure is effective.

What makes the absence of any precise consideration of the relationship between policy measures on the one hand, and the actual or projected outcomes of the policy on the other hand, particularly glaring is the fact that the Charter is not about rights, even further-reaching positive rights. It is about actual linguistic diversity as part of Europe's cultural heritage. Hence, what matters is not whether certain provisions exist, even if these could be interpreted as giving substance to positive rights. Rather, states' periodical reports should at least address the question of whether policy measures are, or can be expected to be, effective in terms of clearly formulated effectiveness criteria. Addressing this question requires, in turn, that procedures for such evaluation be sketched out – showing how this can be done is precisely one of the chief goals of this book.

The Swiss case offers a typical example of reporting confined to a 'supply-side' approach, but remains apparently unconcerned with actual outcomes. Examples of this kind support the view that a policy analysis perspective on language policies is urgently needed, if the action of states under the Charter is to deploy the full effects expected from it. The almost complete absence of an evaluation culture was confirmed in an international conference convened in June 2000 by the European Centre for Minority Issues. The ensuing conference report points out: '[Conference participants] ... noted that the absence of a structured approach to policy made it difficult for them to collect, organise and present information' in terms of effectiveness, cost-effectiveness and democracy. The report further notes that 'policies often seem to be elaborated in a somewhat haphazard way. Once the *standards* are agreed on, ... little attention is devoted to rigorous policy development'.[5]

In this context, it is hardly surprising that hard data about costs and effects are almost entirely lacking, and that cost-effectiveness evaluations are even more difficult to come by. Such developments of, course, cannot take place in a vacuum; they require the development of specialist know-how, as noted on the occasion of the same conference: 'there is very little know-how in the elaboration of language policies. Training in applied policy development needs to be made available, and background research needs to be supported in order to propose quality training suited to the needs of users'.[6] This know-how then needs to be put at the service of language policy development. This brings me to the next point in this assessment, where I discuss the function of language planning bodies.

The role of language planning bodies

Even a cursory examination of the more encouraging stories of language revitalisation suggests that success is difficult to achieve in the absence, among other conditions, of a specialised agency entrusted with the development, implementation and monitoring of language policies. Looking at European cases, one can in particular mention the *Bwrdd yr Iaith Gymraeg* (Welsh Language Board) in Wales, the *Direcció general de política lingüística* (Directorate General of Language Policy) in Catalonia, or the *Hizkuntza Politikarako Sailordetza* (Deputy Ministry for Language Policy) in the Basque Country. Setting up a language policy office is not a guarantee for success, but it certainly helps to establish favourable conditions for language policy development.

Limitations of space prevent me from discussing in detail the functions and operations of language planning offices (LPOs);[7] yet even without an in-depth discussion, the ground covered in the preceding chapters points to five general principles.

1. It is important to establish the profile of an LPO as chiefly concerned with language, rather than, on the one hand 'minority issues' or 'ethnic affairs' or, on the other hand, local and regional development or suchlike labels. A Department of ethnic affairs has to deal with fundamentally political issues of human rights, and an Office for local or regional development typically focuses on matters of labour, training, and infrastructure. The function of an LPO should be, within a given legal and political context regarding minority rights, to focus on those policies that focus on language protection and promotion. This does not mean that an LPO should not be concerned with this legal and political context. In fact, it has a key role to play in the development of draft legislation on language issues, and in supplying information for political debate. However, its role mustn't stop there. Its chief task must be to make sure that political choices translate into good policy decisions, and that policy decisions are followed by results. This is merely a restatement of a distinction made in Chapter 1, where I stressed the specific nature of language policy,

as distinct from the *political* issues within which they are, of course, embedded.

2. Although the remit of an LPO can be more or less broadly defined, it must unambiguously be entrusted with status planning, because a mandate restricted to corpus planning implies only limited, or even negligible competencies for the promotion of a language *vis-à-vis* other languages. Status planning unavoidably raises political questions, whereas the relative share of the 'political' is likely to be less (though certainly not nil) when the questions addressed are confined to typical corpus questions like terminological innovation and spelling. The political context must be provided upstream, and may be illustrated by the very fact that a state *has* subscribed to certain principles, as it can do by signing and ratifying the Charter.

3. The competencies of an LPO must be clearly defined. Efficient operations require, in particular, the position of the language policy authority with respect to other authorities to be identified. For example, if education remains under the authority of a Ministry of Education, what are the competencies of an LPO regarding the number of subjects that may be taught through the medium of regional or minority language? If traffic signs are within the purview of a Ministry of Public Works, what say would the LPO have in the design and installation of bilingual traffic signs? Even if such an office has limited decision-making powers, its remit should include at the very least research, capacity-building and advisory activities.

4. A mechanism needs to be established to ensure that an LPO's recommendations are actually acted upon by the non-specialist departments and ministries as they exercise their authority in their respective areas of competence and their action has an impact on the linguistic environment. If the advice of the language policy office is not used, its role may end up being a purely symbolic or tokenistic one. Although this is generally preferable to nothing at all, it is clearly insufficient in a language revitalisation perspective.

5. A language policy office should work in partnership with public authorities at various tiers of government, business, civil society organisations, and the general public. This 'partnership' approach serves several purposes at once. First, it fosters a permanent exchange of information, which generally enhances the quality of the policy measures eventually adopted. Second, it encourages public support for and compliance with those measures once implemented. Third and most importantly, it reinforces the democratic character of its operations by associating stakeholders to policy

development, as we have seen in Chapter 8; an LPO is in an ideal position to develop modes of governance in which the divide between the governing and the governed becomes less.

The missions, functions, operative processes and formal structures of an LPO must of course be adapted to the historical, political and cultural context of each case. As a general principle, we have already noted that there is no good language policy without good history. These historical, political and cultural circumstances may, in turn, speak in favour of different practical arrangements. For example, one may wish to separate research and long-term strategic planning on the one hand from the accomplishment of certain missions under a Language Act on the other hand; this is what the Province of Québec does under its highly developed language policy, in which five different bodies were instituted by the Charter of the French Language.[8] Some state traditions are better suited to a centralised structure with general competence on language matters, others to a set of co-ordinated LPOs with area-specific competencies; federalism offers an additional dimension of variability. However, although each case is a special case, the setting up of an LPO is an area where the experience acquired by some can be particularly helpful to others.

In practice, local and regional authorities are turning out to play a key role in the implementation of the Charter. In the absence of LPOs, and given the relatively complex and lengthy process that often needs to be completed before an LPO is established and operational, much of the actual responsibility falls to these authorities. There would be a lot to be gained in gathering, systematising and sharing hard data and terrain experience gained by them in different countries that are party to the Charter. An international co-ordination office could collate, process and redistribute this information, which would also be useful to the longer-established LPOs.

The way forward: diversity through '*normalització*'

Although this book is primarily devoted to methodology, it is appropriate, in closing, to take a few steps back and ask ourselves what is, ultimately, the point of protection and promotion of regional or minority languages.

I have already mentioned, in Chapter 2, an article titled, somewhat provocatively, 'Language Maintenance: Why Bother?',[9] which raises the question of whether small languages are really worth all this effort.

This type of question is the subject of endless debate that addresses not only the survival of regional or minority languages, but also the influential position of a language of wider communication such as English or the choice of working languages in international organisations like the European Union.

I have observed on several occasions that one tenet lies at the heart of the Charter or similar enterprises in favour of regional or minority languages, namely, the notion that 'diversity is good'. This may be considered by some as a purely ideological belief. However, as I have tried to show in the introduction to language policy (Chapter 2) there are strong reasons to suppose that because of the phenomenon known as 'market failure', co-ordinated intervention to protect and promote linguistic diversity *is* justified by reasons similar to those on which environmental policy is based. This should not be seen as a 'biologising' analogy, but as a simple application of basic microeconomic theory: diversity carries both benefits and costs, costs tend to increase at an increasing rate, and benefits at a decreasing rate. It follows that a socially preferable level of linguistic diversity is probably not 'infinite' for cost reasons – or, making the same point using another angle, features *other* than diversity also affect our quality of life and require that some resources be spent on them. However, a socially preferable level of linguistic diversity is certainly *positive* (and, therefore, larger than zero).[10] For this general reason, it is not only morally appropriate to preserve threatened languages; it is also a matter of hard-headed, even selfish common sense.

Regional or minority languages do not have a monopoly as incarnations or guardians of linguistic diversity; they are, quite simply, key components of diversity. Given that languages are disappearing at an alarming rate,[11] the matter is urgent.

However, the protection and promotion of those languages must be seen in a broader context, and policy measures in their favour are but part of a larger policy on language – or, more to the point, on languages. This, incidentally, reinforces the point made in the preceding section: language is a fully-fledged area of intervention in its own right, and the setting up of specialised language policy bodies is necessary. If linguistic diversity is to be efficiently preserved, the presence and use of all languages must be considered *normal*. This is why the title of the last section of this book includes the Catalan world '*normalització*'.

Normalització may be translated in English as 'normalisation', but only if its meaning is appropriately explained. One common meaning of the term 'normalisation', in the language disciplines, is that of defining and stabilising the linguistic *norm* – for example, establishing *the* standard for certain grammatical rules or the spelling of certain words. *Normalització*, however, means something quite different, and illuminatingly simple in the context of language policy, namely, *making the use of a particular language 'normal'*.[12] In the Catalan case, this was characterised as requiring (i) the broadening of the demolinguistic base; (ii) the establishment of a context of language rights and freedoms regarding the possibilities to use the language; and (iii) an increased awareness of the population (majority and minority alike) to the social relevance of the language being protected or promoted. These three objectives are strikingly convergent with our three conditions for the long-term vitality of a language, namely, capacity, opportunity and desire. The concept of *normalització* can be used to encapsulate them while at the same time stressing the political legitimacy and social relevance of the enterprise.

In closing, I would like to make a simple, yet often overlooked point: the *normalització* of regional or minority languages is a challenge that states are confronted with throughout Europe, East and West, North and South. Even European countries with a long history of accommodating linguistic diversity in their midst need to critically reassess their practices regarding smaller languages, and often to sharply upgrade the measures they take in order to guarantee the future of these languages. In the philosophy of the Charter, states are therefore invited, first and foremost, to make a contribution to the common effort, by all countries in Europe, towards the preservation and vitality of its linguistic diversity.

Notes

1. Armenia, Austria, Azerbaijan, Croatia, Cyprus, the Czech Republic, Denmark, Finland, France, Germany, Hungary, Iceland, Italy, Liechtenstein, Luxembourg, Malta, Moldova, the Netherlands, Norway, Romania, Russia, Slovakia, Slovenia, Spain, Sweden, Switzerland, the F.Y.R. of Macedonia, Ukraine, and the United Kingdom.
2. Armenia, Austria, Croatia, Cyprus, Denmark, Finland, Germany, Hungary, Liechtenstein, the Netherlands, Norway, Slovakia, Slovenia, Spain, Sweden, Switzerland, and the United Kingdom.
3. Consider for example that part of Hungary's report (published by the Council of Europe on 7 September 1999) which concerns Article 8, paragraphs c.i to c.iv of the Charter, on the use of regional or minority languages in secondary school education. The report describes the legal provisions applying in this respect and quotes the legislative acts in which they are enshrined.
4. On the decline of the Romansch language, see e.g. Furer (1992, 1994), and an assessment of the weaknesses of language policy in Switzerland, Grin (2000a).
5. Grin (2000b: 52).
6. Ibid.

7. The selected internet resources listed in Appendix IV include the addresses of several such bodies. For a particularly clear and language-based mission statement, see for example the site of the Welsh Language Board at: http://www.bwrdd-yr-iaith.org.uk/. For a comparative perspective on language policy in selected Western European countries and in Israel, see *Direcció General de Política Lingüística* (1999).
8. Maurais (1987b).
9. Thieberger (1990).
10. For a more detailed presentation of this point, see e.g. Grin (2000c).
11. Crystal (2000); Skutnabb-Kangas (2000).
12. On *normalització* in Catalonia, see e.g. Vallverdú (1979), Bastardas Boada (1987), Solé i Durany (1995) or Solé i Camardons (1997).

Appendices

Appendix I: Text of the European Charter for Regional or Minority Languages

Appendix II: Explanatory Report on the European Charter

Appendix III: The 'Flensburg Recommendations'

Appendix IV: Selected internet resources

Appendix I

Opening for signature: 5 November 1992
Entry into force (5 ratifications): 1 March 1998

Preamble

The member States of the Council of Europe signatory hereto,

Considering that the aim of the Council of Europe is to achieve a greater unity between its members, particularly for the purpose of safeguarding and realising the ideals and principles which are their common heritage;

Considering that the protection of the historical regional or minority languages of Europe, some of which are in danger of eventual extinction, contributes to the maintenance and development of Europe's cultural wealth and traditions;

Considering that the right to use a regional or minority language in private and public life is an inalienable right conforming to the principles embodied in the United Nations International Covenant on Civil and Political Rights, and according to the spirit of the Council of Europe Convention for the Protection of Human Rights and Fundamental Freedoms;

Having regard to the work carried out within the CSCE and in particular to the Helsinki Final Act of 1975 and the document of the Copenhagen Meeting of 1990;

Stressing the value of interculturalism and multilingualism and considering that the protection and encouragement of regional or minority languages should not be to the detriment of the official languages and the need to learn them;

Realising that the protection and promotion of regional or minority languages in the different countries and regions of Europe represent an important contribution to the building of a Europe based on the principles of democracy and cultural diversity within the framework of national sovereignty and territorial integrity;

Taking into consideration the specific conditions and historical traditions in the different regions of the European States,

Have agreed as follows:

Part I – General provisions

Article 1 – Definitions

For the purposes of this Charter:

a "regional or minority languages" means languages that are:
   i traditionally used within a given territory of a State by nationals of that State who form a group numerically smaller than the rest of the State's population; and

  ii different from the official language(s) of that State;
  it does not include either dialects of the official language(s) of the State or the
  languages of migrants;
b "territory in which the regional or minority language is used" means the geographical area in which the said language is the mode of expression of a number of people justifying the adoption of the various protective and
 promotional measures provided for in this Charter;
c "non-territorial languages" means languages used by nationals of the State
 which differ from the language or languages used by the rest of the State's
 population but which, although traditionally used within the territory of the
 State, cannot be identified with a particular area thereof.

Article 2 – Undertakings

1 Each Party undertakes to apply the provisions of Part II to all the regional or
 minority languages spoken within its territory and which comply with the
 definition in Article 1.
2 In respect of each language specified at the time of ratification, acceptance
 or approval, in accordance with Article 3, each Party undertakes to apply
 a minimum of thirty-five paragraphs or sub-paragraphs chosen from among
 the provisions of Part III of the Charter, including at least three chosen
 from each of the Articles 8 and 12 and one from each of the Articles 9, 10, 11
 and 13.

Article 3 – Practical arrangements

1 Each Contracting State shall specify in its instrument of ratification, acceptance or approval, each regional or minority language, or official language
 which is less widely used on the whole or part of its territory, to which the
 paragraphs chosen in accordance with Article 2, paragraph 2, shall apply.
2 Any Party may, at any subsequent time, notify the Secretary General that it
 accepts the obligations arising out of the provisions of any other paragraph of
 the Charter not already specified in its instrument of ratification, acceptance
 or approval, or that it will apply paragraph 1 of the present article to other
 regional or minority languages, or to other official languages which are less
 widely used on the whole or part of its territory.
3 The undertakings referred to in the foregoing paragraph shall be deemed to
 form an integral part of the ratification, acceptance or approval and will have
 the same effect as from their date of notification.

Article 4 – Existing regimes of protection

1 Nothing in this Charter shall be construed as limiting or derogating from any
 of the rights guaranteed by the European Convention on Human Rights.
2 The provisions of this Charter shall not affect any more favourable provisions
 concerning the status of regional or minority languages, or the legal regime of
 persons belonging to minorities which may exist in a Party or are provided for
 by relevant bilateral or multilateral international agreements.

Article 5 – Existing obligations

Nothing in this Charter may be interpreted as implying any right to engage in any activity or perform any action in contravention of the purposes of the Charter of the United Nations or other obligations under international law, including the principle of the sovereignty and territorial integrity of States.

Article 6 – Information

The Parties undertake to see to it that the authorities, organisations and persons concerned are informed of the rights and duties established by this Charter.

Part II – Objectives and principles pursued in accordance with Article 2, paragraph 1

Article 7 – Objectives and principles

1 In respect of regional or minority languages, within the territories in which such languages are used and according to the situation of each language, the Parties shall base their policies, legislation and practice on the following objectives and principles:

  a the recognition of the regional or minority languages as an expression of cultural wealth;

  b the respect of the geographical area of each regional or minority language in order to ensure that existing or new administrative divisions do not constitute an obstacle to the promotion of the regional or minority language in question;

  c the need for resolute action to promote regional or minority languages in order to safeguard them;

  d the facilitation and/or encouragement of the use of regional or minority languages, in speech and writing, in public and private life;

  e the maintenance and development of links, in the fields covered by this Charter, between groups using a regional or minority language and other groups in the State employing a language used in identical or similar form, as well as the establishment of cultural relations with other groups in the State using different languages;

  f the provision of appropriate forms and means for the teaching and study of regional or minority languages at all appropriate stages;

  g the provision of facilities enabling non-speakers of a regional or minority language living in the area where it is used to learn it if they so desire;

  h the promotion of study and research on regional or minority languages at universities or equivalent institutions;

  i the promotion of appropriate types of transnational exchanges, in the fields covered by this Charter, for regional or minority languages used in identical or similar form in two or more States.

2 The Parties undertake to eliminate, if they have not yet done so, any unjustified distinction, exclusion, restriction or preference relating to the use of a regional or minority language and intended to discourage or endanger the maintenance or development of it. The adoption of special measures in favour

of regional or minority languages aimed at promoting equality between the users of these languages and the rest of the population or which take due account of their specific conditions is not considered to be an act of discrimination against the users of more widely-used languages.

3 The Parties undertake to promote, by appropriate measures, mutual understanding between all the linguistic groups of the country and in particular the inclusion of respect, understanding and tolerance in relation to regional or minority languages among the objectives of education and training provided within their countries and encouragement of the mass media to pursue the same objective.

4 In determining their policy with regard to regional or minority languages, the Parties shall take into consideration the needs and wishes expressed by the groups which use such languages. They are encouraged to establish bodies, if necessary, for the purpose of advising the authorities on all matters pertaining to regional or minority languages.

5 The Parties undertake to apply, **mutatis mutandis**, the principles listed in paragraphs 1 to 4 above to non-territorial languages. However, as far as these languages are concerned, the nature and scope of the measures to be taken to give effect to this Charter shall be determined in a flexible manner, bearing in mind the needs and wishes, and respecting the traditions and characteristics, of the groups which use the languages concerned.

Part III – Measures to promote the use of regional or minority languages in public life in accordance with the undertakings entered into under Article 2, paragraph 2

Article 8 – Education

1 With regard to education, the Parties undertake, within the territory in which such languages are used, according to the situation of each of these languages, and without prejudice to the teaching of the official language(s) of the State:

a i to make available pre-school education in the relevant regional or minority languages; or

ii to make available a substantial part of pre-school education in the relevant regional or minority languages; or

iii to apply one of the measures provided for under i and ii above at least to those pupils whose families so request and whose number is considered sufficient; or

iv if the public authorities have no direct competence in the field of pre-school education, to favour and/or encourage the application of the measures referred to under i to iii above;

b i to make available primary education in the relevant regional or minority languages; or

ii to make available a substantial part of primary education in the relevant regional or minority languages; or

iii to provide, within primary education, for the teaching of the relevant regional or minority languages as an integral part of the curriculum; or iv to apply one of the measures provided for under i to iii above at least to those pupils whose families so request and whose number is considered sufficient;

c   i to make available secondary education in the relevant regional or minority languages; or

    ii to make available a substantial part of secondary education in the relevant regional or minority languages; or

    iii to provide, within secondary education, for the teaching of the relevant regional or minority languages as an integral part of the curriculum; or

    iv to apply one of the measures provided for under i to iii above at least to those pupils who, or where appropriate whose families, so wish in a number considered sufficient;

d   i to make available technical and vocational education in the relevant regional or minority languages; or

    ii to make available a substantial part of technical and vocational education in the relevant regional or minority languages; or

    iii to provide, within technical and vocational education, for the teaching of the relevant regional or minority languages as an integral part of the curriculum; or

    iv to apply one of the measures provided for under i to iii above at least to those pupils who, or where appropriate whose families, so wish in a number considered sufficient;

e   i to make available university and other higher education in regional or minority languages; or

    ii to provide facilities for the study of these languages as university and higher education subjects; or

    iii if, by reason of the role of the State in relation to higher education institutions, sub-paragraphs i and ii cannot be applied, to encourage and/or allow the provision of university or other forms of higher education in regional or minority languages or of facilities for the study of these languages as university or higher education subjects;

f   i to arrange for the provision of adult and continuing education courses which are taught mainly or wholly in the regional or minority languages; or

    ii to offer such languages as subjects of adult and continuing education; or

    iii if the public authorities have no direct competence in the field of adult education, to favour and/or encourage the offering of such languages as subjects of adult and continuing education;

g   to make arrangements to ensure the teaching of the history and the culture which is reflected by the regional or minority language;

h   to provide the basic and further training of the teachers required to implement those of paragraphs a to g accepted by the Party;

i   to set up a supervisory body or bodies responsible for monitoring the measures taken and progress achieved in establishing or developing the teaching of regional or minority languages and for drawing up periodic reports of their findings, which will be made public.

2 With regard to education and in respect of territories other than those in which the regional or minority languages are traditionally used, the Parties undertake, if the number of users of a regional or minority language justifies

it, to allow, encourage or provide teaching in or of the regional or minority language at all the appropriate stages of education.

Article 9 – Judicial authorities

1 The Parties undertake, in respect of those judicial districts in which the number of residents using the regional or minority languages justifies the measures specified below, according to the situation of each of these languages and on condition that the use of the facilities afforded by the present paragraph is not considered by the judge to hamper the proper administration of justice:
   a   in criminal proceedings:
      i   to provide that the courts, at the request of one of the parties, shall conduct the proceedings in the regional or minority languages; and/or
      ii to guarantee the accused the right to use his/her regional or minority language; and/or
      iii to provide that requests and evidence, whether written or oral, shall not be considered inadmissible solely because they are formulated in a regional or minority language; and/or
      iv to produce, on request, documents connected with legal proceedings in the relevant regional or minority language,
      if necessary by the use of interpreters and translations involving no extra expense for the persons concerned;
   b   in civil proceedings:
      i   to provide that the courts, at the request of one of the parties, shall conduct the proceedings in the regional or minority languages; and/or
      ii to allow, whenever a litigant has to appear in person before a court, that he or she may use his or her regional or minority language without thereby incurring additional expense; and/or
      iii to allow documents and evidence to be produced in the regional or minority languages,
      if necessary by the use of interpreters and translations;
   c   in proceedings before courts concerning administrative matters:
      i   to provide that the courts, at the request of one of the parties, shall conduct the proceedings in the regional or minority languages; and/or
      ii to allow, whenever a litigant has to appear in person before a court, that he or she may use his or her regional or minority language without thereby incurring additional expense; and/or
      iii to allow documents and evidence to be produced in the regional or minority languages,
      if necessary by the use of interpreters and translations;
   d   to take steps to ensure that the application of sub-paragraphs i and iii of paragraphs b and c above and any necessary use of interpreters and translations does not involve extra expense for the persons concerned.
2 The Parties undertake:
   a   not to deny the validity of legal documents drawn up within the State solely because they are drafted in a regional or minority language; or
   b   not to deny the validity, as between the parties, of legal documents drawn up within the country solely because they are drafted in a regional or

minority language, and to provide that they can be invoked against interested third parties who are not users of these languages on condition that the contents of the document are made known to them by the person(s) who invoke(s) it; or

c not to deny the validity, as between the parties, of legal documents drawn up within the country solely because they are drafted in a regional or minority language.

3 The Parties undertake to make available in the regional or minority languages the most important national statutory texts and those relating particularly to users of these languages, unless they are otherwise provided.

Article 10 – Administrative authorities and public services

1 Within the administrative districts of the State in which the number of residents who are users of regional or minority languages justifies the measures specified below and according to the situation of each language, the Parties undertake, as far as this is reasonably possible:

a i   to ensure that the administrative authorities use the regional or minority languages; or

   ii   to ensure that such of their officers as are in contact with the public use the regional or minority languages in their relations with persons applying to them in these languages; or

   iii to ensure that users of regional or minority languages may submit oral or written applications and receive a reply in these languages; or

   iv   to ensure that users of regional or minority languages may submit oral or written applications in these languages; or

   v   to ensure that users of regional or minority languages may validly submit a document in these languages;

b to make available widely used administrative texts and forms for the population in the regional or minority languages or in bilingual versions;

c to allow the administrative authorities to draft documents in a regional or minority language.

2 In respect of the local and regional authorities on whose territory the number of residents who are users of regional or minority languages is such as to justify the measures specified below, the Parties undertake to allow and/or encourage:

a the use of regional or minority languages within the framework of the regional or local authority;

b the possibility for users of regional or minority languages to submit oral or written applications in these languages;

c the publication by regional authorities of their official documents also in the relevant regional or minority languages;

d the publication by local authorities of their official documents also in the relevant regional or minority languages;

e the use by regional authorities of regional or minority languages in debates in their assemblies, without excluding, however, the use of the official language(s) of the State;

f the use by local authorities of regional or minority languages in debates in their assemblies, without excluding, however, the use of the official language(s) of the State;

g the use or adoption, if necessary in conjunction with the name in the official language(s), of traditional and correct forms of place-names in regional or minority languages.

3 With regard to public services provided by the administrative authorities or other persons acting on their behalf, the Parties undertake, within the territory in which regional or minority languages are used, in accordance with the situation of each language and as far as this is reasonably possible:

a to ensure that the regional or minority languages are used in the provision of the service; or

b to allow users of regional or minority languages to submit a request and receive a reply in these languages; or

c to allow users of regional or minority languages to submit a request in these languages.

4 With a view to putting into effect those provisions of paragraphs 1, 2 and 3 accepted by them, the Parties undertake to take one or more of the following measures:

a translation or interpretation as may be required;

b recruitment and, where necessary, training of the officials and other public service employees required;

c compliance as far as possible with requests from public service employees having a knowledge of a regional or minority language to be appointed in the territory in which that language is used.

5 The Parties undertake to allow the use or adoption of family names in the regional or minority languages, at the request of those concerned.

Article 11 – Media

1 The Parties undertake, for the users of the regional or minority languages within the territories in which those languages are spoken, according to the situation of each language, to the extent that the public authorities, directly or indirectly, are competent, have power or play a role in this field, and respecting the principle of the independence and autonomy of the media:

a to the extent that radio and television carry out a public service mission:

i to ensure the creation of at least one radio station and one television channel in the regional or minority languages; or

ii to encourage and/or facilitate the creation of at least one radio station and one television channel in the regional or minority languages; or

iii to make adequate provision so that broadcasters offer programmes in the regional or minority languages;

b i to encourage and/or facilitate the creation of at least one radio station in the regional or minority languages; or

ii to encourage and/or facilitate the broadcasting of radio programmes in the regional or minority languages on a regular basis;

c i to encourage and/or facilitate the creation of at least one television channel in the regional or minority languages; or

ii to encourage and/or facilitate the broadcasting of television programmes in the regional or minority languages on a regular basis;

d to encourage and/or facilitate the production and distribution of audio and audiovisual works in the regional or minority languages;

e i to encourage and/or facilitate the creation and/or maintenance of at least one newspaper in the regional or minority languages; or

   ii to encourage and/or facilitate the publication of newspaper articles in the regional or minority languages on a regular basis;

f i to cover the additional costs of those media which use regional or minority languages, wherever the law provides for financial assistance in general for the media; or

   ii to apply existing measures for financial assistance also to audiovisual productions in the regional or minority languages;

g to support the training of journalists and other staff for media using regional or minority languages.

2 The Parties undertake to guarantee freedom of direct reception of radio and television broadcasts from neighbouring countries in a language used in identical or similar form to a regional or minority language, and not to oppose the retransmission of radio and television broadcasts from neighbouring countries in such a language. They further undertake to ensure that no restrictions will be placed on the freedom of expression and free circulation of information in the written press in a language used in identical or similar form to a regional or minority language. The exercise of the above-mentioned freedoms, since it carries with it duties and responsibilities, may be subject to such formalities, conditions, restrictions or penalties as are prescribed by law and are necessary in a democratic society, in the interests of national security, territorial integrity or public safety, for the prevention of disorder or crime, for the protection of health or morals, for the protection of the reputation or rights of others, for preventing disclosure of information received in confidence, or for maintaining the authority and impartiality of the judiciary.

3 The Parties undertake to ensure that the interests of the users of regional or minority languages are represented or taken into account within such bodies as may be established in accordance with the law with responsibility for guaranteeing the freedom and pluralism of the media.

Article 12 – Cultural activities and facilities

1 With regard to cultural activities and facilities – especially libraries, video libraries, cultural centres, museums, archives, academies, theatres and cinemas, as well as literary work and film production, vernacular forms of cultural expression, festivals and the culture industries, including **inter alia** the use of new technologies – the Parties undertake, within the territory in which such languages are used and to the extent that the public authorities are competent, have power or play a role in this field:

a to encourage types of expression and initiative specific to regional or minority languages and foster the different means of access to works produced in these languages;

b to foster the different means of access in other languages to works produced in regional or minority languages by aiding and developing translation, dubbing, post-synchronisation and subtitling activities;

c to foster access in regional or minority languages to works produced in other languages by aiding and developing translation, dubbing, post-synchronisation and subtitling activities;

d to ensure that the bodies responsible for organising or supporting cultural activities of various kinds make appropriate allowance for incorporating the knowledge and use of regional or minority languages and cultures in the undertakings which they initiate or for which they provide backing;

e to promote measures to ensure that the bodies responsible for organising or supporting cultural activities have at their disposal staff who have a full command of the regional or minority language concerned, as well as of the language(s) of the rest of the population;

f to encourage direct participation by representatives of the users of a given regional or minority language in providing facilities and planning cultural activities;

g to encourage and/or facilitate the creation of a body or bodies responsible for collecting, keeping a copy of and presenting or publishing works produced in the regional or minority languages;

h if necessary, to create and/or promote and finance translation and terminological research services, particularly with a view to maintaining and developing appropriate administrative, commercial, economic, social, technical or legal terminology in each regional or minority language.

2 In respect of territories other than those in which the regional or minority languages are traditionally used, the Parties undertake, if the number of users of a regional or minority language justifies it, to allow, encourage and/or provide appropriate cultural activities and facilities in accordance with the preceding paragraph.

3 The Parties undertake to make appropriate provision, in pursuing their cultural policy abroad, for regional or minority languages and the cultures they reflect.

Article 13 – Economic and social life

1 With regard to economic and social activities, the Parties undertake, within the whole country:

a to eliminate from their legislation any provision prohibiting or limiting without justifiable reasons the use of regional or minority languages in documents relating to economic or social life, particularly contracts of employment, and in technical documents such as instructions for the use of products or installations;

b to prohibit the insertion in internal regulations of companies and private documents of any clauses excluding or restricting the use of regional or minority languages, at least between users of the same language;

c to oppose practices designed to discourage the use of regional or minority languages in connection with economic or social activities;

d to facilitate and/or encourage the use of regional or minority languages by means other than those specified in the above sub-paragraphs.

2 With regard to economic and social activities, the Parties undertake, in so far as the public authorities are competent, within the territory in which the regional or minority languages are used, and as far as this is reasonably possible:

a to include in their financial and banking regulations provisions which allow, by means of procedures compatible with commercial practice, the use of regional or minority languages in drawing up payment orders (cheques, drafts, etc.) or other financial documents, or, where appropriate, to ensure the implementation of such provisions;

b   in the economic and social sectors directly under their control (public sector), to organise activities to promote the use of regional or minority languages;

c   to ensure that social care facilities such as hospitals, retirement homes and hostels offer the possibility of receiving and treating in their own language persons using a regional or minority language who are in need of care on grounds of ill-health, old age or for other reasons;

d   to ensure by appropriate means that safety instructions are also drawn up in regional or minority languages;

e   to arrange for information provided by the competent public authorities concerning the rights of consumers to be made available in regional or minority languages.

Article 14 – Transfrontier exchanges

The Parties undertake:

a   to apply existing bilateral and multilateral agreements which bind them with the States in
which the same language is used in identical or similar form, or if necessary to seek to conclude such agreements, in such a way as to foster contacts between the users of the same language in the States concerned in the fields of culture, education, information, vocational training and permanent education;

b   for the benefit of regional or minority languages, to facilitate and/or promote co-operation across borders, in particular between regional or local authorities in whose territory the same language is used in identical or similar form.

Part IV – Application of the Charter

Article 15 – Periodical reports

1   The Parties shall present periodically to the Secretary General of the Council of Europe, in a form to be prescribed by the Committee of Ministers, a report on their policy pursued in accordance with Part II of this Charter and on the measures taken in application of those provisions of Part III which they have accepted. The first report shall be presented within the year following the entry into force of the Charter with respect to the Party concerned, the other reports at three-yearly intervals after the first report.

2   The Parties shall make their reports public.

Article 16 – Examination of the reports

1   The reports presented to the Secretary General of the Council of Europe under Article 15 shall be examined by a committee of experts constituted in accordance with Article 17.

2   Bodies or associations legally established in a Party may draw the attention of the committee of experts to matters relating to the undertakings entered into by that Party under Part III of this Charter. After consulting the Party concerned, the committee of experts may take account of this information in the preparation of the report specified in paragraph 3 below. These bodies or associations can furthermore submit statements concerning the policy pursued by a Party in accordance with Part II.

3   On the basis of the reports specified in paragraph 1 and the information mentioned in paragraph 2, the committee of experts shall prepare a report for the Committee of Ministers. This report shall be accompanied by the comments which the Parties have been requested to make and may be made public by the Committee of Ministers.

4   The report specified in paragraph 3 shall contain in particular the proposals of the committee of experts to the Committee of Ministers for the preparation of such recommendations of the latter body to one or more of the Parties as may be required.

5   The Secretary General of the Council of Europe shall make a two-yearly detailed report to the Parliamentary Assembly on the application of the Charter.

Article 17 – Committee of experts

1   The committee of experts shall be composed of one member per Party, appointed by the Committee of Ministers from a list of individuals of the highest integrity and recognised competence in the matters dealt with in the Charter, who shall be nominated by the Party concerned.

2   Members of the committee shall be appointed for a period of six years and shall be eligible for reappointment. A member who is unable to complete a term of office shall be replaced in accordance with the procedure laid down in paragraph 1, and the replacing member shall complete his predecessor's term of office.

3   The committee of experts shall adopt rules of procedure. Its secretarial services shall be provided by the Secretary General of the Council of Europe.

Part V – Final provisions

Article 18

This Charter shall be open for signature by the member States of the Council of Europe. It is subject to ratification, acceptance or approval. Instruments of ratification, acceptance or approval shall be deposited with the Secretary General of the Council of Europe.

Article 19

1   This Charter shall enter into force on the first day of the month following the expiration of a period of three months after the date on which five member States of the Council of Europe have expressed their consent to be bound by the Charter in accordance with the provisions of Article 18.

2 In respect of any member State which subsequently expresses its consent to be bound by it, the Charter shall enter into force on the first day of the month following the expiration of a period of three months after the date of the deposit of the instrument of ratification, acceptance or approval.

Article 20

1 After the entry into force of this Charter, the Committee of Ministers of the Council of Europe may invite any State not a member of the Council of Europe to accede to this Charter.
2 In respect of any acceding State, the Charter shall enter into force on the first day of the month following the expiration of a period of three months after the date of deposit of the instrument of accession with the Secretary General of the Council of Europe.

Article 21

1 Any State may, at the time of signature or when depositing its instrument of ratification, acceptance, approval or accession, make one or more reservations to paragraphs 2 to 5 of Article 7 of this Charter. No other reservation may be made.
2 Any Contracting State which has made a reservation under the preceding paragraph may wholly or partly withdraw it by means of a notification addressed to the Secretary General of the Council of Europe. The withdrawal shall take effect on the date of receipt of such notification by the Secretary General.

Article 22

1 Any Party may at any time denounce this Charter by means of a notification addressed to the Secretary General of the Council of Europe.
2 Such denunciation shall become effective on the first day of the month following the expiration of a period of six months after the date of receipt of the notification by the Secretary General.

Article 23

The Secretary General of the Council of Europe shall notify the member States of the Council and any State which has acceded to this Charter of:

a any signature;
b the deposit of any instrument of ratification, acceptance, approval or accession;
c any date of entry into force of this Charter in accordance with Articles 19 and 20;
d any notification received in application of the provisions of Article 3, paragraph 2;
e any other act, notification or communication relating to this Charter.

In witness whereof the undersigned, being duly authorised thereto, have signed this Charter.

Done at Strasbourg, this 5th day of November 1992, in English and French, both texts being equally authentic, in a single copy which shall be deposited in the archives of the Council of Europe. The Secretary General of the Council of Europe shall transmit certified copies to each member State of the Council of Europe and to any State invited to accede to this Charter.

Appendix II

EXPLANATORY REPORT

Introduction

1. Many European countries have on their territory regionally based autochthonous groups speaking a language other than that of the majority of the population. This is a consequence of historical processes whereby the formation of states has not taken place on purely language-related lines and small communities have been engulfed by larger ones.

2. The demographic situation of such regional or minority languages varies greatly, from a few thousand speakers to several million, and so does the law and practice of the individual states with respect to them. However, what many have in common is a greater or lesser degree of precariousness. Moreover, whatever may have been the case in the past, nowadays the threats facing these regional or minority languages are often due at least as much to the inevitably standardising influence of modern civilisation and especially of the mass media as to an unfriendly environment or a government policy of assimilation.

3. For many years various bodies within the Council of Europe have been expressing concern over the situation of regional or minority languages. It is true that the Convention for the Protection of Human Rights and Fundamental Freedoms in its Article 14 lays down the principle of non-discrimination, in particular outlawing, at least with respect to the enjoyment of the rights and freedoms guaranteed by the Convention, any discrimination based on such grounds as language or association with a national minority. Important though this is, however, it creates only a right for individuals not to be subjected to discrimination, but not a system of positive protection for minority languages and the communities using them, as was pointed out by the Consultative Assembly as long ago as 1957 in its Resolution 136. In 1961, in Recommendation 285, the Parliamentary Assembly called for a protection measure to supplement the European Convention to be devised in order to safeguard the rights of minorities to enjoy their own culture, to use their own language, to establish their own schools and so on.

4. Lastly, in 1981 the Parliamentary Assembly of the Council of Europe adopted Recommendation 928 on the educational and cultural problems of minority languages and dialects in Europe, and in the same year the European Parliament passed a resolution on the same questions. Both documents concluded that it was necessary to draw up a charter of regional or minority languages and cultures.

5. Acting on these recommendations and resolutions, the Standing Conference of Local and Regional Authorities of Europe (CLRAE) decided to undertake the preparation of a European charter for regional or minority languages, by reason of the part which local and regional authorities must be expected to play in relation to languages and cultures at local and regional level.

6. The preliminary work before the actual drafting of the charter involved a survey of the actual situation of regional and minority languages in Europe and,

in 1984, a public hearing attended by some 250 people representing over 40 languages. The initial drafting was carried out with the assistance of a group of experts. In view of the strong and continuing interest of the Parliamentary Assembly of the Council of Europe and the European Parliament in this topic, the former participated in the drafting and contacts were maintained with competent members of the latter.

7. Finally, in its Resolution 192 (1988), the Standing Conference proposed the text of a charter which was designed to have the status of a convention.

8. Following this initiative, which was supported by the Parliamentary Assembly in its Opinion No. 142 (1988), the Committee of Ministers established an ad hoc committee of experts on regional or minority languages in Europe (CAHLR), with responsibility for drafting a charter bearing the Standing Conference's text in mind. This intergovernmental committee began work at the end of 1989. In view of their important role as promoters of the project, both the CLRAE and the Parliamentary Assembly were represented at its meetings. Before submitting the final text of the draft charter to the Committee of Ministers in 1992, the CAHLR consulted and took into account the opinions of a number of specialised committees within the Council of Europe (culture, education, human rights, legal cooperation, crime problems, local and regional authorities, media), as well as the European Commission for Democracy through Law.

9. The charter was adopted as a convention by the Committee of Ministers at the 478th meeting of the Ministers' Deputies on 25 June 1992 and opened for signature on 5 November 1992 in Strasbourg.

General considerations

Objectives of the charter

10. As is made clear in the preamble, the charter's overriding purpose is cultural. It is designed to protect and promote regional or minority languages as a threatened aspect of Europe's cultural heritage. For this reason it not only contains a non-discrimination clause concerning the use of these languages but also provides for measures offering active support for them: the aim is to ensure, as far as reasonably possible, the use of regional or minority languages in education and the media and to permit their use in judicial and administrative settings, economic and social life and cultural activities. Only in this way can such languages be compensated, where necessary, for unfavourable conditions in the past and preserved and developed as a living facet of Europe's cultural identity.

11. The charter sets out to protect and promote regional or minority languages, not linguistic minorities. For this reason emphasis is placed on the cultural dimension and the use of a regional or minority language in all the aspects of the life of its speakers. The charter does not establish any individual or collective rights for the speakers of regional or minority languages. Nevertheless, the obligations of the parties with regard to the status of these languages and the domestic legislation which will have to be introduced in compliance with the charter will have an obvious effect on the situation of the communities concerned and their individual members.

12. The CLRAE conceived and presented its draft charter before the dramatic changes in central and eastern Europe and in the light of the needs of the countries which at that time were already members of the Council of Europe. Nevertheless,

the relevance of the charter and its approach to the situation of the countries of central and eastern Europe has since been confirmed by the considerable interest expressed by the representatives of a number of these countries in the establishment of European standards on this topic.

13. While the draft charter is not concerned with the problem of nationalities who aspire after independence or alterations to frontiers, it may be expected to help, in a measured and realistic fashion, to assuage the problem of minorities whose language is their distinguishing feature, by enabling them to feel at ease in the state in which history has placed them. Far from reinforcing disintegrating tendencies, the enhancement of the possibility to use regional or minority languages in the various spheres of life can only encourage the groups who speak them to put behind them the resentments of the past which prevented them from accepting their place in the country in which they live and in Europe as a whole.

14. In this context it should be stressed that the charter does not conceive the relationship between official languages and regional or minority languages in terms of competition or antagonism. Rather, it deliberately adopts an intercultural and multilingual approach in which each category of language has its proper place. This approach corresponds fully to the values traditionally upheld by the Council of Europe and its efforts to promote closer relations between peoples, increased European co-operation and a better understanding between different population groups within the state on an intercultural basis.

15. The charter does not deal with the situation of new, often non-European languages which may have appeared in the signatory states as a result of recent migration flows often arising from economic motives. In the case of populations speaking such languages, specific problems of integration arise. The CAHLR took the view that these problems deserved to be addressed separately, if appropriate in a specific legal instrument.

16. Finally, it may be noted that some member states of the Council of Europe already implement policies which go further than some of the requirements of the charter. It is in no way intended that the provisions of the charter should detract from their right to do so.

Basic concepts and approach

Concept of language

17. The concept of language as used in the charter focuses primarily on the cultural function of language. That is why it is not defined subjectively in such a way as to consecrate an individual right, that is the right to speak "one's own language", it being left to each individual to define that language. Nor is reliance placed on a politico-social or ethnic definition by describing a language as the vehicle of a particular social or ethnic group. Consequently, the charter is able to refrain from defining the concept of linguistic minorities, since its aim is not to stipulate the rights of ethnic and/or cultural minority groups, but to protect and promote regional or minority languages as such.

Terminology used

18. In preference to other expressions such as "less widespread languages", the CAHLR opted for the term "regional or minority languages". The adjective

"regional" denotes languages spoken in a limited part of the territory of a state, within which, moreover, they may be spoken by the majority of the citizens. The term "minority" refers to situations in which either the language is spoken by persons who are not concentrated on a specific part of the territory of a state or it is spoken by a group of persons, which, though concentrated on part of the territory of the state, is numerically smaller than the population in this region which speaks the majority language of the state. Both adjectives therefore refer to factual criteria and not to legal notions and in any case relate to the situation in a given state (for instance, a minority language in one state may be a majority language in another state).

Absence of distinction between different "categories" of regional or minority languages

19. The authors of the charter were confronted by the problem of the major differences which exist in the situations of regional or minority languages in Europe. Some languages cover a relatively large territorial area, are spoken by a substantial population and enjoy a certain capability of development and cultural stability; others are spoken only by a very small proportion of the population, in a restricted territory, or in a very marked minority context and already with greatly impaired potential for survival and development.
20. Nevertheless, it was decided not to attempt to define different categories of languages according to their objective situation. Such an approach would not do justice to the diversity of language situations in Europe. In practice, each regional or minority language constitutes a special case and it is pointless to try and force them into distinct groups. The solution adopted was to preserve the single notion of regional or minority language, while enabling states to adapt their undertakings to the situation of each regional or minority language.

Absence of a list of regional or minority languages in Europe

21. The charter does not specify which European languages correspond to the concept of regional or minority languages as defined in its first article. In fact the preliminary survey of the linguistic situation in Europe carried out by the Standing Conference of Local and Regional Authorities of Europe prompted the authors of the charter to refrain from appending a list of regional or minority languages. However expert its compilers, such a list would certainly be widely disputed on linguistic and other grounds. Moreover, its value would be limited, since at any rate with respect to the specific measures in Part III of the charter it is left largely up to the parties to determine which provisions shall apply to which language. The charter puts forward appropriate solutions for the different situations of individual regional or minority languages but does not prejudge what is the specific situation in concrete cases.

The structure of the charter

22. On the one hand, the charter establishes a common core of principles, set out in Part II, which apply to all regional or minority languages. On the other hand,

Part III of the charter contains a series of specific provisions concerning the place of regional or minority languages in the various sectors of the life of the community: the individual states are free, within certain limits, to determine which of these provisions will apply to each of the languages spoken within their frontiers. In addition, a considerable number of provisions comprise several options of varying degrees of stringency, one of which must be applied "according to the situation of each language".

23. This flexibility takes account of the major differences in the de facto situations of regional or minority languages (number of speakers, degree of fragmentation, etc). It also has regard to the costs entailed by many of the provisions and the varying administrative and financial capacity of the European states. In this respect it is important that the parties are allowed to add to their commitments at a later stage, as their legal situation develops or their financial circumstances allow.

24. Finally, Part IV of the charter contains implementing provisions, including in particular the establishment of a European expert committee to monitor the application of the charter.

Commentary on the Provisions of the Charter

Preamble

25. The preamble sets out the reasons for having the charter drawn up and explains its basic philosophical approach.

26. The aim of the Council of Europe is to achieve a greater unity between its members in order to promote their common heritage and ideals. Linguistic diversity is one of the most precious elements of the European cultural heritage. The cultural identity of Europe cannot be constructed on the basis of linguistic standardisation. On the contrary, the protection and strengthening of its traditional regional and minority languages represents a contribution to the building of Europe, which, according to the ideals of the members of the Council of Europe, can be founded only on pluralist principles.

27. The preamble refers to the United Nations International Covenant on Civil and Political Rights and to the European Convention on Human Rights. In addition, it cites the commitments of a political nature adopted within the framework of the Conference on Security and Co-operation in Europe. Having regard to the present weakness of some of the historical regional or minority languages of Europe, however, the mere prohibition of discrimination against their users is not a sufficient safeguard. Special support which reflects the interests and wishes of the users of these languages is essential to their preservation and development.

28. The approach of the charter respects the principles of national sovereignty and territorial integrity. Each state is required to take into account a cultural and social reality and there is no question of challenging any political or institutional order. On the contrary, it is because the member states accept territorial and state structures as they are, that they believe it is necessary, within each state, but in a concerted manner, to take measures to promote languages of a regional or minority nature.

29. The affirmation of the principles of interculturalism and multi lingualism serves to remove any misapprehension as to the aims of the charter, which by no

means seeks to foster any kind of partitioning off of linguistic groups. On the contrary, it is recognised that in every state it is necessary to know the official language (or one of the official languages); consequently, none of the charter's provisions should be interpreted as intending to raising obstacles to the knowledge of official languages.

Part I – General provisions

Article 1 – Definitions

Definition of "regional or minority languages" (Article 1, paragraph a)

30. The definition employed in the charter emphasises three aspects:

Languages traditionally used by nationals of the state:

31. The purpose of the charter is not to resolve the problems arising out of recent immigration phenomena, resulting in the existence of groups speaking a foreign language in the country of immigration or sometimes in the country of origin in case of return. In particular, the charter is not concerned with the phenomenon of non-European groups who have immigrated recently into Europe and acquired the nationality of a European state. The expressions "historical regional or minority languages of Europe" (see second paragraph of the preamble) and languages "traditionally used" in the state (Article 1, paragraph a) show clearly that the charter covers only historical languages, that is to say languages which have been spoken over a long period in the state in question.

Different languages:

32. These languages must clearly differ from the other language or languges spoken by the remainder of the population of the state. The charter does not concern local variants or different dialects of one and the same language. However, it does not pronounce on the often disputed question of the point at which different forms of expression constitute separate languages. This question depends not only on strictly linguistic considerations, but also on psycho-sociological and political phenomena which may produce a different answer in each case. Accordingly, it will be left to the authorities concerned within each state, in accordance with its own democratic processes, to determine at what point a form of expression constitutes a separate language.

Territorial base:

33. The languages covered by the charter are primarily territorial languages, that is to say languages which are traditionally used in a particular geographical area. That is why the charter seeks to define the "territory in which the regional or minority language is used". It is not only the territory within which that language is dominant or spoken by the majority, since many languages have become minority languages even in the areas where they have their traditional territorial base. The reason why the charter is mainly concerned with languages which have a territorial base is that most of the measures which it advocates necessitate the

definition of a geographical field of application other than the state as a whole. Obviously there are situations in which more than one regional or minority language is spoken on a given territory; the charter also covers these situations.

Definition of the territory of a regional or minority language (Article 1, paragraph b)

34. The territory referred to is that where a regional or minority language is spoken to a significant extent, even if only by a minority, and which corresponds to its historical base. Since the terms used in the charter in this respect are inevitably fairly flexible, it is up to each state to define more precisely, in the spirit of the charter, the notion of regional or minority languages' territory, taking into account the provisions of Article 7, paragraph 1.b, regarding protection of the territory of regional or minority languages.

35. A key expression in this provision is "number of people justifying the adoption of the various protective and promotional measures". The authors of the charter avoided establishing a fixed percentage of speakers of a regional or minority language at or above which the measures laid down in the charter should apply. They preferred to leave it up to the state to assess, within the spirit of the charter, according to the nature of each of the measures provided for, the appropriate number of speakers of the language required for the adoption of the measure in question.

Definition of "non-territorial languages" (Article 1, paragraph c)

36. "Non-territorial languages" are excluded from the category of regional or minority languages because they lack a territorial base. In other respects, however, they correspond to the definition contained in Article 1, paragraph a, being languages traditionally used on the territory of the state by citizens of the state. Examples of non-territorial languages are Yiddish and Romany.

37. In the absence of a territorial base, only a limited part of the charter can be applied to these languages. In particular, most of the provisions of Part III aim to protect or promote regional or minority languages in relation to the territory in which they are used. Part II can more easily be applied to non-territorial languages, but only mutatis mutandis and on the terms set out in Article 7, paragraph 5.

Article 2 – Undertakings

38. Article 2 distinguishes between the two main parts of the charter, namely Part II and Part III.

Implementation of Part II (Article 2, paragraph 1)

39. Part II is general in scope and applies in its entirety to all regional or minority languages spoken on the territory of a State Party. It will be noted, however, that the use of the expression "according to the situation of each language" shows that this part is drafted so as to cater for the very great variety of language situations

that may be encountered in the various European countries and within each country. In particular, in the first paragraph the States Parties are required to undertake to match their policy, legislation and practice to a number of principles and objectives. These are fairly generally defined and allow the states concerned a broad measure of discretion as regards interpretation and application (see explanations below concerning Part II).

40. Although the States Parties are not free to grant or to refuse a regional or minority language the status which it is guaranteed under Part II of the charter, they are responsible, as authorities for the application of the charter, for deciding whether the form of expression used in a particular area of their territory or by a particular group of their nationals constitutes a regional or minority language within the meaning of the charter.

Implementation of Part III (Article 2, paragraph 2)

41. The purpose of Part III is to translate the general principles asserted in Part II into precise rules. It is binding on those contracting states which, in addition to the provisions of Part II, undertake to apply the provisions of Part III which they have chosen. In order to enable the charter to be adapted to the variety of linguistic situations encountered in the various European states, the authors of the charter have provided for a twofold modulation: firstly, the states are free to name the languages to which they agree to Part III of the charter being applied and, secondly, for each of the languages for which they accept that the charter shall apply, they can determine the provisions of Part III to which they subscribe.

42. It is possible for a contracting state, without offending the letter of the charter, to recognise that a particular regional or minority language exists on its territory but consider it preferable, for reasons which lie within its discretion, not to extend to that language the benefit of the provisions of Part III of the charter. Clearly, however, the reasons which prompt a state to exclude a recognised regional or minority language completely from the benefit of Part III must be reasons compatible with the spirit, objectives and principles of the charter.

43. Once a state has agreed to apply Part III to a regional or minority language spoken on its territory, it will still have to determine which paragraphs of Part III are to be applied to that particular regional or minority language. Under paragraph 2 of Article 2, the parties undertake to apply at least 35 paragraphs or subparagraphs chosen from among the provisions of Part III. The role of the state in the choice between these different paragraphs will consist in matching the charter as closely as possible to the particular context of each regional or minority language.

44. For this purpose the conditions stipulated by Article 2, paragraph 2 are kept to a minimum designed to provide for a reasonable distribution of the parties' undertakings among the different articles of the charter and thus ensure that they do not ignore any of the major fields of protection of regional or minority languages (education, judicial authorities, administrative authorities and public services, media, cultural activities and facilities, economic and social life).

45. The expression "paragraphs or sub-paragraphs" refers to distinct provisions of the charter which stand on their own. Thus, if a state chooses paragraph 3 of Article 9, this paragraph will count as one unit for the purposes of Article 2, paragraph 2; the same applies if a state accepts sub-paragraph g of Article 8, paragraph 1.

Where a given paragraph or sub-paragraph contains several options, the choice of one option will constitute a sub-paragraph for the purposes of Article 2, paragraph 2. For example, in Article 8, if a state chooses option a.iii in paragraph 1, this text will count as a "sub-paragraph". The position is different when the options are not necessarily alternatives but may be accepted cumulatively. Thus in Article 9, if a state chooses options a.iii and a.iv in paragraph 1, these texts will count as two sub-paragraphs within the meaning of Article 2.

46. The aim of these options is to introduce a further element of flexibility into the charter so as to take account of the wide disparities in the de facto situation of regional or minority languages. It is clear that certain provisions which are perfectly well adapted to a regional language practised by a large number of speakers are not suited to a minority language used only by a small group of persons. The role of the states will be, not to choose arbitrarily between these alternatives, but to seek for each regional or minority language the wording which best fits the characteristics and state of development of that language. The purpose of these alternative wordings is clearly expressed in the very text of the relevant articles or paragraphs of Part III, which provide that they are applicable "according to the situation of each language". Broadly speaking, and in the absence of other relevant factors, this would imply, for instance, that the larger the number of speakers of a regional or minority language and the more homogeneous the regional population, the "stronger" the option which should be adopted; a weaker alternative should be adopted only when the stronger option cannot be applied owing to the situation of the language in question.

47. It will therefore be for the states to choose in Part III provisions forming a coherent framework adapted to the specific situation of each language. They may also, if they prefer, adopt a general framework applying to all the languages or to a group of languages.

Article 3 – Practical arrangements

48. Article 3 describes the procedure for the implementation of the principles just outlined in Article 2: each Contracting State specifies in its instrument of ratification, acceptance, approval or accession, firstly, those regional or minority languages to which Part III applies and, secondly, the paragraphs of Part III chosen for application to each language, it being understood that the paragraphs chosen need not be the same for each language.

49. The charter, in its Article 2, does not compel acceptance of both Parts II and III, since a state could confine itself to ratifying the convention without selecting any language for the purposes of the application of Part III. In such a case, only Part II would apply. In general, the spirit of the charter would require that states make use of the possibilities offered by Part III, which constitutes the essence of the protection afforded by the charter.

50. It is also clear that, at any time, a party may accept new obligations, for example by extending to an additional regional or minority language the benefit of the provisions of Part III of the charter or by subscribing, in respect of a language or all the minority or regional languages spoken on its territory, to paragraphs of the charter not previously accepted.

51. The wording of Article 3 takes account of the position in certain member states whereby a national language which has the status of an official language of the

state, either on the whole or on part of its territory, may in other respects be in a comparable situation to regional or minority languages as defined in Article 1, paragraph a, because it is used by a group numerically smaller than the population using the other official language(s). If a state wishes such a less widely used official language to benefit from the measures of protection and promotion provided for by the charter, it is therefore enabled to determine that the charter shall apply to it. Such an extension of the application of the charter to an official language then holds good for all articles of the charter, including Article 4, paragraph 2.

Article 4 – Existing regimes of protection

52. This article relates to the combination of the charter with domestic legislation or international agreements laying down a legal status for linguistic minorities.
53. Where certain languages or the minorities who practise them already enjoy a status defined in domestic law or under international agreements, the purpose of the charter is clearly not to reduce the rights and guarantees recognised by those provisions. However, the protection afforded by the charter is additional to the rights and guarantees already granted by other instruments. For the application of all these undertakings, where competing provisions exist on the same subject the most favourable provisions should be applied to the minorities or languages concerned. Thus the existence of more restrictive provisions in domestic law or under other international undertakings must not be an obstacle to the application of the charter.
54. Paragraph 1 of this article is concerned with the specific case of the rights guaranteed by the European Convention on Human Rights. It seeks to exclude the possibility that any of the provisions of the charter might be so interpreted as to detract from the protection accorded thereby to the human rights of individuals.

Article 5 – Existing obligations

55. As is already indicated in the preamble, the protection and promotion of regional or minority languages which is the objective of the charter must take place within the framework of national sovereignty and territorial integrity. This article makes explicit in this respect that the existing obligations of the parties remain unchanged. In particular the fact that, by ratifying the charter, a state has entered into undertakings with respect to a regional or minority language may not be used by another state having a special interest in that language or by the users of the language as a pretext for taking any action prejudicial to the sovereignty and territorial integrity of that state.

Article 6 – Information

56. The motive for the undertaking to provide information which is established by this article lies in the fact that the charter can never become fully effective if the competent authorities and interested organisations and individuals are not aware of the obligations which derive from it.

Part II – Objectives and principles

(Article 7)

List of objectives and principles included in the charter
(Article 7, paragraph 1)

57. These provisions concern essentially objectives and principles and not precise implementing rules. These objectives and principles are considered to constitute the necessary framework for the preser-vation of regional or minority languages. They fall under six main headings.

Recognition of regional or minority languages *(Article 7, paragraph 1.a)*

58. This is a question of recognition of the existence of these languages and of the legitimacy of their use. Such recognition must not be confused with recognition of a language as an official language. Admitting the existence of a language is a pre-condition for taking its specific features and needs into consideration and for action on its behalf.

Respect for the geographical area of each regional or minority language *(Article 7, paragraph 1.b)*

59. Although the charter considers it desirable to ensure a consistency between the territory of a regional or minority language and an appropriate territorial administrative entity, it is clear that this objective cannot be achieved in all cases, since settlement patterns may be too complex and the determination of territorial administrative entities may legitimately depend on other considerations than the use of a language. Accordingly, the charter does not require that the territory of a regional or minority language should in all cases coincide with an administrative unit.

60. On the other hand, it does condemn practices which devise territorial divisions so as to render the use or survival of a language more difficult or to fragment a language community among a number of administrative or territorial units. If administrative units cannot be adapted to the existence of a regional or minority language, they must at least remain neutral and not have a negative effect on the language. In particular, local or regional authorities must be in a position to discharge their responsibilities in relation to these languages.

Need for positive action for the benefit of regional or minority languages *(Article 7, paragraph 1.c and d)*

61. It is clear today that, by reason of the weakness of numerous regional or minority languages, the mere prohibition of discrimination is not sufficient to ensure their survival. They need positive support. This is the idea expressed in paragraph 1.c. In this paragraph it is left up to the states to determine the manner in which they intend acting to promote regional or minority languages in order to preserve them, but the charter emphasises that such action must be resolute.

62. Furthermore, as stated in paragraph 1.d, this effort of promotion must include action in favour of the possibility to use regional or minority languages freely, both orally and in writing, not only in private life and in individual relations, but also in community life, that is to say within the framework of institutions, social activities and economic life. The place which a regional or minority language may occupy in public contexts will obviously depend on its own particular features and will vary from one language to another. The charter does not lay down precise objectives in this respect but is content to call for an effort of promotion.

Guarantee of the teaching and study of regional or minority languages (Article 7, paragraph 1.f and h)

63. A crucial factor in the maintenance and preservation of regional or minority languages is the place they are given in the education system. The charter is content in Part II to affirm the principle, leaving it to the states to define implementing measures. However, it requires that regional or minority languages be present "at all appropriate stages" of the education system. The arrangements for the teaching of the regional or minority language will obviously vary according to the level of education concerned. In particular, in some cases, provision will need to be made for teaching "in" the regional or minority language and in others only for teaching "of" the language. Only the teaching of the regional or minority language at levels for which the language would not be appropriate, in view of its own particular characteristics, could be left out of account.

64. While paragraph 1.f is concerned to establish or safeguard teaching in or of the language as an instrument of transmission of the language, paragraph 1.h provides for the promotion of studies and research on regional or minority languages in a university or equivalent setting; for such work is essential to the development of such languages in terms of vocabulary, grammar and syntax. The promotion of such studies is part of the general effort to promote regional or minority languages in order to encourage their intrinsic progress.

Facilities afforded to non-speakers of regional or minority languages to acquire a knowledge of them (Article 7, paragraph 1.g)

65. The speakers of regional or minority languages know that, for their own personal fulfilment, they need to know the official language. However, in accordance with the emphasis placed in the preamble on the value of interculturalism and multilingualism, it is desirable that this spirit of receptiveness to several languages should not be confined to the speakers of regional or minority languages. In order to facilitate communication and understanding between language groups, the parties are called upon, in territories where a regional or minority language exists, to provide facilities for persons who are not native speakers of that language to learn it if they so desire.

66. It is well known that in some states the objective of the appropriate authorities is that the regional language should be the language normally and generally spoken in the region, and measures are taken to ensure that the language is known even by people for whom it is not their native language. Such a policy is not contrary to the charter, but does not constitute the purpose of paragraph 1.g. This paragraph seeks only to ensure greater mutual permeability between language groups.

*Relations between groups speaking a regional or minority language
(Article 7, paragraph 1.e and i)*

67. It is necessary that groups speaking the same regional or minority language have the possibility of engaging in cultural exchanges and in general of developing their relations, in order to contribute together to the preservation and enrichment of their language. To this end, the charter seeks to prevent fragmented patterns of settlement, administrative divisions within a state or the fact that such groups are settled in different states from constituting an obstacle to relations between them.

68. Admittedly, such awareness of a shared identity between speakers of a regional or minority language must not be reflected negatively in exclusiveness or marginalisation in relation to other social groups. The objective of promoting cultural relations with speakers of different regional or minority languages therefore serves the goal both of cultural enrichment and of enhanced understanding between all groups in the state.

69. Paragraph 1.i adds a further dimension: the idea that such relations must also be able to develop across national frontiers if groups speaking the same or similar regional or minority languages are spread over several states. By definition, regional or minority languages are spoken in the state concerned by a relatively small number of speakers: for the purpose of mutual enrichment in the cultural sphere, the latter may need to be able to rely on the cultural resources available, across frontiers, to other groups speaking the same or a similar language. This is particularly important where a regional language in one state corresponds to a major cultural language, or even the national language, of another state and where transfrontier co-operation can enable the regional community to benefit from cultural activity in that more widespread language. It is important that states should recognise the legitimacy of such relations and not consider them suspect in terms of the loyalty which every state expects of its nationals or regard them as a threat to their territorial integrity. A language group will feel all the more integrated in the state of which it is a part if it is recognised as such and if cultural contacts with its neighbouring communities are not hindered.

70. However, the states are left free to work out the most suitable arrangements for bringing such transnational exchanges about, especially bearing in mind the domestic and international constraints which some of them may face. More specific commitments are set out in Article 14 in Part III.

Elimination of discrimination (Article 7, paragraph 2)

71. The prohibition of discrimination in respect of the use of regional or minority languages constitutes a minimum guarantee for the speakers of such languages. For this reason, the parties undertake to eliminate measures discouraging the use or jeopardising the maintenance or development of a regional or minority language.

72. However, the purpose of this paragraph is not to establish complete equality of rights between languages. As is indicated by its wording, and in particular by the insertion of the term "unjustified", it is in fact quite compatible with the spirit of the charter that in the pursuit of policies which relate to regional or minority languages certain distinctions could be made between languages. In particular, the measures laid down by each state in favour of the use of a national

or official language do not constitute discrimination against regional languages on the sole grounds that these same measures are not taken for their benefit. However, such measures must not constitute an obstacle to the maintenance or development of the regional or minority languages.

73. At the same time, precisely because disparities exist between the situation of official languages and that of regional or minority languages and because those who practise the latter are often at a disadvantage, the charter accepts that positive measures may be necessary with the aim of preserving and promoting such languages. Provided that the measures have such an aim, and that they seek to do no more than promote equality between languages, they are not to be regarded as discriminatory.

Promotion of mutual respect and understanding between linguistic groups (Article 7, paragraph 3)

74. Respect for regional or minority languages and the development of a spirit of tolerance towards them are part of a general concern to develop understanding for a situation of language plurality within a state. The development of this spirit of tolerance and receptiveness through the educational system and the media is an important factor in the practical preservation of regional or minority languages. The encouragement of the mass media to pursue such objectives is not considered to constitute illegitimate state influence; indeed respect for human rights, tolerance of minorities and avoidance of incitement to hatred are the kinds of objective which most European states do not hesitate to impose as obligations upon the media. In the same spirit, for speakers of regional or minority languages, this principle constitutes an important factor causing them to be receptive to majority languages and cultures.

Establishment of bodies to respresent the interests of regional or minority languages (Article 7, paragraph 4)

75. The CAHLR thought it important that in each state mechanisms should exist whereby the public authorities take account of the needs and wishes expressed by the speakers of regional or minority languages themselves. Consequently, it is recommended that for each regional or minority language there should be a promoting body responsible for representing the interests of the language at national level, carrying out practical measures to promote it, and monitoring the implementation of the charter in relation to that particular language. The expression "if necessary" indicates inter alia that, where such institutions already exist in one form or another, it is not intended to encourage states to establish new ones which would duplicate them.

Application of the charter's principles to non-territorial languages (Article 7, paragraph 5)

76. Although the charter is primarily concerned with languages which are historically identified with a particular geographical area of the state, the CAHLR did

not wish to ignore those languages traditionally spoken within the state but which have no precise territorial base.

77. However, it is recognised that, owing to the territorial field of application of a number of principles and objectives laid down in Part II and the practical difficulty of taking measures to implement them without defining their geographical scope, these provisions cannot without certain adjustments be applied to non-territorial languages. Paragraph 5 accordingly specifies that they are to be applied only so far as possible to these languages.

78. Some of the provisions contained in paragraphs 1 to 4 can be applied without difficulty also to non-territorial languages; this is the case regarding the recognition of these languages, the measures to develop a spirit of respect, understanding and tolerance towards them, the prohibition of discrimination and the action to afford them positive support, the possibility for the groups speaking those languages to develop links with each other within the state and abroad, and the promotion of language research and study. On the other hand, it will not be possible to apply to non-territorial languages the provisions concerning administrative divisions and the facilities provided for non-speakers of these languages to acquire some knowledge of them, since such measures are capable of being taken only in a specified territory. Lastly, the objectives of making provision for the teaching and study of these non-territorial languages and the promotion of their use in public life can probably, for practical reasons, be implemented only with certain adjustments.

Part III – Measures to promote the use of regional or minority languages in public life in accordance with the undertakings entered into under Article 2, paragraph 2

Article 8 – Education

79. The provisions of paragraph 1 of this article relate only to the territory in which each regional or minority language is used. They are also to be applied "according to the situation of each of these languages". As indicated with reference to Article 2, paragraph 2 above, this stipulation is especially relevant to the choice of which option to accept for which language in sub-paragraphs a to f.

80. The phrase "and without prejudice to the teaching of the official language(s) of the state" is intended to avert any possiblity of interpreting the provisions of Article 8, paragraph 1 – and in particular the first option in each of sub-paragraphs a to f – as excluding the teaching of the language(s) spoken by the majority. Such a tendency to form linguistic ghettos would be contrary to the principles of interculturalism and multilingualism underlined in the preamble and inimical to the interests of the population groups concerned. In the special circumstances of those countries where the charter applies to less widely used official languages, this phrase should be interpreted as meaning that the provisions of paragraph 1 are without prejudice to the teaching of other official languages.

81. Article 8 deals with several levels of education: pre-school, primary, secondary, technical and vocational, university and adult education. For every one of these levels, different options are presented according to the situation of each regional or minority language.

82. Some of the sub-paragraphs employ the expression "in a number considered sufficient". This recognises that the public authorities cannot be required to take the measures concerned where the situation of the linguistic group makes it difficult to attain the minimum number of pupils required to form a class. On the other hand, given the particular circumstances of regional or minority languages, it is suggested that the normal quota required to constitute a class may be applied flexibly and a lower number of pupils may be "considered sufficient".

83. The wording of option iv in sub-paragraphs c and d takes account of the fact that national situations vary with regard to both the age of majority and the age at which such education may be completed. Depending on these circumstances, the wishes to be taken into account may be either those of the pupils themselves or those of their families.

84. It is recognised that not all education systems distinguish between secondary education and vocational education, the latter being merely regarded as a particular type of secondary education. Nevertheless, as made in sub-paragraphs c and d, this distinction takes account of the differences in systems of vocational training. In particular, in the case of countries where vocational training is largely carried out by means of apprenticeship and measures in favour of regional or minority languages are therefore difficult to apply, it enables the parties at least to accept the more stringent requirements in the field of general secondary education.

85. The provisions concerning university and adult education are comparable to those for other levels of education in as much as they offer an alternative between teaching in the regional or minority language and teaching of it as a subject of education. Morever, as in the case of pre-school education, a further solution is offered for those cases in which the public authorities have no direct competence for the type of education concerned. In certain states, the number of speakers of a regional or minority language might be judged insufficient for the provision of university education in or of that language. In this connection, the example has been cited of states which, by virtue either of a specific agreement or of a general agreement on the recognition of diplomas, recognise the university degree obtained by a speaker of a regional or minority language at a university of another state in which the same language is used.

86. Paragraph 1.g is motivated by a concern not to isolate the teaching of regional or minority languages from their cultural context. These languages are often related to a separate history and specific traditions. This history and regional or minority culture constitutes a component of Europe's heritage. It is accordingly desirable that non-speakers of the languages concerned should have access to it too.

87. Where a state undertakes to guarantee that a regional or minority language is taught, it must see that the necessary means are available in terms of finance, staff and teaching aids. This necessary consequence does not need to be specified in the charter. However, where staff are concerned, the question also arises of their competence and therefore of their training. This is a fundamental aspect, which is why specific provision is made for it in paragraph 1.h.

88. Considering the fundamental importance of teaching and, more specifically, of the school system, for the preservation of regional or minority languages, the CAHLR considered it necessary to provide for a specific body or bodies to monitor what was being done in this field. The characteristics of such a supervisory institution are not specified in paragraph 1.i. It could accordingly be an education authority body or an independent institution. This function could also be

conferred on the body provided for in Article 7, paragraph 4, of the charter. In any case, the charter requires the findings of the monitoring to be made public.

89. The charter normally confines the protection of regional or minority languages to the geographical area where they are traditionally spoken. But paragraph 2 of Article 8 constitutes an exception to this rule. It is motivated by the realisation that in modern circumstances of mobility the principle of territoriality may no longer be sufficient in practice for the effective protection of a regional or minority language. In particular, a substantial number of speakers of such languages have migrated to the major cities. However, in view of the difficulties involved in the extension of educational provision for regional or minority languages outside their traditional territorial base, Article 8, paragraph 2, is drafted flexibly in terms of the undertakings involved and in any case applies only where such measures are justified by the number of users of the language concerned.

Article 9 – Judicial authorities

90. Paragraph 1 of this article applies to those judicial districts in which the number of residents using the regional or minority languages justifies the measures concerned. This stipulation corresponds in part to the general rule in most of the provisions of the charter, which is concerned to protect regional or minority languages within the territory in which they are traditionally used. For higher courts located outside the territory in which the regional or minority language is used, it is then a matter for the state concerned to take account of the special nature of the judicial system and its hierarchy of instances.

91. The wording of the introductory sentence of Article 9, paragraph 1, also reflects the concern of the CAHLR to protect fundamental principles of the judicial system, such as equality of the parties and avoidance of undue delays in the process of law, against possible misuse of the facilities for recourse to regional or minority languages. This legitimate concern does not, however, justify any general restriction of a party's undertakings under this paragraph; rather, abuse of the possibilities offered will have to be determined by the judge in individual cases.

92. A distinction is made between criminal, civil and administrative proceedings and the options provided for are adapted to the particular nature of each. As is indicated by the words "and/or", some of these options may be adopted cumulatively.

93. The provisions of Article 9, paragraph 1, relate to proceedings before courts of law. Depending on the particular arrangements for the administration of justice obtaining in each state, the term "courts" should, where appropriate, be understood as covering other bodies exercising a judicial function. This is especially relevant in the case of sub-paragraph c.

94. The first option of sub-paragraphs a, b and c of Article 9, paragraph 1, employs the expression "conduct the proceedings in the regional or minority languages". This expression implies, at any rate, that the relevant regional or minority language is used in the courtroom and in those proceedings in which the party speaking this language takes part. However, it is up to each state, in the light of the particular characteristics of its judicial system, to determine the precise scope of the expression "conduct the proceedings".

95. It should be noted that paragraph 1.a.ii, whereby the parties undertake to guarantee the accused the right to use his/her regional or minority language, goes beyond the right of the accused, as laid down in Article 6, paragraph 3.e, of the

European Convention on Human Rights, to have the free assistance of an interpreter if he cannot understand or speak the language used in court. Like subparagraphs b.ii and c.ii, it is based on the consideration that even if speakers of a regional or minority language are able to speak the official language, when it comes to justifying themselves before a court of law, they may feel the need to express themselves in the language which is emotionally closest to them or in which they have greater fluency. It would therefore run counter to the purpose of the charter for its application to be limited to situations of practical necessity. On the other hand, given that this provision goes beyond the strictly human rights aspect by in effect giving a free choice to the accused and requires facilities to be provided in accordance with his or her decision, it was considered reasonable to allow states some discretion as to whether to accept it or not and to limit its application to certain judicial districts.

96. The purpose of paragraph 1.d is to provide that the translation or interpretation which may be rendered necessary by the application of Article 9, paragraphs 1.b and c, shall be free of charge. In the case of those states which do not choose this sub-paragraph, it is up to them to resolve this question either according to the existing legal provisions or by adopting new, specific provisions which would take account of the need to promote regional or minority languages. Consequently, the costs could be borne wholly or partly by the person who makes the request for a given act, or shared among the parties, etc.

97. Paragraph 2 concerns the validity of legal documents drawn up in a regional or minority language. Its scope is in fact limited in as much as it does not indicate all the conditions for the validity of a legal document but confines itself to stipulating that the fact that a document is drafted in a regional or minority language cannot by itself alone be a ground for denying its validity. Moreover, it does not preclude a state from providing for additional formalities in such a case, for example the need for a particular formula of certification to be added in the official language. Paragraph 2.b implies that the contents of the document invoked by the party using the regional or minority language are made known, directly or indirectly (advertisement, state information service, etc.), to the other party or to interested third parties who do not speak the regional or minority language, in a form they can understand.

98. The application of Article 9, paragraph 2, is without prejudice to the application of treaties and conventions on mutual assistance in legal matters, in each of which the question of the languages to be used is explicitly dealt with.

99. Paragraph 3 concerns the translation of legislative texts into regional or minority languages. The phrase "unless they are otherwise provided" refers to cases where the text already exists in a regional or minority language because it has already been translated into a similar or identical language which is the official language of another state.

Article 10 – Administrative authorities and public services

100. The purpose of this article is to allow the speakers of regional or minority languages to exercise their rights as citizens and fulfil their civic duties in conditions that respect their mode of expression.

101. The provisions are mainly designed to improve communication between the public authorities and those who use regional or minority languages. It is true

that social and cultural situations have evolved in such a way that the very great majority of the people speaking these languages are bilingual and able to use an official language in order to communicate with the public authorities. However, allowing the use of regional or minority languages in relations with those authorities is fundamental to the status of these languages and their development and also from a subjective standpoint. Clearly, if a language were to be completely barred from relations with the authorities, it would in fact be negated as such, for language is a means of public communication and cannot be reduced to the sphere of private relations alone. Furthermore, if a language is not given access to the political, legal or administrative sphere, it will gradually lose all its terminological potential in that field and become a "handicapped" language, incapable of expressing every aspect of community life.

102. Article 10 distinguishes, in the types of action taken by the public authorities, three categories:

– action by administrative authorities of the state: that is to say the traditional acts of the public authorities, especially in the form of the exercise of public prerogatives or powers under ordinary law (paragraph 1);

– action by local and regional authorities, that is general sub-national territorial authorities with powers of self-government (paragraph 2);

– action by bodies providing public services, whether under public or private law, where they remain under public control: postal services, hospitals, electricity, transport, and so on (paragraph 3).

103. In each field, with suitable adaptations to the specific nature of the authorities or bodies concerned, account is taken of the diversity of linguistic situations. In some cases the characteristics of the regional or minority language allow it to be recognised as a "quasi-official" language, thus making it, on its territory, a working language, or the normal means of communication, of the public authorities. (Recourse to the official or most widely-spoken language remains the norm in contacts with persons who do not speak the regional or minority language.) Alternatively, the language may at least be used in relations which such authorities may have with persons who address them in that language. Where, however, the objective situation of a regional or minority language makes such solutions impracticable, minimum undertakings are provided to safeguard the position of the speakers of the language concerned: oral or written applications or documents may legitimately be submitted in the regional or minority language, but without entailing any obligation to reply in that language.

104. The undertakings of the parties in paragraphs 1 and 3 are qualified by the phrase "as far as this is reasonably possible". This proviso is not intended to be a substitute for the exercise of the faculty, accorded to the parties by Articles 2, paragraph 2 and 3, paragraph 1, of omitting some of the provisions of Part III of the charter from their undertakings in respect of each particular language. However, it does seek to take account of the fact that some of the measures provided for have significant implications In terms of finance, staffing or training. An acceptance of a particular provision with respect to a given language necessarily entails a commitment to provide the resources and make the administrative arrangements required to render it effective. Nevertheless, it is recognised that there may be some circumstances in which total and unqualified application of the provision in question is not, or not yet, realistic. The phrase "as far as this is reasonably possible" allows the parties, in the implementation of the

relevant provisions, to determine in individual cases whether such circumstances obtain.

105. The terms of paragraph 2, and in particular the undertaking of the parties to "allow and/or encourage", are drafted so as to take account of the principle of local and regional autonomy. They do not signify that less importance is attached to the application of the provisions set out therein, which concern the public authorities closest to the citizen. More generally, the CAHLR was aware that the application of some of the charter's provisions falls within the competence of local or regional authorities and may entail substantial costs for those concerned. The parties should ensure that the implementation of the charter respects the principle of local autonomy as defined in the European Charter of Local Self-Government, and in particular its Article 9, paragraph 1, which stipulates that: "Local authorities shall be entitled, within national economic policy, to adequate financial resources of their own, of which they may dispose freely within the framework of their powers."

106. Paragraph 2.a provides for the use of regional or minority languages "within the framework" of the regional or local authority. This formulation is intended to indicate that a regional or minority language may be used as a working language by the authority concerned; however, it does not imply that the regional or minority language may be used when communicating with central government.

Article 11 – Media

107. The time and space which regional or minority languages can secure in the media is vital for their safeguard. Today no language can keep its influence unless it has access to the new forms of mass communications. The development of these throughout the world and the progress of technology are leading to the weakening of the cultural influence of less widely-spoken languages. For the major media, especially television, the size of the audience is generally the decisive factor. But regional and minority languages represent a small cultural market. Despite the new opportunities offered them by the advances in broadcasting technology, it remains true that to have access to the media they need public support. However, the media constitute a field where public intervention is limited and action by means of regulations is not very effective. The public authorities act in this field essentially by encouragement and the provision of aid. With a view to ensuring that such encouragement and aid is provided in support of regional or minority languages, the charter asks states to give undertakings on various levels.

108. The measures provided for in this article are for the benefit of the users of regional or minority languages within the respective geographical areas of those languages. However, the wording of paragraph 1 in this respect, which differs from the formulation in other articles, takes account of the special nature in particular of the audio-visual media. Thus even if the measures are taken with reference to a particular territory, their effects may extend well beyond it; on the other hand, the measures need not be taken within the territory in question, provided that they benefit those who live there.

109. It is recognised that the public authorities in the different states have varying degrees of control over the media. For this reason it is specified in paragraphs 1 and 3 that the extent of their commitment is determined by the extent of their competence, powers or legitimate role in this field. It is underlined, moreover, that in

every country the legitimate role of the state in creating the legal framework and conditions within which the purpose of this article can be achieved is circumscribed by the principle of the autonomy of the media.

110. Paragraph 1 of Article 11 makes a distinction between the undertakings which are proposed for the benefit of regional or minority languages in the field of radio and television, according to whether or not the latter carry out a public service mission. Such a mission, which may be performed by a public or private broadcasting body, involves the provision of a broad range of programmes including the consideration of minority tastes and interests. In this context the state can make provision (for instance, in legislation or in the broadcaster's specifications) for the broadcasting of programmes in regional or minority languages. Sub-paragraph a deals with this situation. On the other hand, where broadcasting is conceived as a purely private-sector function, the state can do no more than "encourage and/or facilitate" (sub-paragraphs b and c). Only the latter situation applies to the written press (sub-paragraph e). Where relevant, the undertaking given by the parties includes the allocation of the necessary frequencies to those broadcasting in regional or minority languages.

111. However minimal the role of the state may be in relation to the media, it normally at least retains the power to guarantee freedom of communication or take measures involving the elimination of obstacles to such freedom. For this reason, paragraph 2 does not contain the same proviso as paragraph 1 concerning the extent of the competence of public authorities. The undertaking to guarantee freedom of reception relates not only to obstacles deliberately placed in the way of the reception of programmes broadcast from neighbouring countries but also to passive obstacles resulting from the failure of the competent authorities to take any action to make such reception possible.

112. In view of the fact that broadcasts from a neighbouring state may not be subject to the same legitimate conditions as those produced on the relevant party's own territory, the third sentence of this paragraph introduces a safeguard which is worded in the same terms as Article 10, paragraph 2, of the European Convention on Human Rights concerning freedom of expression. It should be pointed out, however, with respect to television, that for those states which are parties to the European Convention on Transfrontier Television, the circumstances and conditions under which the freedoms guaranteed by Article 11, paragraph 2, of the charter can be restricted will be determined by that convention, in particular by the principle of non-restriction of the retransmission on their territories of programme services which comply with the terms of the Convention on Transfrontier Television. Moreover, the provisions of this paragraph do not affect the need for copyright to be respected.

113. Article 11, paragraph 3, provides for the representation of the interests of the users of regional or minority languages in the bodies responsible for ensuring media pluralism. Such structures exist in most European countries. The words "or taken into account" were inserted in response to the possible difficulties involved in determining who were the representatives of the users of these languages. However, the CAHLR considered that it was sufficient that the linguistic groups be represented on similar terms to other categories of the population. This could be arranged, for example, through the bodies representing regional or minority languages which are provided for in Article 7, paragraph 4, of the charter.

Article 12 – Cultural activities and facilities

114. In this field, as in the case of Article 11, states are asked to commit themselves to the extent to which the public authorities have competence, powers or a legitimate role, enabling them to take effective action. However, since the public authorities have an undoubted influence on the conditions in which cultural facilities are used, the charter requires them to see that regional or minority languages have an appropriate place in the functioning of such facilities.

115. In paragraph 1.a states are asked in general to encourage initiatives typical of the modes of cultural expression specific to regional or minority languages. The means for this support are those usually drawn on for cultural promotion purposes. The expression "the different means of access to works ..." covers – depending on the type of cultural activity concerned – publication, production, presentation, diffusion, transmission, and so on.

116. By reason of their limited number of speakers among the population, regional and minority languages do not have the same cultural productivity as the more widely-spoken languages. In order to promote their use and also allow their speakers access to a vast cultural heritage, it is therefore necessary to have recourse to the techniques of translation, dubbing, post-synchronisation and subtitling (paragraph 1.c). The avoidance of cultural barriers implies, however, a two-way process. It is therefore essential to the viability and status of regional or minority languages that important works produced in them should become known to a wider public. That is the purpose of paragraph 1.b.

117. With regard to the functioning of cultural institutions, that is to say of bodies whose function it is to undertake or support cultural activities in a variety of forms, states are asked to see that such institutions accord sufficient importance in their programmes to the knowledge and use of regional or minority languages and to their attendant cultures (Article 12, paragraph 1.d to f). The charter cannot of course specify how regional or minority languages are to be incorporated in the activities of these institutions. It speaks simply of making "appropriate allowance" for them. The role of states in this sphere is generally one of guidance and supervision; they are not asked to further this objective themselves, but merely to "ensure" that it is pursued.

118. The charter also provides for the creation for each regional or minority language of a body responsible for collecting, keeping a copy of and disseminating works in that language (Article 12, paragraph 1.g). Having regard to the weak situation in which many regional or minority languages find themselves, it is necessary to organise this type of work systematically, the manner of its organisation being left to states to decide. For the purposes of the implementation of this paragraph g, it may be necessary for certain states to adapt their legislation on legal deposit and archives so that the body envisaged can take part in the conservation of works in regional or minority languages.

119. The application of Article 12, paragraph 1, relates to the territory in which regional or minority languages are used, even though it is recognised that in practice many of its provisions have implications extending beyond that territory. However, having regard to the nature of cultural promotion and to needs arising outside of the areas in which the languages are traditionally used (in particular as a result of internal migration), Article 12, paragraph 2, introduces provisions corresponding to those of Article 8, paragraph 2.

120. All countries seek to promote their national culture abroad. In order to give a complete and faithful picture of that culture, such promotion should not neglect regional or minority languages and cultures. This undertaking, which is provided for in Article 12, paragraph 3, constitutes one way of applying the principle of the recognition of regional or minority languages embodied in Article 7, paragraph 1.a, of Part II of the charter.

Article 13 – Economic and social life

121. In the economic and social systems which characterise the Council of Europe countries, intervention by the public authorities in economic and social life is mainly confined to the promulgation of laws and regulations. In these circumstances, the possibilities of action on the part of the authorities to see that regional or minority languages receive due consideration in these sectors are limited. Nevertheless, the charter provides for a certain number of measures in this field. It seeks, on the one hand, to eliminate measures to ban or discourage the use of such languages in economic and social life and proposes, on the other hand, a number of positive measures.

122. The provisions of Article 13, paragraph 1, give concrete application to the principle of non-discrimination. This is why they are intended to apply throughout the territory of contracting states and not only in the parts of that territory where regional or minority languages are used.

123. Article 13, paragraph 2, of the charter lists various concrete measures in support of regional or minority languages in this sector. For practical reasons, they are confined to the geographical areas in which these languages are used. With regard to the proviso "as far as this is reasonably possible", reference should be made to the explanations under Article 10 above (see paragraph 104). Finally, the undertakings of the parties extend only as far as the public authorities have competence, a proviso which, however, is relevant only to sub-paragraph c.

Article 14 – Transfrontier exchanges

124. This article expands and develops the idea set out in Article 7, paragraph 1.i, and reference is therefore made to the explanations given above (see paragraphs 69–70).

125. In many fields, transfrontier co-operation develops between the neighbouring regions of different states. It is noted that in certain cases such a situation could still be seen as a problem in terms of territorial integrity. With European states now moving closer together, however, it now presents an opportunity for the states concerned to employ a "cultural factor" to enhance their mutual understanding. The Council of Europe has drawn up an outline convention on transfrontier co-operation at local and regional level. While it is desirable that such co-operation should develop in a general manner, paragraph b underlines that this is particularly the case where one and the same regional language is spoken on either side of the border.

126. The co-operation envisaged may extend to such matters as school twinnings, teacher exchanges, the mutual recognition of diplomas and qualifications, the joint organisation of cultural activities, the further circulation of cultural assets (books, films, exhibitions, etc) and the transfrontier activities of cultural

agencies (theatre companies, lecturers, etc). In some circumstances, it may also be a satisfactory (and less expensive) means of implementing undertakings entered into under other articles of the charter: for example, with respect to the provision of higher education facilities as laid down in Article 8, paragraph 1.e, a bilateral agreement could make arrangements for the students concerned to attend appropriate institutions in a neighbouring state.

Part IV – Application of the charter

(Articles 15–17)

127. To enable its application to be monitored by the Council of Europe, its member states and the general public, the charter has opted for a system of periodical reports by the parties on the action taken in pursuance of its provisions. The reports are triennial; however the first report, which is intended to describe the situation of the regional or minority languages at the time when the charter enters into force for the state concerned, is to be presented within one year of that date.

128. In order to ensure the efficiency of this system for monitoring the implementation of the charter, the latter provides for the setting up of a committee of experts to examine the reports submitted by the various parties. It will also be possible for the committee of experts to be approached by bodies or associations wishing to supply further information or describe specific situations relating to the application of the charter, especially Part III thereof (Article 16, paragraph 2). Only bodies legally established in one of the parties will have access to this committee of experts for matters concerning that party. The purpose of this rule is to prevent groups whose headquarters is outside the party concerned by the application of the charter from using the monitoring system set up under it to generate discord among the parties.

129. It should be emphasised that this is not a quasi-judicial complaints procedure. The committee of experts is merely instructed to monitor the implementation of the charter and receive information to that end. The bodies referred to in Article 16 may not ask it to act as a more or less judicial appeal body.

130. The committee of experts may verify any information submitted with the states concerned and must call on them for further explanations or information for the purposes of carrying out its investigations. The results will be communicated to the Committee of Ministers, together with the comments of the states concerned, on the occasion of the presentation of the experts' reports. Although it might appear that, in the interests of openness, these reports should be published automatically, it was felt that, since they might contain proposals for recommendations which the Committee of Ministers might make to one or more states, it should be left up to the Committee of Ministers to judge case by case to what extent the reports should be published.

131. The number of members of the committee of experts will be the same as the number of parties to the charter. They must be persons of recognised competence in the field of regional or minority languages. At the same time, by placing emphasis on the intrinsically personal trait of the "highest integrity", the charter makes clear that the experts appointed to the committee, in carrying out their task, should be free to act independently and not be subject to instructions from the governments concerned.

132. This machinery for the monitoring of the application of the charter by a committee of experts will make it possible to assemble a body of objective information concerning the situation of regional or minority languages, while respecting to the full the specific responsibilities of states.

Part V – Final provisions

133. The final clauses contained in Articles 18 to 23 are based on the model final clauses for conventions and agreements concluded within the Council of Europe.
134. It was decided not to include among these final provisions a territorial clause enabling states to exclude part of their territories from the scope of the charter. This is because it is already an intrinsic characteristic of the present charter that it is concerned especially with particular territories, namely those on which regional or minority languages are used; moreover, contracting states already have the right, under Article 3, paragraph 1, to specify those regional or minority languages to which their detailed undertakings will apply.
135. Under Article 21, the parties have the right to make reservations only in respect of paragraphs 2 to 5 of Article 7 of the charter. The CAHLR considered that contracting states should not have the possibility to make reservations with regard to Article 7, paragraph 1, since this paragraph contains objectives and principles. As far as Part III is concerned, it took the view that, in a text which already allowed the parties so much choice as to the undertakings they entered into, reservations would be inappropriate.
136. In view of the importance of the subject-matter of the charter for many states which are not, or not yet, members of the Council of Europe, it was decided that the charter should be an open convention, to which non-member states may be invited to accede (Article 20).

Appendix III

European Centre for Minority Issues (ECMI)

Flensburg Recommendations

on the Implementation of Policy Measures for Regional or
Minority Languages

(Adopted 24 June 2000)

EXPLANATORY NOTE

With support from the European Commission, and in close co-operation with the Council of Europe and the European Bureau for Lesser Used Languages, the *European Centre for Minority Issues* (ECMI) organised, on 23 and 24 June 2000, an international conference on "Evaluating policy measures for minority languages in Europe: Towards effective, cost-effective and democratic implementation". Participants included noted scholars in minority issues, representatives from major international organisations, non-governmental organisations, and member countries of the Council of Europe. The conference is an important element in a larger project on the analysis of policies adopted in favour of minority languages, particularly, but not exclusively, in the context of the *European Charter for Regional or Minority Languages*.

The European Charter for Regional or Minority Languages is a novel instrument in international law, in that its focus is not on the rights of minorities, but on languages themselves – although languages are, of course, used by individuals who belong to groups defined, among other possible criteria, by language. Hence, in the conference convened by ECMI, legal standards were taken as given, with debates emphasising instead issues of implementation.

Owing to the extreme degree of variability of situations between different regional or minority languages (and, of course, between the states in which these regional or minority languages are traditionally used), the purpose of the conference was not to make general recommendations regarding the set of specific measures that should be adopted in order to protect or revitalise these languages – this diversity of situations also explains the structure of the Charter itself, which gives states a wide range of options to choose from. Accordingly, the conference focused not on the specific measures that should adopted by states (whether such measures are adopted explicitly in order to comply with Charter obligations or not), but on *how* authorities at various levels choose policy measures in favour of regional or minority languages, because some very practical issues of decision-making arise in all cases. More precisely, emphasis was placed on how states can meet *principles* of good public policy, in particular: (i) aiming at *effective* policies; (ii) aiming at *cost-effective* policies; (iii) aiming at *democratic* policies.

The concepts of effectiveness and cost-effectiveness, as well as the characteristics of genuinely democratic policies in the context of language policy implementation, were discussed at length during the conference, generating consensus around the view that effectiveness, cost-effectiveness and democracy are among the core principles of "good practice".

The following *Recommendations*, reflecting the results of discussions during the conference, are intended as a means to draw attention to relevant principles in the selection, design, implementation and evaluation of policies in favour of regional or minority languages, as well as an instrument assisting authorities in implementing the *Charter*, with a view to helping states that have not yet ratified (or signed) the *Charter* to assess the practical implications of doing so, and to offering assistance to other organisations, particularly NGOs, involved in minority language policies.

The following recommendations will be forwarded to:

- the members of the Committee of Ministers and members of the Parliamentary Assembly of the Council of Europe
- the Secretary General of the Council of Europe
- the European Commission and members of the European Parliament
- the participating States of the OSCE and members of the Parliamentary Assembly of the OSCE
- the OSCE High Commissioner on National Minorities
- language planning bodies and language boards in charge of promoting regional or minority languages in Europe
- non-governmental organisations whose activity addresses minority issues, in particular minority languages
- other relevant minority organisations

Recommendations

Preamble

With the active help of the participants at the International Conference on *Evaluating Policy Measures for Minority Languages in Europe: Towards Effective, Cost-Effective and Democratic Implementation*, convened on 22 to 25 June by the *European Centre for Minority Issues* (ECMI) in Flensburg, Germany, the ECMI has formulated the following Recommendations.

These Recommendations are based on the firm conviction:

(a) that regional or minority languages constitute a crucial element of Europe's linguistic and cultural heritage;
(b) that linguistic and cultural diversity is valuable resources contributing to the overall quality of life of all residents in Europe, and must therefore be recognised as a contribution to general welfare;
(c) that the maintenance and revitalisation of regional or minority languages, allowing for their vitality in the long term, represents a core element of the identity of individual speakers of these languages, and as such represents a relevant policy goal in a human rights perspective;

(d) that the maintenance and revitalisation of regional or minority languages requires committed and tangible support from states and international organisations;

(e) that the maintenance and revitalisation of regional or minority languages is an issue taking on increasing saliency, as evidenced among others by the declaration of 2001 as the *European Year of Languages*, both by the Council of Europe and the European Union.

Participants at the Conference further note that there is a need, beyond the political dimensions and legal issues involved, for developing analytical and technical guidelines for the selection, design, implementation and evaluation of policy measures. While these guidelines must take account of the considerable diversity of cases and conditions, it is possible to formulate general principles and guidelines of good governance towards the management of linguistic diversity, with particular regard for regional or minority languages. These Recommendations therefore aim at contributing to the necessary bridge-building between analytical principles of good policy and practical modalities for the selection, design, implementation and evaluation of policies.

Participants at the Conference share the view that the resulting guidelines can be useful for states considering, planning or evaluating policy measures for regional or minority languages. Furthermore, such guidelines can also be useful for the communities using the regional or minority languages concerned, as well as for the civil society organisations also concerned with the preservation and promotion of linguistic diversity in Europe.

These ECMI Recommendations are formulated with particular reference to the implementation of the *European Charter for Regional or Minority Languages* of the Council of Europe opened for signature on 5 November 1992. States are therefore urged to accede to the *Charter* as soon as possible while ensuring that accession is rapidly followed by the adoption of policies reflecting the guidelines in these Recommendations, in compliance with the spirit and letter of the *Charter*.

It is the belief of the participants that the principles for the selection, design, implementation and evaluation of policy measures outlined in the present Recommendations can also be relevant in a broader range of policy contexts. The Participants at the Conference therefore underline the relevance of:

(a) the Framework Convention for the Protection of National *Minorities*;

(b) the *Oslo Recommendations Regarding the Linguistic Rights of National Minorities*;

(c) the *Hague Recommendations Regarding the Education Rights of National Minorities*;

(d) the *Lund Recommendations on the Effective Participation of National Minorities in Public Life*;

(e) the relevant resolutions of the European Parliament;

(f) the relevant recommendations of the Parliamentary Assembly of the Council of Europe.

In order to meet the obligations to which they subscribe by acceding to the *Charter*, states are urged to take into consideration the following guidelines.

I. Recognising the role and importance of minority language policy[1]

1. MINORITY LANGUAGES AND LINGUISTIC AND CULTURAL DIVERSITY: In addition to their relevance in the definition of human rights and minority rights standards, regional or minority languages should be explicitly recognised as essential elements of linguistic and cultural diversity as well as an important aspect of the identity of users of the regional or minority languages.
2. IMPORTANCE OF MINORITY LANGUAGE POLICY: In line with the standards developed in international instruments as mentioned in the *Preamble*, and taking account of the intrinsic value of linguistic and cultural diversity, governments should recognise the selection, design, implementation and evaluation of policies in favour of regional or minority languages as necessary tasks making a crucially important contribution to the good governance of modern societies.

II. Identification of and agreement on clear aims and principles

3. CLARITY OF AIMS: The successful implementation of minority language policies requires their aims to be clearly identified, defining in particular the criteria to be used to assess the attainment of policy goals by a particular set of measures.
4. CLARITY OF PRINCIPLES: Realising these aims requires good policy principles for the selection, design, implementation and evaluation of the corresponding policies, as described in particular in the following paragraphs of these Recommendations.

III. Recognising and applying good policy principles

5. PRINCIPLES OF GOOD POLICY AND THEIR ADAPTATION: "Good policy" is to be understood as an approach to public policy stressing in particular, though not exclusively, the effectiveness, the cost-effectiveness and the democratic nature of policies.
6. EFFECTIVENESS: Policies selected should be demonstrably effective, promising to result in a significant improvement in the position, status, use (or other relevant criterion) of the regional or minority language(s) being promoted.
7. ANALYSING AND SPELLING OUT EFFECTIVENESS: Effective policies require proper identification of the aims pursued, of the resources used, and of the processes through which policies can realise these aims. This requires in particular the proper identification of the needs and demands of the regional or minority languages for which policies are intended, and the supply, by the state or its surrogates, of appropriately defined facilities for minority language learning and use.
8. RECOGNISING URGENCY: The issue of the effectiveness of policies must be given particularly sustained attention in the case of particularly threatened

---

1. Throughout the four Sections of these Recommendations, the expression "minority language(s)" refers to "regional or minority language(s)" in the sense of the *European Charter for Regional or Minority Languages*. The same applies to the expression "minority language policy/policies".

languages, with a view to restoring, wherever possible, the conditions for the natural maintenance and development of all regional or minority languages.

9. COST-EFFECTIVENESS: Policies should be demonstrably cost-effective. The principle of cost-effectiveness, which is only a means to an end, is entirely compatible with adequate provisions for regional or minority languages, and requires a well-managed use of resources towards achieving desirable results. Cost-effectiveness favours the transparent use of resources allocated to minority language policy and demonstrates the authorities' commitment to good policies; it is therefore a key factor for the acceptability, among majority opinion, of minority language policies. Demonstrated cost-effectiveness should be seen as an opportunity for increasing the aggregate volume of resources made available to minority language promotion.

10. DEMOCRATIC PROCESSES: Policy measures must be adopted through a *demonstrably democratic policy process*. Throughout the policy process, it is necessary to ensure broad consultation and participation, including through non-formal channels complementing the normal institutions of democratic states. Civil society organisations, including in particular non-governmental organisations, as well as the general public should therefore be encouraged to play an active role at all stages of this process, ensuring that the dynamic evolution of social and economic needs over time is duly taken into account.

11. AVAILABLE EXPERIENCE: Throughout the policy process in any given context, it is important to learn from the experience in good practices and from the successes already achieved in other contexts through appropriate measures in favour of regional or minority languages.

IV. Establishing the necessary structures

12. ANALYSIS AND RESEARCH: In order to develop States' capacity to adopt appropriate policy measures in favour of minority languages, particularly in the context of the *European Charter for Regional or Minority Languages*, it is important for the authorities to provide facilities and support, including through applied academic research, for the study of the corresponding policies.

13. SHARING, EXCHANGING AND DISSEMINATING INFORMATION: Civil servants and other social actors involved in the selection, design, implementation and evaluation of minority language policies can gather considerable and valuable information and experience in the course of their activities. It is essential for this information and experience to be regularly exchanged and disseminated through widely accessible publications, meetings, etc. In particular, the attention of public opinion must be drawn to success already achieved in the revitalisation of regional or minority languages.

14. EXPERT ADVICE: The Council of Europe, possibly with participation of the *European Bureau for Lesser Used Languages* (EBLUL), the OSCE, UNESCO, and other relevant organisations and research institutions, should establish a panel of independent experts whose services would be available to help governments and communities in the selection, design, implementation and evaluation of regional or minority language policies.

15. INDEPENDENT EVALUATION AND MONITORING: All policies should be evaluated at appropriate intervals, and their implementation and effects monitored by

independent experts. As a general rule, these independent evaluations should be made widely accessible to the public and the media.

16. DEMOCRATIC DEBATE: States should establish the institutions and structures, for example in the form of regularly held *Estates General* of minority language policy, which will provide the necessary fora for such discussion. These fora must be open and accessible to individuals and organisations, including those emanating from the minority language communities concerned, and place particular emphasis on ensuring that relatively powerless individuals and groups have unrestricted access to these fora.

17. INTEGRATION IN ACTUAL POLICIES: Authorities, with the support of international organisations, in particular the Council of Europe, should ensure that the inputs from academic research, expert panels, independent evaluators, as well as from open democratic debate on successive stages of the policy process, are efficiently integrated into the actual selection, design, implementation and evaluation of policy measures.

V. Further recommendations

18. SIGN LANGUAGES: Due recognition should also be given to Sign Languages. The Council of Europe and other international organisations should consider the desirability and feasibility of preparing a legal instrument to safeguard these languages and the rights of their users. Likewise, the European Commission is requested to sympathetically consider the inclusion of actions to support Sign Languages in their language programmes.

The ECMI is a non-partisan, bi-national institution founded in 1996 by the Governments of the Kingdom of Denmark, the Federal Republic of Germany, and the Land of Schleswig-Holstein. Its three main missions are information, constructive conflict management, and practice-oriented research in minority–majority relations.

ECMI – Schiffbrücke 12 – D-24939 Flensburg, Germany tel.: (+49) 461-141-490 – fax: (+49) 461 141-4919 – internet: http:www.ecmi.de

Appendix IV: Selected Internet Resources

The following is a selection of web sites offering relevant information on regional or minority language policy and related topics. This list is not an exhaustive one. First, it had to be restricted to resources that are relatively directly connected with policy issues and the corresponding background; with a few exceptions, the sites of non-official organisations devoted to specific languages are therefore excluded. Second, the Internet is a rapidly changing reality, and new resources regularly come into existence, while others are no longer maintained or updated. In all cases, the opinions and information provided in the web sites listed below remain the sole responsibility of the persons and organisations who run them, and do not necessarily reflect the views of the author and co-authors of this book or the institutions to which they are affiliated. This list was updated on 1 August 2002.

General information, academic and other research institutions

Aménagement linguistique dans le monde
http://www.tlfq.ulaval.ca/axl/

This site presents the linguistic portrait and language policy of 226 States or autonomous regions spread over 131 countries. This source is linked to Laval University's Centre interdisciplinaire de recherches sur les activités langagières (CIRAL) at http://www.ciral.ulaval.ca/, which contains a wealth of specialist information on language research.

Centre for Multilingual Multicultural Research (CMMR)
http://www.usc.edu/dept/education/CMMR

The CMMR, located at the University of Southern California, seeks to facilitate the research collaboration, dissemination and professional development activities of students and educational institutions. The Centre provides a base for those interested in multilingual education, multicultural education and related areas.

COMIR
http://lgi.osi.hu/comir/

COMIR is an Internet-based cooperative project of some 14 institutions. It develops and promotes virtual libraries, mailing lists, a database of full-text documents, training materials, etc. The COMIR site provides access to co-ordinated mailing lists, a meta-search engine across founders' web sites, a Minority Rights Practitioners Resource Pack, a best practice database, legal documentary sources, etc.

eLandnet: Europe
http://www.elandnet.org/

This site provides information on national minorities and offers different categories of links on culture, language, history, religion, etc.; it also offers extensive general links.

Endangered Languages Fund
http://sapir.ling.yale.edu/~elf

The Endangered Language Fund, hosted at Yale University, is devoted to the scientific study and the maintenance of endangered languages. It supports efforts originated by the native community or the scholar planning to work with a language. The ELF site also proposes a list of endangered languages links.

Ethnologue
http://www.sil.org/ethnologue.introduction.html

Extensive information on an unparalleled range of languages can be found here. Ethnologue is linked to SIL International, formerly known as the Summer Institute of Linguistics (SIL), http://www.sil.org/, which is a religious organisation.

Eurolang
http://www.eurolang.net/

This site informs on current developments on minority languages and inter-ethnic issues across Europe. It also provides background information on lesser-used languages in EU member states. In addition, an Archives section offers special reports.

Euromosaic
http://campus.uoc.es/euromosaic/

The Euromosaic website is linked to the report of the same name that was commissioned by the European Union in the early 1990s to provide detailed information on each language community of the EU. The site contains information and links about 39 regional or minority languages in the EU.

European Centre for Minority Issues (Flensburg, Germany)
http://www.ecmi.de/

The ECMI web site provides information about the activities of the centre in the field of majority–minority relations across Europe. Specialised publications can be downloaded free. The site maintains a growing list (currently over 450) of internet links to other websites dealing with minority issues.

European Language Council/Conseil Européen pour les Langues
http://www.solki.jyu.fi/elc/elcm.htm

The European Language Council aims to contribute to the quantitative and qualitative improvement of knowledge on the languages and cultures of the European Union and beyond. Its also aims to play a role in language policy making at a European level, while creating the framework and conditions necessary for common policy development. The website offers information about conferences organised by the ELC.

European Languages Resources Association (ELRA)
http://www.icp.inpg.fr/ELRA/home.html

The ELRA was established in order to promote the creation, verification, and distribution of language resources in Europe, with an emphasis on language engineering and language technology, in cooperation with the ELDA (European Language resources Distribution Agency).

European Minority Languages
http://www.smo.uhi.ac.uk/saoghal/mion-chanain/en/

This website provides access to further links on about over 80 European languages, including a broad range of lesser-used languages. The information is often philological, rather than sociolinguistic, institutional or policy-oriented.

European Research Centre on Migration and Ethnic Relations (ERCOMER)
http://www.ercomer.org/

ERCOMER, located at the University of Utrecht (Netherlands), is a research centre with a strong interest in comparative research in the fields of international migration, ethnic relations, racism and ethnic conflict within the European context. An affiliated group of researchers from the Department of Cross-Cultural Studies in Utrecht focuses on family policy and family relations including also ethnic minority families. The site provides access to research projects information and a rich list of publications.

Foundation for Endangered Languages
http://www.ogmios.org/

The Foundation aims to raise awareness of endangered languages, to support their use, to monitor linguistic policies and practices, and to support the documentation of endangered languages. It organises conferences, offers financial assistance, training, or facilities for the publication of results. The Foundation does not have a specifically European focus. The site reports on these activities.

GeoNative
http://www.geocities.com/Athens/9479/tables.html

The GeoNative websites provides information on some 233 minority languages in Europe, the former Soviet Union, and the Americas.

Gesellschaft für bedrohte Sprachen
http://www.uni-koeln.de/gbs/index.html

The goal of this German non-profit society is to promote the use, the preservation, and the documentation of endangered languages and dialects. The website reports on the activities of the society and contains a valuable set of links to other relevant websites.

I love languages
http://www.ilovelanguages.com/

A comprehensive catalogue of internet resources covering some 200 languages, with a focus on language learning, and an extensive collection of links to other organisations.

INCORE: Initiative on Conflict Resolution and Ethnicity
http://www.incore.ulst.ac.uk/

INCORE, based at the University of Ulster, is part of the United Nations University. It undertakes research and policy work on the resolution of ethnic, political and religious conflicts; it includes a Policy and Evaluation Unit which investigates 'best practice' in conflict management. The site offers in particular a valuable Information Bank in Conflict Resolution and Ethnicity on the Internet as well as further documentary resources.

Language futures Europe
http://web.inter.nl.net/users/Paul.Treanor/eulang.html

This very original (and somewhat idiosyncratic) privately-run website contains useful links on language policy, multilingualism, the dominance of English, and global language structures.

Linguasphere
http://www.linguasphere.org/

The Linguasphere Observatory is an independent and transnational research network devoted to the study and promotion of multilingualism and the exploration of our global linguistic environment. The site contains extracts from the *Linguasphere Register of the World's Languages and Speech Communities* and further access to a wide spectrum of documentary resources.

Mercator-Education
http://www.mercator-education.org/

The Mercator Project was set up in 1987 with the help of the European Commission to collect documentation and information and to carry out research on minority or regional languages. Mercator-Education, based in Friesland, is one of its three thematic networks. The site provides a wealth of information, particularly in the form of annotated links , on-line data bases (register of organisations and a bibliography of over 4,000 titles) and 24 dossiers on education in the minority languages of the EU.

Mercator-Legislation
http://www.troc.es/ciemen/mercator/index-gb.htm

Mercator – Linguistic Law and Legislation, based in Barcelona, has as its main goal to build a comprehensive data base of legal and/or normative documents making up Europe's linguistic frame, especially from the European Union institutions and languages. In addition to a rich set of links to other sites and access do on-line data bases, the site is particularly valuable as a source of international legal texts and national constitutions and legislation.

Mercator-Media
http://www.aber.ac.uk/~merwww/

Mercator-Media concentrates on information gathering and research about minority language media (including radio, television, film, newspapers, magazine and book publishing, archives and libraries and electronic data storage and networks). The site provides a list of the network's specialised publications, as well as access to a data base (http://mercator.inf.aber.ac.uk/) of minority language radio and television stations, publishers, etc.

MINELRES – Minority Electronic Resources
http://www.riga.lv/minelres/

MINELRES, based in Riga, is a directory of resources on minority human rights and related problems of the transition period in Central and Eastern Europe. It also offers a very active e-mail information service carrying news about minorities in the region (http://lists.delfi.lv/mailman/listinfo/minelres).

Minorities at Risk Project
http://www.geocities.com/~patrin/marp.htm

The Minorities at Risk Project, based at the University of Maryland, contains extensive information about Roma communities.

Minority Languages Links
http://biblioteca.udg.es/fl/aucoc/min_link.htm

This website based at the University of Girona (Catalonia) contains a collections of links to information sources about a wide range of European minority languages, and further links to information sources about minorities and linguistic diversity.

Minority languages of Russia on the Net
http://www1.peoples.org.ru/eng_index.html

A rich source of regularly updated information in English and in Russian on the Russian Federation.

MOST Clearing House
http://www.unesco.org/most/

The UNESCO's 'MOST' Programme (Management of Social Transformation) addresses issues such as language rights, democratic governance in multilicultural and multiethnic societies, etc.). The site provides information on the related research activities and publications, as well as links to relevant documentary sources.

Red Book of the Peoples of the Russian Empire
http://www.eki.ee/books/redbook/

This site contains information on a wide range of threatened languages and cultures in the Russian Federation.

Terralingua: Language Diversity and Biological Diversity
http://www.terralingua.org/

The association Terralingua aims to support the perpetuation and continued development of the world's linguistic diversity and to explore the connections between linguistic, cultural and biological diversity. The regularly updated website offers a varied set of links, including to the very informative *Langscape* quarterly newsletter.

UCLA Languages Materials Project
http://www.lmp.ucla.edu/default.htm

The Language Materials Project of the University of California in Los Angeles contains more than 11,000 citations covering over 900 languages, providing bibliographic references to language teaching materials for the less commonly taught languages. 40 of the languages are accompanied by detailed linguistic profiles that contain a map showing the geographical distribution of the language and a description of key dialects, grammatical features, and a historical background.

UC Linguistic Minority Research Institute
http://lmri.ucsb.edu/abtlmri/tocabout.htm

The Linguistic Minority Research Institute is a multi-campus research unit of the University of California. The web site provides information to researchers, students, practitioners, and policymakers interested in issues of language, education, and public policy, especially as they relate to linguistic minorities in the USA.

UNESCO Red Book on Endangered Languages: Europe
http://www.helsinki.fi/~tasalmin/eur_index.html

An extensive set of links to other websites on endangered languages, autochthonous European languages, non-regional languages and diaspora dialects.

Yamada Language Centre
http://babel.uoregon.edu/yamada/guides.html

The *Yamada Language Guides* contain information on 115 languages and 112 special fonts for 40 languages. The languages are listed alphabetically.

Selected internet journals on language and/or education

Annual Review of Applied Linguistics
(Editor: Mary McGroarty)
http://uk.cambridge.org/journals/apl/

The journal provides a comprehensive, up-to-date review of research in key areas in the broad field of applied linguistics.

Bilingual Family Newsletter
(Editor: Marjukka Grover)
http://www.multilingualmatters.com/

This Newsletter publishes short informative articles on current thoughts on language learning, bilingualism, biculturalism, mother tongue, schools, etc. It also publishes descriptions of how particular families have handled particular multilingual situations, assessing problems encountered and how these were overcome.

Current Issues in Language Planning
(Editors: Robert B. Kaplan & Richard B. Baldauf Jr.)
http://cilp.arts.usyd.edu.au/

This journal provides substantial review studies focusing on the very diverse language policy and language planning literature.

Current Issues in Language & Society
(Editor: Sue Wright)
http://www.multilingualmatters.com/

This journal publishes the proceedings of the regularly held Aston Symposium. An invited audience of experts on a particular subject area devote a full day to the consideration and constructive criticism of an invited discussion paper.

DiversCité Langues – Revue et forums interdisciplinaires sur la dynamique des langues
http://www.teluq.uquebec.ca/diverscite/entree.htm
(Editor: Angéline Martel)

This site (in French) contains an on-line journal and an interdisciplinary forum to promote discussion on the dynamics of language. The aim is to increase interest in the interrelations between linguistic and sociocultural phenomena.

Estudios de Sociolingüística
(Editors: Xoan Paolo Rodrigues-Yanez, Anxo M. Lorenzo Suarez, Fernando Ramallo)
http://www.linguistlist.org/issues/11/11-2619.html

EdS targets a specialised national and international readership. In addition to sociolinguistics, *EdS* leaves room for contributions about interactional linguistics, linguistic anthropology, language acquisition and socialisation, etc.

Evaluation & Research in Education
(Editor: Steve Higgins)
http://www.multilingualmatters.com/

This journal aims to make methods of evaluation and research in education available to teachers, administrators and research workers. The journal publishes report evaluations and research findings focusing on conceptual and methodological issues.

International Journal of Bilingual Education and Bilingualism
(Editor: Colin Baker)
http://www.multilingualmatters.com/multi/

This journal aims to spread international developments, initiatives, ideas and research on bilingualism and bilingual education, and to ensure collaboration between scholars and practitioners from different continents.

International Journal of the Sociology of Language
(General editor: Joshua A. Fishman)
http://www.degruyter.de/journals/ijsl/

The *IJSL* is dedicated to the development of the sociology of language and seeks to contribute to the growth of language-related knowledge, applications, values, and sensitivities. Contributions are particularly invited on small languages and small language communities.

Journal of Multilingual & Multicultural Development
(Editor: John Edwards)
http://www.multilingualmatters.com/

The *JMMD* publishes a broad range of articles on different aspects of multilingualism and multiculturalism (research studies, descriptions of educational policies and systems, accounts of teaching or learning strategies and assessment procedures).

Journal of Sociolinguistics
(Editors: Allan Bell and Nikolas Coupland)
http://www.blackwellpublishers.co.uk/journals/JOSL/descript.htm

The *Journal of Sociolinguistics* is an international forum for multi-disciplinary research on language and society, which promotes sociolinguistics as a thoroughly linguistic and thoroughly social-scientific endeavour.

Language Awareness
(Editor: Peter Garrett)
http://www.multilingualmatters.com/

The journal encourages and disseminates work on the role of targeted knowledge about language learning, language teaching and language use processes.

Language, Culture and Curriculum
(Editor: Eoghan Mac Aogáin)
http://www.multilingualmatters.com/

This journal provides a forum for the discussion of social, cultural, cognitive and organisational factors relevant to the formulation and implementation of language curricula. Second languages, minority and heritage languages are a special concern.

Language and Education
(Editor: Viv Edwards)
http://www.multilingualmatters.com/

Language & Education provides a forum for the discussion of recent topics and issues in the language disciplines which have an immediate bearing upon thought and practice in education.

Language and Intercultural Communication
(Editors: Michael Kelly and Alice Tomic)
http://www.multilingualmatters.com/

This journal aims to promote understanding of the relationship between language and intercultural communication, and seeks to make an effective contribution to disseminating new ideas and examples of good practice in educating students in language and intercultural communication.

Language Policy
(Editors: Bernard Spolsky and Elana Shohamy)
http://www.kluweronline.com/issn/1568-4555/current

A new journal that aims to contribute to the maturity of language policy as a scientific field through high-quality analytical and theoretical contributions.

Language Problems and Language Planning
(Editors: Probal Dasgupta and Humphrey Tonkin)
http://www.benjamins.com/jbp/journals/Lplp_info.html

The journal publishes articles primarily on political, sociological, and socioeconomic aspects of language and language use. It is especially concerned with interlingualism and relationships between and among language communities.

Language, Society and Culture
(Editors: Thao Lê and Quynh Lê)
http://www.educ.utas.edu.au/users/tle/JOURNAL/JournalF.html

Language, Society and Culture is an on-line journal publishing articles and reports dealing with theoretical as well as practical issues focusing on the link between language, society and culture within a socio-cultural context or beyond its boundaries.

Llengua i Ús
http://cultura.gencat.es/llengcat/publicacions/liu.htm

Llengua i ús, published in Catalan only, may be the most specialised of all the journals listed here; it defines itself as a technical review of language policy, and has a clear, though not exclusive focus on language planning in Catalan-speaking regions.

Mercator Media Forum
(Editor: George Jones)
http://www.aber.ac.uk/~merwww/engintro.htm

This annual journal promotes discussion and the flow of information between those who work in or on the non-state languages of the European Union in the field of media. The journal is published on behalf of the Mercator-Media programme at the University of Wales, Aberystwyth, with support from the European Union.

MOST Journal on Multicultural Societies
(Editor: Matthias Koenig)
http://www.unesco.org/most/jmshome.htm

MOST, which is published on-line, offers quality theme issues on ethnic, linguistic and cultural diversity and related issues.

Multilingua
(Editor: Richard Watts)
http://www.degruyter.de/journals/multilin/

Multilingua is an international interdisciplinary journal aimed at the enhancement of cross-cultural understanding through the study of interlanguage communication; its focus is on pragmatic linguistics rather than sociolinguistics or language policy issues.

The Linguist List – Journals
http://www.linguistlist.org/journal.html#languages

This web site gives a useful list of journals on languages and languages groups, sociolinguistics, general linguistics, and other related areas.

Selected international organisations dealing with regional or minority language issues

Council of Europe
http://www.coe.int/

The Council of Europe web site contains the texts of all Conventions and Charters together with updated listings of the countries that sign and ratify them. Also relevant on the Council of Europe web site is the home page of the Congress of Local and Regional Authorities at http://www.coe.fr/cplre/indexe.htm.

The Council of Europe also maintains the European Centre for Modern Languages in Graz (Austria) (http://www.ecml.at/) whose mission is the implementation of language policies and the promotion of innovative approaches to the learning and teaching of modern languages.

European Bureau for Lesser-Used Languages
http://www.eblul.org/

The Bureau is a key player in the field of regional and minority languages. It is actively engaged, with support from the European Union, in the conservation and preservation of the autochthonous regional or minority languages in EU member states. *Contact Bulletin*, the newsletter of the Bureau can be found in this site.

European Union
http://europa.eu.int/comm/education/langmin.html

Europa is the main internet portal to EU institutions, policy programmes, and news releases. The above address informs about EU activity in the field of RML protection and promotion.

Organisation for Security and Cooperation in Europe
http://www.osce.org/

The web site of the OSCE contains information on the organisation's activities concerning (mostly 'national') minorities in Central and Eastern Europe. Through its Office for Democratic Institutions and Human Rights (ODIHR), the OSCE also offers the 'Legislation on line' service (http://www.legislationline. org/). This free-of-charge online service compiles international texts and domestic legislation in the OSCE region (55 countries located in the Caucasus, Central Asia, Europe and North America) dealing with the rule of law and the protection of human rights and fundamental freedoms.

United Nations
http://www.un.org/

The United Nations' web pages provide access to relevant UN legal documents.

Selected official or semi-official language policy bodies in Europe

In this last section, only a small number of institutions has been retained. The selection criteria applied are that the action of these offices takes place in Europe, that they focus on language policy, or that language issues significantly impacts on their activity in other areas (e.g. regional development).

Bwrdd yr Iaith Gymraeg/Welsh Language Board/(Wales, UK)
http://www.bwrdd-yr-iaith.org.uk

The Welsh Language Board aims to promote and facilitate the use of the Welsh language on a basis of equality with English; its mission is also to help ensure a healthy future for the language.

Comunn na Gàidhlig (Scotland, UK)
http://www.cnag.org.uk/

Comunn na Gàidhlig (CnaG) was established with support from the Scottish Office as a co-ordinating Gaelic development agency. CnaG is a company with charitable status operating at regional and national levels.

Délégation générale à la langue française et aux langues de France/General Delegation to the French Language and languages of France (France)
http://www.dglf.culture.gouv.fr/

The DGLF is an administrative structure linked to France's Ministry of Culture, whose remit includes not only the promotion of the French, but also of plurilingualism; it covers the regional languages of France and of France's overseas territories. This structure, which operates as a think tank, provides studies and documents for the ministries, other publics bodies, and associations dealing with linguistic matters.

Direcció General de Política Lingüística / Directorate General of Language Policy (Catalonia)
http://cultura.gencat.net/llengcat/

The DGPL is the General Directorate of Linguistic Policy of the autonomous government of Catalonia. Its aims are to give impetus to the development of linguistic legislation and to monitor the implementation of linguistic policy. It is linked to other state structures (the Consortium for Language Normalisation; the Terminological Centre; the Social Council for the Catalan Language; and the Institute of Catalan Studies), which together constitute what may be the most active hub of language policy worldwide.

Hizkuntza Politikarako Sailburuordetza/Viceconsejería de política lingüística/Deputy Ministry for Language policy (Basque Country)
http://www.euskadi.net/euskara_hps/indice_c.htm

The Deputy Ministry is in charge of the various programmes that make up the strongly structured policy for the promotion of the Basque language in the Autonomous Basque region of Spain.

Údarás na Gaeltachta/Gaeltacht Authority
http://www.udaras.ie/

The Údaras is a Regional Development Agency with responsibility for the economic, social and cultural development of the Gaeltacht (historically Irish-speaking regions), in order to encourage continuing use of the Irish language in these regions.

Bibliography

Albanese, Ferdinando, 1999: 'The position of the European Charter for Regional or Minority Languages in the general context of the protection of minorities', in *Implementation of the European Charter for Regional or Minority Languages*. Strabourg: Council of Europe, 25–9.

Ambrose, John, and Williams, Colin, 1989: 'On the Spatial Definition of Minority: Scale as an Influence on the Geolinguistic Analysis of Welsh', in E. Haugen (ed.), *Minority Languages Today*. Edinburgh: Edinburgh University Press, 53–71.

Anderson, Benedict, 1991: *Imagined Communities* (2nd edn). London: Verso.

Baggioni, Daniel, 1997: *Langues et nations d'Europe*. Paris: Payot.

Baker, Colin, 1992: *Attitudes and Language*. Clevedon: Multilingual Matters.

Baker, Colin, 2001: *Foundations of Bilingual Education and Bilingualism*. Clevedon: Multilingual Matters.

Bastardas Boada, Albert, 1987: 'L'aménagement linguistique en Catalogne au XXe siècle', in J. Maurais (ed.), *Politique et aménagement linguistiques*. Paris: Le Robert, 121–58.

Becker, Gary, 1976: *The Economic Approach to Human Behavior*. Chicago: University of Chicago Press.

Benhabib, Seyla (ed.), 1996: *Democracy and Difference. Contesting the Boundaries of the Political*. Princeton: Princeton University Press.

Benoît-Rohmer, Florence, 1999: *Les minorités, quels droits?* Strasbourg: Éditions du Conseil de l'Europe.

Blumentwitz, Dieter, 1996: 'Das Recht auf Gebrauch der Minderheitensprache. Gegenwärtiger Stand und Entwicklungstendenzen im Europäischen Völkerrecht', in Bott-Bodenhausen, Karin (ed.), *Unterdrückte Sprachen. Sprachverbote und das Recht auf Gebrauch der Minderheitensprachen*. Frankfurt/ Main: Peter Lang, 159–203.

Breathnach, Diarmaid (ed.), 1998: *Mini guide to the lesser used languages of the European union – mini-manuel des langues moins répandues de l'Union européenne*. Dublin: European Bureau for Lesser Used Languages.

Brunner, Georg and Meissner, Boris (eds), 1999: *Das Recht der nationalen Minderheiten in Osteuropa*. Berlin: Berlin Verlag Arno Spitz.

Calvet, Louis-Jean, 1987: *La guerre des langues et les politiques linguistiques*.

Calvet, Louis-Jean, 1996: *Les politiques linguistiques*. Paris: Presses Universitaires de France.

Capotorti, Francesco, 1991: *Study on the Rights of Persons Belonging to Ethnic, Religious and Linguistic Minorities*. New York: United Nations.

Cardinal, Linda, and Hudon, Marie-Ève, 2001: *The Governance of Canada's Official Language Minorities: a Preliminary Study*. Ottawa: Office of the Commissioner of Official Languages.

Churchill, Stacey, 1986: *The Education of Linguistic and Cultural Minorities in the OECD Countries*. Clevedon: Multilingual Matters.

Coimisiún na Gaeltachta [Gaeltacht Commission], 2002: Report/Tuarascáil. Baile Átha Cliath [Dublin]: Department of Arts, Heritage, Gaeltacht and Islands.

Cornes, Richard, and Sandler, Todd, 1996: *The Theory of Externalities, Public Goods and Club Goods* (2nd edn). Cambridge: Cambridge University Press.

Council of Europe, 1998a: *International conference on the European Charter for Regional or Minority Languages*. Strasbourg: Council of Europe.

Council of Europe, 1998b: *Les langues vivantes: apprendre, enseigner, évaluer. Un cadre européen commun de référence* (Conseil de la coopération culturelle, Comité de l'éducation). Strasbourg: Council of Europe.

Council of Europe, 1999: *Implementation of the European Charter for Regional or Minority Languages*. Strasbourg: Council of Europe.

Cooper, Robert, 1989: *Language Planning and Social Change*. Cambridge: Cambridge University Press.

Crystal, David, 2000: *Language Death*. Cambridge: Cambridge University Press.

Cullis, John and Jones, Philip, 1998: *Public Finance and Public Choice* (2nd edn). Oxford: Oxford University Press.

Cunningham, Denis, 2002: *Civil Society and Language Policy: a Role for Associations*. Paper presented at the World Congress on Language Policies, Barcelona, 16–20 April 2002.

Daftary, Farimah, and Gál, Kinga, 2002: 'The New Slovak Language Law: Internal or External Politics?' in F. Daftary and F. Grin (eds), *Nation-Building, Ethnicity and Language Politics in Transition Countries*. Budapest: LGI (Open Society Institute) (forthcoming).

De Swaan, Abram, 2001: *Words of the World*. Cambridge: Polity Press.

De Witte, Bruno, 1989: 'Droits fondamentaux et protection de la diversité linguistique', in P. Pupier and J. Woehrling (eds), *Langue et Droit/Language and Law*. Montreal: Wilson & Lafleur, 85–101.

De Witte, Bruno, 1992: 'Le principe d'égalité et la pluralité linguistique', in H. Giordan (ed.), *Les minorités en Europe: Droits linguistiques et Droits de l'Homme*. Paris: Kimé, 50–62.

Direcció General de Política Lingüística, 1999: *Polítiques lingüístiques a països plurilingües*. Barcelona: Institut de Scoiolingüística Catalana.

Dunbar, Robert, 1991: *Language Rights in International Law: Useful Tools for Language Revitalisation?* Paper presented at the 7th International Conference on Minority Languages, Bilbao, 1–3 December 1999.

Dunbar, Robert, 2001: 'Minority Language Rights in International Law', *International & Comparative Law Quarterly*, Vol. 50, Part 1, 90–121.

Dunn, William, 1994: *Public Policy Analysis. An Introduction*. Englewood Cliffs: Simon & Schuster.

Durand, Charles, 2001: *La mise en place des monopoles du savoir*. Paris: L'Harmattan.

Edwards, John (ed.), 1994a: *Linguistic Rights of Minorities*. London: Harcourt Brace Jovanovich.

Edwards, John, 1994b: *Multilingualism*. London: Routledge.

Estébanez, María Amor Martín, and Gál, Kinga, 1999: *Implementing the Framework Convention for Protection of National Minorities*. ECMI Report No. 3. Flensburg: European Centre for Minority Issues.

Euskal Kultur Erakundea, 1996: *Enquête sociolinguistique au Pays Basque, 1996. La continuité de la langue basque. II*. Gasteiz/Vitoria: Kultura Saila & Pamplona: Nafarroako Gobernua.

Fabà, Albert, López, Pilar, Solé, Joan and Ubach, Noemí, 2000: 'Ofercat: indicadors sobre l'oferta de català a Santa Coloma de Gramenet', *Revista de llengua i dret*, 33, 143–69.

Falcon, Xabier, 1995: 'Avaluació i seguiment de la planficació lingüística: necessitat i metodologia', in *Actes del Congrés Europeu sobre Planificació Lingüística*. Barcelona: Institut de Sociolingüística Catalana, 298–304.

Fishman, Joshua, 1977: 'Language and Ethnicity', in H. Giles (ed.), *Language and Ethnicity in Intergroup Relations*. New York: Academic Press: 83–98.

Fishman, Joshua, 1989: *Language and Ethnicity in Minority Sociolinguistic Perspective*. Clevedon: Multilingual Matters.

Fishman, Joshua, 1991: *Reversing Language Shift. Theoretical and Empirical Foundations of Assistance to Threatened Languages*. Clevedon: Multilingual Matters.

Fishman, Joshua (ed.), 1993: *The Earliest Stage of Language Planning. The 'First Congress' Phenomenon*. Berlin: Mouton de Gruyter.

Fishman, Joshua (ed.), 2001: *Can Threatened Languages be Saved?* Clevedon: Multilingual Matters.

Foundation on Inter-Ethnic Relations, 1999: The Lund Recommendations on the Effective Participation of Minorities in Public Life & Explanatory Note. The Hague: FIER.

Furer, Jean-Jacques, 1992: 'Plurilinguisme en Suisse: un modèle?' in H. Giordan (ed.), *Les minorités en Europe, droits linguistiques et droits de l'homme*. Paris: Kimé.

Furer, Jean-Jacques, 1994: 'Vous avez dit frontière linguistique romanche-allemand?', *Babylonia* 1/94, 44–55.

Gellner, Ernest, 1997: *Nationalism*. New York: New York University Press.

Genro, Tarso and de Souza, Ubiratan, 1998: *Quand les habitants gèrent vraiment leur ville. Le budget participatif: l'expérience de Porto Alegre au Brésil*. Paris: Éditions Charles Léopold Meyer (1st published by Editora Fundação Perseu Abramo, 1997).

Grin, François, 1990: 'The Economic Approach to Minority Languages', *Journal of Multilingual and Multicultural Development*, 11, 153–73.

Grin, François, 1992: 'Towards a Threshold Theory of Minority Language Survival', *Kyklos*, 45, 69–97.

Grin, François, 1993: 'The Relevance of Thresholds in Language Shift and Reverse Language Shift', *Journal of Multilingual and Multicultural Development*, 14, 375–92.

Grin, François, 1994: 'L'identification des bénéfices de l'aménagement linguistique: la langue comme actif naturel', in C. Phlipponneau and A. Boudreau (eds), *Sociolinguistique et aménagement des langues*. Moncton (N.-B.): Centre de recherche en linguistique appliquée, 67–101.

Grin, François, 1996: 'The Economics of Language: Survey, Assessment and Prospects', *International Journal of the Sociology of Language*, 121, 17–44.

Grin, François, 1997: 'Diversité linguistique et théorie économique de la valeur', in J. Hatem (ed.), *Lieux de l'intersubjectivité*. Paris: L'Harmattan, 155–74.

Grin, François, 1999a: *Compétences et récompenses. La valeur des langues en Suisse*. Fribourg: Editions Universitaires Fribourg.

Grin, François, 1999b: 'Market forces, language spread and linguistic diversity', in Kontra, M., Phillipson R., Skutnabb-Kangas T. and Varady T. (eds), *Language: a Right and a Resource*. Budapest: Central European University Press, 169–86.

Grin, François, 2000a: 'Language Policy in Multilingual Switzerland: Overview and recent developments', in K. Deprez et T. du Plessis (dir.), *Multilingualism and Government*. Pretoria: Van Schaik, 71–81.

Grin, François, 2000b: *Evaluating Policy Measures for Minority Languages in Europe: Towards Effective, Cost-Effective and Democratic Implementation*. ECMI Report No. 6. Flensburg: European Centre for Minority Issues.

Grin, François, 2000c: 'On the Economics of Diversity Governance', in J. Dacyl and C. Westin (eds), *Governance of Cultural Diversity*. Stockholm: Swedish National Commission for UNESCO and CEIFO, Stockholm University, 355–78.

Grin, François, 2001: 'On effectiveness and efficiency in education: operationalizing the concepts', in J. Oelkers (ed.), *Futures of Education*. Bern: Peter Lang, 203–16.

Grin, 2002a: 'La Suisse comme non-multination', in M. Seymour (ed.), *États-nations, multinations et organisations supranationales*. Montréal: Liber, 265–81.

Grin, François, 2002b: *Using Language Economics and Education Economics in Language Education Policy*. Strasbourg: Council of Europe, Directorate of School, Out-of-School and Higher Education.

Grin, François, 2003: 'Diversity as Paradigm, Analytical Device, and Policy Goal', in W. Kymlicka and A. Patten (eds), *Language Rights and Political Theory*. Oxford: Oxford University Press, 169–88.

Grin, François, Moring, Tom, Gorter, Durk, Häggman, Johan, Ó Riagáin, Dónall and Strubell, Miquel, 2002: *Support for Minority Languages in Europe*. Final Report to the European Commission (EAC), No. 2000-1288/001-001 EDU-MLCEV http://europa.eu.int/comm/education/langmin/support.pdf

Grin, François and Sfreddo, Claudio, 1997: *Dépenses publiques pour l'enseignement des langues secondes en Suisse*. Aarau (Switzerland): Schweizerische Koordinationsstelle für Bildungsforschung.

Grin, François and Vaillancourt, François, 1997: 'The Economics of Multilingualism: Overview of the Literature and Analytical Framework', in W. Grabe (ed.), *Multilingualism and Multilingual Communities* (ARAL XVII). Cambridge, MA.: Cambridge University Press, 43–65.

Grin, François and Vaillancourt, François, 1998: *Language Revitalisation Policy: an Analytical Survey. Part I: Analytical framework*, 66 p. *Part II: Policy Experience*, 115 p. *Part III: Application to Te Reo Maori*, 35 p. Report to the Treasury, Gouvernment of New-Zealand, Wellington. Published on http://www.treasury.govt.nz.

Grin, François and Vaillancourt, François, 1999: *The Cost-Effectiveness Evaluation of Minority Language Policies. Case Studies on Wales, Ireland, and the Basque Country*. ECMI Monograph No. 2. Flensburg: European Centre for Minority Issues.

Grin, François, and Vaillancourt, François, 2000: 'On the financing of language policies and distributive justice', in R. Phillipson (ed.), *Rights to Language: Equity, Power and Education*. New York: Lawrence Erlbaum Associates, 102–10.

Guillorel, Hervé and Koubi, Geneviève (eds), 1999: *Langues et droits. Langues du droit, droit des langues*. Bruxelles: Bruylant.

Habermas, Jürgen, 1994: 'Struggles for recognition in the democratic constitutional state', in A. Gutmann (ed.), *Multiculturalism: Multicultural and Multilingual Policies in Education*. Princeton: Princeton University Press, 107–48.

Hamers, Josiane and Blanc, Michel, 2000: *Bilinguality and Bilingualism* (2nd edn). Cambridge: Cambridge University Press.

Hannum, Hurst, 1990: *Autonomy, Sovereignty, and Self-Determination*. Philadelphia: University of Pennsylvania Press.

Hannum, Hurst (ed.), 1993: *Documents on Autonomy and Minority Rights*. Dordrecht: Martinus Nijhoff.

Hanushek, Eric, 1986: 'The economics of schooling: production and efficiency in public schools', *Journal of Economic Literature*, XXIV, 1141–77.

Hanushek, Eric, 1987: 'Educational production functions', in G. Psacharopoulos (ed.), *Economics of Education. Research and Studies*. Oxford: Pergamon Press, 36–42.

Henrard, Kristin, 2000: *Devising an Adequate System of Minority Protection*. The Hague: Martinus Nijhoff.

Henrard, Kristin, 2001: 'Devising an Adequate System of Minority Protection: Individual Human Rights, Minority Rights and the Right to Self-Determination. Focus on Human Rights'. Paper presented at the *European Science Foundation Exploratory Workshop* 'Minority Languages in Europe: Frameworks – Status – Prospects'. University of Bath, 8–10 June 2001.

Héraud, Guy, 1997: 'Les instruments de la coopération transfrontalière pour la protection des minorités', in N. Labrie (ed.), *Etudes récentes en linguistique de contact*. Bonn: Dümmler.

Herberts, Kjell and Turi, Joseph (eds), 1999: *Multilingual Cities and Language Politics*. Turku/Åbo (Finland): Åbo Akademi University, Social Science Research Unit, No. 36.

High Commissioner on National Minorities, 1999: *Report on the Linguistic Rights of Persons Belonging to National Minorities in the OSCE Area*. The Hague: OSCE, HCNM.

Holmes, Janet, 1992: *An Introduction to Sociolinguistics*. New York: Longman.

Hornberger, Nancy, 1994: 'Literacy and Language Planning', *Language and Education*, 8(1 & 2), 75–86.

Hutchinson, John and Smith, Antony (eds), 1994: *Nationalism*. Oxford: Oxford University Press.

Jernudd, Björn, 1971: 'Notes on Economic Analysis for Solving Language Problems', in B. Jernudd and J. Rubin (eds), *Can Language Be Planned?* Honolulu: University Press of Hawaii, 263–76.

Jernudd, Björn, 1983: 'Evaluation of Language Planning. What has the Last Decade Accomplished?', in J. Cobarrubias and J. Fishman (eds), *Progress in Language Planning*. Berlin: Mouton, 345–78.

Jernudd, Björn, 2001: *Language Planning on the Eve of the 21st Century*. Paper presented at the 2nd European Congress on Language Policy, Andorra, 14–16 November 2001.

Johnes, Geraint, 1993: *The Economics of Education*. London: Macmillan.

Jones, Eric, 2000: 'The Case for a Shared World Language', in M. Casson and A. Godley (eds), *Cultural Factors in Economic Growth*. Berlin: Springer, 210–35.

Kaldor, Mary (ed.), 1991: *Europe From Below. An East–West Dialogue*. London: Verso.

Kaplan, Robert and Baldauf, Richard, 1997: *Language Planning from Practice to Theory*. Clevedon: Multilingual Matters.

Kellas, James, 1991: *The Politics of Nationalism and Ethnicity*. Basingstoke: Macmillan – now Palgrave Macmillan.

Kloss, Heinz, 1969: *Research Possibilities on Group Bilingualism: a Report*. Québec: Centre international de recherche sur le bilinguisme.

Kontra, Miklós, Phillipson, Robert, Skutnabb-Kangas, Tove and Várady, Tibor (eds), 1999: *Language: a Right and a Resource*. Budapest: Central European University Press.

Kriesi, Hanspeter, 1994: *Les démocraties occidentales. Une approche comparée*. Paris: Economica.

Kriesi, Hanspeter, 1995: *Le système politique suisse*. Paris: Economica.

Kymlicka, Will, 1989: *Liberalism, Community, and Culture*. Oxford: Clarendon Press.

Kymlicka, Will, 1995a: *Multicultural Citizenship. A Liberal Theory of Minority Rights*. Oxford: Clarendon Press.

Kymlicka, Will (ed.), 1995b: *The Rights of Minority Cultures*. Oxford: Oxford University Press.

Labrie, Normand, 1993: *La construction linguistique de la Communauté européenne*. Paris: Honoré Champion.

Lapidoth, Ruth, 1996: *Autonomy. Flexible Solutions to Ethnic Conflicts*. Washington: United States Institute of Peace.

Lapierre, Jean-William, 1988: *Le pouvoir politique et les langues*. Paris: Presses Universitaires de France.

Laponce, Jean, 1992: *Language and Politics*, in Encyclopedia of Government and Politics. Volume 1. London: Routledge, 587–602.

Lauvaux, Philippe, 1990: *Les grandes démocraties contemporaines*. Paris: Presses Universitaires de France.

Layard, P.R.G. and Walters, Alan, 1978: *Microeconomic Theory*. New York: McGraw-Hill.

Lemelin, Clément, 1998: *L'économiste et l'éducation*. Montréal: Presses Universitaires du Québec.

Lijphart, Arend, 1977: *Democracy in plural societies*. New Haven: Yale University Press.

Martel, Angéline, 1991: *Official Language Minority Education Rights in Canada: from Instruction to Management*. Ottawa: Office of the Commissioner of Official Languages.

Martel, Angéline, 2002: *Rights, Schools and Communities in Minority Contexts: 1986–2002*. Ottawa: Office of the Commissioner of Official Languages.

Maurais, Jacques (ed.), 1987a: *Politique et aménagement linguistiques*. Paris: Le Robert.

Maurais, Jacques, 1987b: 'L'expérience québécoise d'aménagement linguistique', in J. Maurais (ed.), *Politique et aménagement linguistiques*. Paris: Le Robert, 361–416.

May, Stephen, 1994: *Making Multicultural Education Work*. Clevedon: Multilingual Matters.

May, Stephen, 2000: 'Uncommon Languages: the Challenges and Possibilities of Minority Language Rights', *Journal of Multilingual and Multicultural Development*, 21(5), 366–85.

May, Stephen, 2001: *Language and Minority Rights. Ethnicity, Nationalism and the Politics of Language*. Harlow (UK): Longman (Pearson).

McGarry, John and O'Leary, Brendan (eds), 1993: *The Politics of Ethnic Conflict Regulation. Case Studies of Protracted Conflicts*. London: Routledge.

McLeod, Wilson, 2001: 'Gaelic in the New Scotland: Politics, Rhetoric, and Public Discourse', *Journal on Ethnopolitics and Minority Issues in Europe*, http://www.ecmi.de/publications/jemie/index.html.

Mitchell, Robert, and Carson, Richard, 1989: *Using Surveys to Value Public Goods: the Contingent Valuation Method*. Washington: Resources for the Future.

Moutouh, Hughes, 1999: 'Vers un statut des langues régionales en droit français?', in H. Guillorel and G. Koubi (eds), *Langues et Droits. Langues du droit, droit des langues*. Bruxelles: Bruylant, 221–49.

Mühlhäusler, Peter, 2000: 'Language Planning and Language Ecology', *Current Issues in Language Planning*, 3, 306–67.

Nelde, Peter, Strubell, Miquel, and Williams, Glyn, 1996: *Euromosaic. The Production and Reproduction of the Minority Language Groups in the European Union*. Brussels: European Commission.

Nelde, Peter, and Rindler-Schjerve, Rosita (eds), 2001: *Minorities and Language Policy*. St Augustin: Asgard.

North, Brian, 1994: *Scales of Language Proficiency: a Survey of Some Existing Systems*. Strasbourg: Council of Europe.

North, Brian, 1999: 'The European Common Reference Levels and the Portfolio', *Babylonia*, 99/1, 25–8.

OECD (Organisation for Economic Development and Cooperation), 2001: *Education at a Glance*. Paris: Centre for Educational Research and Innovation (OECD/CERI).

O'Reilly, Camille (ed.), 2001: *Language, Ethnicity, and the State*. Vol. 1: *Minority Languages in the European Union*. Basingstoke & New York: Palgrave – now Palgrave Macmillan.

Ó Riagáin, Dónall (ed.), 1998: *Vade-Mecum. A guide to the legal, political and other documents pertaining to the lesser used languages of Europe*. Dublin: European Bureau for Lesser Used Languages.

Ó Riagáin, Pádraig, 1995: 'Evaluating Language Policies: Some Theoretical Considerations', in *Actes del Congrés Europeu sobre Planificació Lingüística*. Barcelona: Institut de Sociolingüística Catalana, 374–84.

OSCE, 1999: *Report on the Linguistic Rights of Persons Belonging to National Minorities in the OSCE Area*. The Hague: High Commissioner on National Minorities.

Patrinos, Harry and Velez, Eduardo, 1996: *Costs and Benefits of Bilingual Education in Guatemala. A Partial Analysis*. Human Capital Development Paper No. 74, The World Bank.

Pattanayak, D.P., 1990: *Multilingualism in India*. Clevedon: Multilingual Matters.

Patten, Alan, 2002: 'Political Theory and Language Policy', *Political Theory*, 29, 683–707.

Peters, Guy, 2001: 'Globalization, Institutions, and Governance', in G. Peeters, and D. Savoie (eds), *Governance in the Twenty-First Century: Revitalizing the Public Service*. Ottawa, Montreal & Kingston: Canadian Centre for Management Development/McGill-Queens University Press, 29–57.

Phillipson, Robert, 1992: *Linguistic Imperialism*. Oxford: Oxford University Press.

Pool, Jonathan, 1991a: 'The Official Language Problem', *American Political Science Review*, 85, 495–514.

Pool, Jonathan, 1991b: *A Tale of Two Tongues*. Unpublished Manuscript, Department of Political Science, University of Washington, Seattle.

Psacharopoulos, George (ed.), 1987: *Economics of Education: Research and Studies*. Oxford: Pergamon Press.

Ricento, Thomas (ed.), 2000a: *Ideology, Politics and Language Policies. Focus on English*. Amsterdam: John Benjamins.

Ricento, Thomas, 2000b: 'Ideology, Politics and Language Policies: Introduction', in T. Ricento (ed.), *Ideology, Politics and Language Policies. Focus on English*. Amsterdam: John Benjamins, 1–8.

Rossiaud, Jean, 1996: *Mouvement social et État dans la mondialisation. Une illustration: le Helsinki Citizens Assembly*. PhD Dissertation, University of Geneva.

Rossiaud, Jean, 1997: *'MoNdernisation' et subjectivation. Éléments pour la sociologie des mouvements sociaux*. Florianópolis (BR): Universidade Federal de Santa Catarina.

Rubin, Joan, 1983: 'Evaluating Status Planning', in J. Cobarrubias and J. Fishman (eds), *Progress in Language Planning*. Berlin: Mouton, 329–43.

Rubin, Joan and Jernudd, Björn (eds), 1971: *Can Language be Planned? Sociolinguistic Theory and Practice for Developing Nations*. The Hague: Mouton.

Sanguin, André-Louis (ed.), 1993: *Les minorités ethniques en Europe*. Paris: L'Harmattan.

Saward, Michael, 1994: 'Democratic Theory and Indices of Democratization', in D. Beetham (ed.), *Defining and Measuring Democracy*. London: Sage, 6–24.

Schärer, Rolf (ed.), 2000: *European Language Portfolio II*. Theme issue of *Babylonia*, 4/2000.

Scharpf, Fritz, 1997: *Games Real Actors Play. Actor-Centered Institutionalism in Policy Research*. Boulder: Westview Press.

Schiffman, Harold, 1996: *Linguistic Culture and Language Policy*. London: Routledge.

Schmid, Carol, 2001: *The Politics of Language. Conflict, Identity, and Cultural Pluralism in Comparative Perspective*. Oxford: Oxford University Press.

Schneider, Günther, and North, Brian, 1997: 'Portfolio européen des langues pour jeunes et adultes', in Conseil de l'Europe, *Portfolio européen des langues. Propositions d'élaboration* (CC-LANG (97) 1). Strasbourg: Council of Europe, 75–88.

Schoch, Bruno, 1999: *Switzerland – a Model for Solving Nationality Conflicts?* PRIF Report No. 54, Peace Research Institute, Frankfurt.

Schöpflin, George, 2000: *Nations, Identity, Power*. New York: New York University Press.

Sen, Amartya, 1999: 'Democracy as a Universal Value', *Journal of Democracy*, 10(3), 3–17.

Shapiro, Ian and Kymlicka, Will (eds), 1997: *Ethnicity and Group Rights* (Nomos No. XXXIX). New York: New York University Press.

Simonnot, Philippe, 1998: *Trente-neuf leçons de théorie économique*. Paris: Gallimard.

Skutnabb-Kangas, Tove, 2000: *Linguistic Genocide in Education – or Worldwide Diversity and Human Rights?* Mahwah, NJ: Lawrence Erlbaum.

Skutnabb-Kangas, Tove, and Phillipson, Robert (eds), 1994: *Linguistic Human Rights. Overcoming Linguistic Discrimination*. Berlin: Mouton de Gruyter.

Smith, Dennis and Wright, Sue (eds), 1999: *Whose Europe? The Turn Towards Democracy*. Oxford: Blackwell.

Solé i Durany, Joan Ramon, 1995: 'La Llei de normalització lingüística i la seva reforma', in *Actes del Congrés Europeu sobre Planificació Lingüística*. Barcelona: Institut de Sociolingüística Catalana, 218–39.

Solé i Camardons, Joan, 1997: 'Planning Multilingualism: the Catalan Case', *Sociolinguistica* 11, 43–52.

Stokey, Edith and Zeckhauser, Richard, 1978: *A Primer for Policy Analysis*. New York: Norton & Co.

Stoker, Gerry, 1998: 'Cinq propositions pour une théorie de la gouvernance', *Revue iunternational des sciences sociales*, 155, 19–30.

Taylor, Charles,1992: *Multiculturalism and the 'Politics of Recognition'*, Princeton: Princeton University Press.

Taylor Fitz-Gibbon, Carol, and Tymms, Peter, 2002: 'Technical and Ethical Issues in Indicator Systems: Doing Things Right and Doing Wrong Things', *Education Policy Analysis Archives*, 10(6).

Thieberger, Nicholas, 1990: 'Language Maintenance: Why Bother?', *Multilingua*, 9, 333–58.

Tollefson, James, 1991: *Planning Language, Planning Inequality*. New York: Longman.

Tomuschat, Christian (ed.), 1993: *Modern Law of Self-Determination*. Dordrecht: Martinus Nijhoff.

Tovey, Hillary, Hannan, Damian, and Abramson, Hal, 1989: *Why Irish? Irish Identity and the Irish Language*. Baile Átha Cliath/Dublin: Bord na Gaeilge.

Vaillancourt, François, 1978: 'La Charte de la langue française au Québec: un essai d'analyse', *Canadian Public Policy/Analyse de Politiques*, 4, 284–308.

Vaillancourt, François, 1996: 'Language and Socioeconomic Status in Quebec: Measurement, Findings, Determinants, and Policy Costs', *International Journal of the Sociology of Language*, 121, 69–92.

Vaillancourt, François and Grin, François, 2000: *The Choice of a Language of Instruction: the Economic Aspects*. Unpublished manuscript. Washington: The World Bank Institute.

Vallverdú, Francesc, 1986: *La normalització lingüística a Catalunya*. [First published 1979]. Barcelona: Laia.

Van Parijs, Philippe, 2001: 'If You're an Egalitarian, How Come You Speak English?', Unpublished Conference Paper, Yale University, 11–12 May 2001.

Van Parijs, Philippe, 2002: 'Linguistic Justice', *Politics, Philosophy & Economics*, 1(1), 59–74.

de Varennes, Fernand, 1996: *Language, Minorities and Human Rights*. The Hague: Martinus Nijhoff.

de Varennes, Fernand, 1999a: 'Les droits de l'Homme et la protection des minorités linguistiques', in H. Guillorel and H. Koubi (eds), *Langues et Droit. Langues du droit, droit des langues*. Brussels: Bruylant, 129–41.

de Varennes, Fernand, 1999b: 'The Existing Rights of Minorities in International Law', in M. Kontra *et al.* (eds), *Language: a Right and a Resource*. Budapest: Central European University Press, 117–46.

Varian, Hal, 1999: *Intermediate Microeconomics*. New York: Norton.

Verry, David, 1987: 'Educational Cost Functions', in G. Psacharopoulos (ed.), *Economics of Education. Research and Studies*. Oxford: Pergamon Press, 400–9.

de Villiers, Bertus (ed.), 1994: *Evaluating Federal Systems*. Dordrecht: Martinus Nijhoff.

Voyame, Joseph, 1996: 'La situation en Suisse', Proceedings of seminar on *Autonomies locales, intégrité territoriale et protection des minorités*, in collaboration with the European Committee for Democracy through Law of the Council of Europe ('Commission de Venise'), Lausanne, 25–27 April 1996, 267–77.

Weber, Peter (ed.), 1999: *Language Planning and Minorities* [Contact + Conflict series]. Bonn: Dümmler.

Weinstock, N., Sephiha, H. and Barrera-Schoonheere, A., 1997: *Yiddish and Judeo-Spanish – a European Heritage*. Brussels: European Bureau for Lesser-Used Languages.

Williams, Colin (ed.), 1988: *Language in Geographic Context*. Clevedon: Multilingual Matters.

Williams, Colin (ed.), 1991: *Linguistic Minorities, Society and Territory*. Clevedon: Multilingual Matters.

Wimberley, James, 2000: *Is Rational Policy Compatible with Democracy?* Unpublished manuscript, Council of Europe.

Woodhall, Maureen, 1987: 'Cost Analysis in Education', in G. Psacharopoulos (ed.), *Economics of Education. Research and Studies*. Oxford: Pergamon Press, 393–9.

Wright, Sue, 2001: 'Language and Power: Background to the Debate on Linguistic Rights', *MOST Journal on Multicultural Societies*, Vol. 3, No. 1, http://www.unesco.org/most/vl3n1wri.htm

Wydra, Harald, 1999: 'Democracy in Eastern Europe as a civilising process', in D. Smith and S. Wright (eds), *Whose Europe? The Turn Towards Democracy*. Oxford: Blackwell, 288–310.

Zajac, Edward, 1995: *Political Economy of Fairness*. Cambridge: The MIT Press.

Subject Index

Note: references to the definition or core explanation of an analytical concept are printed in bold.

acquisition planning, 170–1; *see also* language competence
Asturian, 189 (n. 5)

Basque, 90, 174–5, 189 (n. 5, 12, 13), 190 (n. 21)
  Deputy Ministry for Language Policy (Hizkuntza politikarako sailordetza), 199
'best practice', 86, 89, 91–6, 98 (n. 19), 147, 195
  see also Flensburg Recommendations
Breton, 189 (n. 5)

Canada
  Canada-Community agreements, 154–5
  Canadian Charter of Rights and Freedoms, 158
capacity (to use a language), 43, 45, 100, 105–6, 170
Catalan, 90, 107, 175, 189 (n. 5)
  Consortium for Language Normalisation (Consorci per a la normalització lingüística), 107
  Directorate General of Language Policy (Direcció general de política lingüística), 107, 115 (n. 4), 199, 204 (n. 7)
  OFERCAT, 107
  see also normalisation (normalització)
Committee of Experts
  in the implementation of the *Charter*, 74–6
  'on-the-spot' visits, 76
conditions
  'capacity, opportunity and desire', **43–4**, 85, 100, 103, 170
  for democracy, 160
  'seven success conditions', 33, 116 (n. 9), 168; *see also SMiLE Report*

contingent valuation, 123, 146 (n. 10)
cost, 93, **117–32**, 195
  average, 124–5, 146 (n. 11, 14)
  and discounting, 127–32
  estimates of minority language education, 179–85, 190 (n. 23)
  v expenditure, 117, 146 (n. 13)
  macroeconomic, 120
  marginal, 125–7, 146 (n. 12)
  market *v* non-market, 122–3
  opportunity cost, 119; *see also* counterfactual
cost-benefit analysis, 87–8
  v cost-effectiveness analysis, **133–4**
cost-effectiveness, **93**, 98 (n. 21), **132–45**, 196
  estimates of minority language education, 186–7
  indicators, 135
Council of Europe
  Bordeaux Declaration, 56
  CAHLR (Comité *ad hoc* langues régionales), 58
  Convention for the Protection of Human Rights and Political Freedoms, 56, 59, 62, 81
  Framework Convention for the Protection of National Minorities, 83, 85
  Galway Declaration, 56
  language competence levels, 170, 189 (n. 4, 9)
  Parliamentary Assembly, 56–8
  Recommendations, 56
  Secretary General, 76
  see also Committee of Experts; local and regional authorities (Congress of); European Charter for Regional or Minority Languages
counterfactual, **114**, 119, 121, 135, 145 (n. 5), 178–9, 195
  see also cost (marginal)

democracy, 95–6, 148
  consociational democracy,
    161 (n. 4)
  and democratisation, 152
  and governance, 152
  participatory democracy, 149–53,
    151, 157, 161 (n. 8), 196;
    examples of, 161 (n. 15, 16);
    and minority protection,
    157–60
Denmark, 161 (n. 16)
desire (to use a language), 43, 45,
    100, 105–6
distribution of resources, 86, 144
  and resource allocation, 25, 188
  see also equality
diversity, value of, 26, 34, 194, 202

education, *see* language policy
    (in education)
  education economics, 173, 178
  see also acquisition planning
effectiveness, **91–2**, 98 (n. 21)
  boundary, 133
  and cross-effects, 100, 112
  external, **174–8**
  indicators, **104–9**, 136
  internal, **172–4**
  measured in time units, 110,
    136–7
  and policy-specific effects, 113,
    186, 195
  see also generalised effectiveness
    comparison
equality, 65, 82, 84, 96 (n. 3), 158
equity, 25, 159
  see also distribution of resources;
    equality
Euromosaic Report, 42, 50 (n. 43),
    189 (n. 5)
European Centre for Minority Issues
    (ECMI), 98 (n. 20), 198
  see also Flensburg Recommendations
*European Charter for Regional or
    Minority Languages*
  contents of, 58–67
  explanatory report on, 221–45
  history of, 55–8
  signatures, 203 (n. 1)

ratifications, 203 (n. 2)
  full text of, 207–20
European Union, 202
expenditure, 117–18, 178
externalities, 35, 97 (n. 15), 121

fairness, 162 (n. 23)
  see also equality; equity
Fédération internationale des
    professeurs de langues vivantes
    (FIPLV), 161 (n. 25)
Flensburg Recommendations, **246–51**
Franco-provençal, 189 (n. 5)
French Language Charter, 97 (n. 7),
    120, 201
Frisian, 72
Friulian, 189 (n. 5)

Gaelic (Scottish), 146 (n. 17)
Gaeltacht Commission (Coimisiún
    na Gaeltachta, Ireland), 155–6,
    162 (n. 19)
generalised effectiveness comparison,
    109
'good practice/policy', *see* 'best practice'
governance, 152–3, 200–1
Graded Intergenerational Disruption
    Scale (GIDS), 41–2, 50 (n. 40), 92,
    167, 189 (n. 5)
Guatemala, 185

Hungary, 203 (n. 3)

India, 153, 161 (n. 14)
indicators, **104–9**, 135–43, 145
    (n. 2)
  see also effectiveness; OFERCAT;
    Office de la langue française
interest rate, 130
*International Covenant on Civil and
    Political Rights*, 56, 59, 81
International Centre on Language
    Planning (Centre international de
    recherché sur l'aménagement lin-
    guistique, Québec), 161 (n. 14)
international standard classification of
    education (ISCED), 189 (n. 6)
interpretation, 65
Irish, 28–9, 61, 155–6, 189 (n. 5)

Ladin, 90, 189 (n. 5)
language
  attitudes, 45
  competence, 43, 170, 189 (n. 4)
  conflict *v* threat, 3–4
  corpus, 28–9, 166
  v dialect, 60
  domains, 42, 50 (n. 41), 104; *see also*
    indicators
  dynamics and reproduction, 41–3,
    47, 99, 189 (n. 10)
  lesser-used *v* minority, 20
  non-territorial, 21, 61, 63
  and oppression, 37–8
  planning, *see* language policy
  politics assessment ('LPA'), 168–9,
    189 (n. 8)
  as public good, 35–6
  regional, 20
  regional or minority, 20–1, **60**
  rights, 9, 18 (n. 11), 23, 25, 84
  status, 28, 199
  see also language policy; territoriality
language policy
  acceptability of, 95, 98 (n. 18), 123,
    133, 144–5, 168, 188
  agencies/bodies in charge of, 154,
    199–201
  definition of 28, **30–2**
  direct *v* indirect effects of, 45–6,
    100, 112, 137
  in education (Language Education
    Planning), **163–88**, 189 (n. 5)
  goals of, 42–4, 169–70, 175–7,
    202–3
  history of, 27, 97 (n. 6)
  and politics, 21, 23, **29**, 46, 49
    (n. 21), 168–9, 187, 188 (n. 1)
  and quality, 112, 156
  and success conditions, *see*
    conditions
  training in, 198–9
  see also acquisition planning;
    effectiveness; policy-to-
    outcome path
legal discourse
  limits of, 7–8, 196–7
  nature of, 22–3
linguistic environment, 31, 36, 122, 134

linguistic human rights, *see* language
    (rights); *see also* rights
local and regional authorities, 71, 201
  Congress of, 57
  and democracy, 153

market failure, 35, 98 (n. 15), 144
minority, 20, 60
  see also language (regional or
    minority)
Mirandese, 189 (n. 5)

Netherlands, 197
non-governmental organisations
    (NGOs), role of, 75, 161
normalisation (normalització), 107,
    175, 201–3, 204 (n. 12)
normative political theory, 8, 18 (n. 12)
  see also positive *v* normative

opportunity (to use a language), 43,
    45, 82, 100, 105–6
opportunity cost, *see* cost (opportunity)
OSCE
  Copenhagen meeting (Document of
    the), 59, 97 (n. 5)
  Hague Recommendations Regarding
    the Educational Rights of
    National Minorities, 97 (n. 5)
  Helsinki Final Act, 59
  High Commissioner for National
    Minorities, 18 (n. 5)
  Lund Recommendations on the
    Effective Participation of
    National Minorities in Public
    Life, 97 (n. 14)
  Oslo Recommendations Regarding the
    Linguistic Rights of National
    Minorities, 97 (n. 5)

Pareto optimality, 86, 95, 98 (n. 15, 17)
participatory budget, 153–4
policy
  comparisons 133–7, 175–8, 185–7
  and compensation, 25; *see also*
    language policy (acceptability of)
  and externalities, 35; *see also*
    externalities
  outcomes *v* outputs, 92, 132–4, 171

policy – *continued*
  v politics, 21, 29, 163,
    168–9, 199; *see also*
    positive *v* normative
    (discourse)
  and resources, **137–43**
  see also effectiveness; equality;
    democracy
policy analysis
  application of, **86–7**, 99
  and democracy, 95–6, 149
  ex ante *v* ex post, 30, 39, 103,
    120, 186
  principles of, 7, 23, **39–40**,
    86–7, 193–4
  see also policy-to-outcome path
policy-to-outcome path
  (P-TOP), **44–7**, 92, 99, 100–4,
    163, 194
  and effectiveness indicators,
    105–7, 109
positive *v* normative (discourse), 7,
  17 (n. 1), 22–3

Québec, 83, 104, 122, 145
  (n. 9), 201
  Office de la langue française (OLF),
    104, 115 (n. 4)
  see also French Language Charter

rights
  group or collective, 83, 84, 97
    (n. 4, 7), 158–9
  positive *v* negative, 81–2, 198
  see also language (rights)
Romansch, 48 (n. 9), 90, 197–8,
  203 (n. 4)

Sámi, 76
Saskatchewan, 155
sign languages, 61
skills development, *see* language
  (competence)
SMiLE Report (*Support for Minority
  Languages in Europe*), 151 (n. 454),
  115 (n. 2), 116 (n. 9)
Sorab/Sorbian, 90, 189 (n. 5)
success conditions, *see* conditions
State
  reports (on the implementation of
    the Charter), 74–5, 197–8, 203
    (n. 3)
  role of, **33–5**, 85, 144, 157–9, 202
  sovereignty, 62, 123, 169
  see also language policy
    (agencies/bodies in charge of)
subjectivity, 161 (n. 9)
Swedish, 90
Switzerland, 49 (n. 27), 153, 182, 190
  (n. 17), 197–8, 203 (n. 4)

territoriality, 20, 61, 72, 108
translation, 65, 127

Universal Declaration of Human Rights,
  55, 81

welfare, 24–5, 31–2, 49 (n. 23), 134
  see also Pareto optimality
Welsh, 115 (n. 1), 175
  Welsh Language Board (Bwrdd yr
    Iaith Gymraeg), 98 (n. 22), 103,
    157, 199, 204 (n. 7)
  language initiatives (Mentrau Iaith),
    156–7, 162 (n. 20)

Name Index

Abramson, Hal, 97 (n. 13)
Ambrose, John, 189 (n. 10)
Anderson, Benedict, 18 (n. 1)
Arfé, Gaetano, 68 (n. 7)
Arrow, Kenneth, 96, 98 (n. 23)

Baggioni, Daniel, 18 (n. 13)
Baldauf, Richard, 17 (n. 3), 48 (n.12), 49 (n. 16), 113, 189 (n. 1)
Baker, Colin, 51 (n. 48), 115 (n. 3), 189 (n. 4), 190 (n. 22)
Bastardas Boada, Albert, 204 (n. 12)
Becker, Gary, 116 (n. 8)
Benhabib, Seyla, 18 (n. 12), 161 (n. 4)
Benoît-Rohmer, Florence, 17 (n. 4), 97 (n. 9)
Blanc, Michel, 115 (n. 3)
Blumentwitz, Dieter, 18 (n. 11), 51 (n. 47)
Breathnach, Diarmaid, 18 (n. 13)
Brunner, Georg, 161 (n. 2)

Calvet, Louis-Jean, 49 (n. 16, 20), 188 (n. 1)
Capotorti, Francesco, 20
Cardinal, Linda, 161 (n. 10, 11), 162 (n. 17)
Carson, Richard, 146 (n. 10)
Churchill, Stacey, 115 (n. 3)
Cooper, Robert 17 (n. 3), 49 (n. 16), 116 (n. 10), 189 (n. 1, 8)
Cornes, Richard, 50 (n. 30), 146 (n. 10)
Crystal, David, 204 (n. 11)
Cullis, John, 17 (n. 2), 98 (n. 17, 21)
Cunningham, Dennis, 162 (n. 25)

Daftary, Farimah, 48 (n. 13)
de Souza, Ubiratan, 161 (n. 15)
de Swaan, Abram, 49 (n. 18), 50 (n. 31)
de Varennes, Fernand, 18 (n. 11), 96 (n. 1, 3), 97 (n. 12), 161 (n. 2)
de Villiers, Bertus, 161 (n. 2)

de Witte, Bruno, 96 (n. 3), 97 (n. 6)
Dunbar, Robert, 18 (n. 7), 96 (n. 1, 2)
Dunn, William, 39, 50 (n. 35, 36), 50 (n. 39)
Durand, Charles, 48 (n. 11), 145 (n. 7)

Edwards, John, 18 (n. 11), 51 (n. 47)
Estébanez, María Amor Martin, 17 (n. 14)

Fabà, Albert, 116 (n. 7)
Falcon, Xabier, 17 (n. 3)
Fishman, Joshua, ix, 34, 48 (n. 3), 41, 49 (n.18), 51 (n.47), 167, 189 (n. 1)
Friedman, Milton, 34
Furer, Jean-Jacques, 203 (n. 4)

Gál, Kinga, 17 (n. 4), 48 (n. 13)
Gellner, Ernest, 161 (n. 3)
Genro, Tarso, 161 (n. 15)
Grin, François 18 (n. 6), 48 (n. 6), 49 (n. 19, 20, 27), 50 (n. 28, 31), 51 (n. 45), 98 (n. 16, 20, 21), 115 (n. 2), 116 (n. 8, 9), 145 (n. 3, 4), 146 (n. 10, 16), 161 (n. 13), 189 (n. 2, 4, 5, 10), 190 (n. 16, 18, 19), 203 (n. 4, 5, 6), 204 (n. 10)
Guillorel, Hervé, 188 (n. 1)

Habermas, Jürgen, 84, 97 (n. 11)
Hamers, Josiane, 115 (n. 3)
Hannan, Damian, 97 (n. 13)
Hannum, Hurst, 161 (n. 2)
Hanushek, Eric, 189 (n. 11)
Holmes, Janet, 50 (n. 41), 51 (n. 48)
Henrard, Kristin, 18 (n. 11), 51 (n. 47), 96 (n. 1), 97 (n. 4, 8, 9, 14)
Héraud, Guy, 115 (n. 2)
Hornberger, Nancy, 115 (n. 3)
Hudon, Marie-Ève, 161 (n. 10, 11), 162 (n. 17)
Hutchinson, John, 161 (n. 3)

Jernudd, Björn, 17 (n. 3), 48 (n. 7), 49 (n.18)
Johnes, Geraint, 189 (n. 11)
Jones, Philip, 17 (n. 2), 98 (n. 17, 21)

Kaldor, Mary, 161 (n. 6)
Kaplan, Robert, 17 (n. 3), 48 (n.12), 49 (n. 16), 113, 189 (n. 1)
Kellas, James, 18 (n. 1)
Kloss, Heinz , 28
Kontra, Miklos, 188 (n. 1)
Koubi, Geneviève, 188 (n. 1)
Kymlicka, Will, 18 (n. 12), 48 (n. 3), 84, 97 (n. 8, 10, 12), 161 (n. 4)

Labrie, Normand, 188 (n. 1)
Lapidoth, Ruth, 161 (n. 2)
Lapierre, Jean-William, 49 (n. 16)
Laponce, Jean, 49 (n. 18)
Lauvaux, Philippe, 148
Lemelin, Clément, 145 (n. 1), 189 (n. 11), 190 (n. 5)
Lijphardt, Arend, 161 (n. 4)

Martel, Angéline, 162 (n. 21)
Maurais, Jacques, 49 (n. 18), 189 (n. 1), 204 (n. 8)
May, Stephen, 18 (n. 11), 37, 48 (n. 1), 97 (n. 10, 11), 115 (n. 3), 189 (n. 1)
McGarry, John, 161 (n. 3)
McLeod, Wilson, 146 (n. 17)
Meissner, Boris, 161 (n. 2)
Mitchell, Robert, 146 (n. 10)
Moring, Tom, 50 (n. 28), 51 (n. 45), 115 (n. 2), 116 (n. 9), 145 (n. 4), 189 (n. 2, 5)
Moutouh, Hugues, 48 (n. 14)
Mühlhäusler, Peter, 51 (n. 46)

Nelde, Peter, 18 (n. 13), 48 (n. 18), 51 (n. 43), 189 (n. 5)
North, Brian, 189 (n. 4, 9)
Nozick, Robert, 34

O'Leary, Brendan, 161 (n. 3)
O'Reilly, Camille, 161 (n. 3)
Ó Riagáin, Dónall, 18 (n. 11)
Ó Riagáin, Pádraig, 17 (n. 3)

Patrinos, Harry, 190 (n. 16, 20)
Pattanayak, D.P., 161 (n. 14)
Patten, Alan, 18 (n. 12), 48 (n. 3)
Pareto, Vilfredo, 86
Peters, Guy, 162 (n. 24)
Phillipson, Robert, 49 (n. 15), 189 (n. 1)
Pool, Jonathan, 98 (n. 16), 162 (n. 23), 187, 189 (n. 3), 190 (n. 24)
Psacharopoulos, George, 145 (n. 1)

Ricento, Thomas, 48 (n. 7), 49 (n. 15), 189 (n. 1)
Rindler-Schjerve, Rosita, 49 (n. 18)
Rossiaud, Jean, 161 (n. 9)
Rubin, Joan, 17 (n. 3)

Sandler, Todd, 50 (n. 30), 146 (n. 10)
Sanguin, André-Louis, 18 (n. 3)
Saward, Michael, 162 (n. 22)
Schärer, Rolf, 189 (n. 9)
Scharpf, Fritz, 50 (n. 36), 189 (n. 7)
Schiffman, Harold, 48 (n. 14, 15, 21), 189 (n. 1)
Schneider, Günther, 189 (n. 4, 9)
Schoch, Bruno, 49 (n. 27), 161 (n. 13)
Schöpflin, George, 161 (n. 3)
Sen, Amartya, 161 (n. 7)
Sfreddo, Claudio, 145 (n. 3), 190 (n. 16, 18)
Shapiro, Ian, 161 (n. 4)
Skutnabb-Kangas, Tove, 50 (n. 32), 115 (n. 3), 189 (n. 1, 5), 204 (n. 11)
Smith, Anthony, 161 (n. 3)
Smith, Dennis, 161 (n. 1)
Solé, Pilar, 116 (n. 7)
Solé i Camardons, Joan, 204 (n. 12)
Solé i Durany, Joan, 204 (n. 12)
Sonntag, Selma, 49 (n. 24)
Stoker, Gerry, 161 (n. 12)
Stokey, Edith, 50 (n. 36), 117
Strubell, Miquel, 18 (n. 13), 51 (n. 43), 189 (n. 5)

Taylor, Charles, 18 (n. 12), 161 (n. 4)
Taylor Fitz-Gibbon, Carol, 116 (n. 5)
Thieberger, Nicholas, 48 (n. 4), 204 (n. 9)
Tollefson, James, 49 (n. 15, 26), 189 (n. 1)

Tomuschat, Christian, 161 (n. 2)
Tovey, Hillary, 97 (n. 13)
Tymms, Peter, 116 (n. 5)

Vaillancourt, François, 48 (n. 6), 50
    (n. 28, 31), 51 (n. 45), 98 (n. 16),
    116 (n. 8, 9), 145 (n. 4, 6), 146
    (n. 16), 189 (n. 2), 190 (n. 16, 19)
Vallverdú, Francesc, 204 (n. 14)
van Parijs, Philippe, 98 (n. 16),
    162 (n. 23)
Velez, Eduardo, 190 (n. 16, 20)
Verry, David, 190 (n. 5)
Voyame, Joseph, 161 (n. 13)

Weber, Peter, 49 (n. 18)
Williams, Colin, 49 (n. 18),
    189 (n. 10)
Williams, Glyn, 18 (n. 13), 51 (n. 43),
    189 (n. 5)
Wimberley, James, 50 (n. 33)
Woodhall, Maureen, 190 (n. 5)
Wright, Sue, 49 (n. 25), 161 (n. 1)
Wydra, Harald, 161 (n. 6)

Zajac, Edward, 17 (n. 2),
    98 (n. 17, 21, 22)
Zeckhauser, Richard,
    50 (n. 36), 117